Letters from Barcelona

Also by Gerd-Rainer Horn

EUROPEAN SOCIALISTS RESPOND TO FASCISM
THE SPIRIT OF '68
WESTERN EUROPEAN LIBERATION THEOLOGY
LEFT CATHOLICISM (*Co-edited with Emmanuel Gerard*)
1968 UND DIE ARBEITER (*Co-edited with Bernd Gehrke*)
TRANSNATIONAL MOMENTS OF CHANGE (*Co-edited with Padraic Kenney*)

Letters from Barcelona

An American Woman in Revolution and Civil War

Lois Orr

With Some Materials by Charles Orr

Edited by

Gerd-Rainer Horn
Senior Lecturer in Twentieth-Century History, Department of History, University of Warwick

© Gerd-Rainer Horn 2009

Softcover reprint of the hardcover 1st edition 2009 978-0-230-52739-3

All rights reserved. No reproduction, copy or transmission of this publication may be made without written permission.

No portion of this publication may be reproduced, copied or transmitted save with written permission or in accordance with the provisions of the Copyright, Designs and Patents Act 1988, or under the terms of any licence permitting limited copying issued by the Copyright Licensing Agency, Saffron House, 6-10 Kirby Street, London EC1N 8TS.

Any person who does any unauthorized act in relation to this publication may be liable to criminal prosecution and civil claims for damages.

The author has asserted his right to be identified as the author of this work in accordance with the Copyright, Designs and Patents Act 1988.

First published 2009 by
PALGRAVE MACMILLAN

Palgrave Macmillan in the UK is an imprint of Macmillan Publishers Limited, registered in England, company number 785998, of Houndmills, Basingstoke, Hampshire RG21 6XS.

Palgrave Macmillan in the US is a division of St Martin's Press LLC, 175 Fifth Avenue, New York, NY 10010.

Palgrave Macmillan is the global academic imprint of the above companies and has companies and representatives throughout the world.

Palgrave® and Macmillan® are registered trademarks in the United States, the United Kingdom, Europe and other countries.

ISBN 978-1-349-35812-0   ISBN 978-0-230-23449-9 (eBook)
DOI 10.1057/9780230234499

This book is printed on paper suitable for recycling and made from fully managed and sustained forest sources. Logging, pulping and manufacturing processes are expected to conform to the environmental regulations of the country of origin.

A catalogue record for this book is available from the British Library.

Library of Congress Cataloging-in-Publication Data
Orr, Lois.
   Letters from Barcelona : an American woman in revolution and civil war / Lois Orr ; with some materials by Charles Orr ; edited by Gerd-Rainer Horn.
     p. cm.
   Includes bibliographical references and index.
   1. Orr, Lois. 2. Orr, Lois—Correspondence. 3. Spain—History—Civil War, 1936–1939—Personal narratives, American. 4. Barcelona (Spain)—History—20th century 5. Spain—History—Civil War, 1936–1939—Women. 6. Spain—History—Civil War, 1936–1939—Foreign public opinion, American. 7. Americans—Spain—Barcelona—History—20th century I. Horn, Gerd-Rainer. II. Title.
DP269.9.O66 2009
946.081092—dc22
[B]
                                                                 2008042642

10 9 8 7 6 5 4 3 2 1
18 17 16 15 14 13 12 11 10 09

Contents

List of Illustrations		vii
Acknowledgements		viii
Introduction Gerd-Rainer Horn		x
1	The Catalan Revolution Gerd-Rainer Horn	1
2	Women's Autobiographies: History and Meaning Gerd-Rainer Horn	19
3	The Language of Symbols and the Barriers of Language: Foreigners' Perceptions of Social Revolution (Barcelona 1936–1937) Gerd-Rainer Horn	31
4	Letters from Barcelona (Autumn)	67
5	Letters from Barcelona (Winter)	113
6	Letters from Barcelona (Spring)	147
7	Reminiscences by Charles Orr	176
	Homage to Orwell – As I knew him in Catalonia	177
	The repentant spy	181
8	In Stalin's Secret Barcelona Jail	183
	Some facts on the persecution of foreign revolutionaries in 'Republican' Spain (*by Charles A. Orr*)	184
	The May Days and My Arrest (*by Lois Orr*)	189

List of foreign detainees – facsimiles (*by Lois and Charles Orr*)	196
Letter fragment from Paris, January 1938 (*by Lois Orr*)	199
9 (Auto-)Biographical Notes by Lois Orr	**202**
Index	208

List of Illustrations

1	Large excerpt from *Barcelona*	57
2	Large excerpt from *Barricades*	58
3	Large excerpt from *The Defense of the Faith*	59
4	Large excerpt from *To the Front*	60
5	Large excerpt from *Trade Unions*	60
6	*Live Forces* (*Fuerzas Vivas*)	61
7	*The League of Nations*	62
8	Large excerpt from *Arrival of Soviet Smoke* (*Llegada del humo soviético*), or *Up in Soviet Smoke*	63
9	*The Trade Union Leader and His Wife*	64
10	Large excerpt from *May '37*, or *The Barcelona May Days*	65
11	*Passage to France*	66
12	'Celebrating Franco' – Excerpt from *L'Uruguay*	66

Acknowledgements

In the course of preparing this book, I have incurred many debts to friends and colleagues. I first encountered the Orr Papers in the University of Michigan's Labadie Collection when preparing a graduate seminar paper, which was eventually published as 'The Language of Symbols and the Barriers of Language: Foreigners' Perceptions of Social Revolution (Barcelona 1936–1937)', in the Spring 1990 edition of *History Workshop Journal*, here reprinted as Chapter 3. I thank Oxford University Press for permission to reproduce this article. Bruce Lincoln, whose 'Revolutionary Exhumations in Spain, July 1936', *Comparative Studies in Society and History*, 27 (1985), provided a much-needed anthropological corrective to the demonization of anarchist-led anti-clerical violence in the course of the Spanish Civil War, first suggested the desirability to publish the letters from which my article had drawn much information and most of its inspiration. Some years later, Michael Löwy repeated this idea. It took almost 20 years for their suggestion to become reality.

Tom Buchanan, Andy Durgan, Ernest Erber, Jay Gertzman, Ursula Langkau-Alex, Dieter Nelles, Hans Schafranek and Reiner Tosstorff helped provide difficult-to-find information for the annotations of this work. Laura Orr and Elisabeth Cusick, niece and daughter of Lois Orr, provided me with supporting materials and additional information. Ellen Poteet was of additional indispensable help during her repeated visits to Ann Arbor in recent years. I 'abused' her friendship at those moments to suggest that she take a closer look at some of Lois' materials again. The interview transcription, excerpted at the very end of this book, is entirely her work. If Lois' frequent misspellings of Catalan and Castilian words in her letters have been reduced to a minimum in this selection of her epistolary output, then this is entirely the work of Reiner Tosstorff. Any remaining orthographic errors are entirely my fault. Charles Orr and Laura Orr, Lois' niece, gave me permission to reproduce materials from the Orr Papers in the Labadie Collection many years ago. Julie Herrada, Curator, added her permission for the reproduction of various letters and supporting materials included in the Lois Orr Papers, Labadie Collection, University of Michigan.

When crossing the Pyrenees on foot in September 2005, I happened to stumble across an exhibition of drawings by a Catalan artist named Josep Bartolí, then unknown to me, in the Musée de la Cerdagne in

Saint-Léocadie. Consisting mostly of political cartoons Bartolí drew in the course of the civil war years, it immediately struck me that his drawings provided a most evocative pictorial parallel to the situations and events described in the copious letters by Lois Orr. Some months later, I obtained a copy of the richly illustrated collection of biographical essays: Pilar Parcerisas (ed.), *Josep Bartolí. Un creador. Dibuixant, pintor, escriptor a l'exili* (Barcelona: Diputació Barcelona, 2002), which provided background information on the long and productive life of the Catalan artist. A visit to the Barcelona Municipal Archive in October 2006 helped me select the most pertinent images for inclusion in this text. I thank Bernice Bromberg, Josep Bartolí's widow, for her permission to reproduce a selection of Josep Bartolí's *dibuixos de guerra* (war drawings). Xavier Tarraubella i Mirabet, Director of the Barcelona Municipal Archives, granted permission for the use of the materials housed in his archive. Christoph Mick carried out the actual work of transforming the digitalized images into the appropriate size and format for reproduction in this book. Given that virtually all of the pictures Bartolí drew are so brimming with evocative and rich detail, the reproduction of the entirety of each work of art in the reduced format of a book page would have rendered most vital details virtually unrecognizable. I have therefore repeatedly chosen selected representative portions of the chosen cartoons, rather than the entire drawings, for reproduction in this book. In all but one instance, however, I should add, virtually all component parts of the respective drawings are included in the images reproduced in this book. I trust that this selection mechanism has done justice to the wealth of meaning included within each of the full-size original drawings.

I dedicate this book to Charles Orr, whom I met in the summer of 1998 in Geneva, where he proved to be a knowledgeable, charming and fast-paced tour guide and an equally pleasant host in Divonne. But Barcelona is where I got to know Birgit in the early autumn of 2006, after a first encounter on the GR 128. Barcelona, the erstwhile city of revolutionary prophets and activist dreamers, will forever be etched in our memory.

Introduction

In the summer of 1936, a 19-year-old American woman from Louisville, Kentucky, and her newly-wed husband, 30-year-old Charles, decide on a honeymoon spent hitch-hiking through Europe, to be followed by a sea voyage to India. While exploring Nazi Germany, they learn of the outbreak of the Spanish Civil War. The two Americans, who had been active socialists in the Left wing of Norman Thomas' American Socialist Party back home, eventually decide to thumb their way down to revolutionary Spain. After an eventful border crossing, they take up residence in Barcelona, where Charles becomes an editor for the POUM's English-language bulletin, *The Spanish Revolution*, and broadcasts English-language news on Radio POUM. After briefly working for the POUM, Lois takes up paid employment for the Catalan Regional Government's Propaganda Office. But their stay is cut short when, in July 1937, they are arrested by the Stalinist-controlled secret police in the wake of the Barcelona 'May Days'. After nine days in jail, they are released and move to Paris, where they take up solidarity work for imprisoned comrades in Spain.

This paragraph, in a nutshell, summarizes the exterior circumstances out of which emerged the series of letters, postcards and memoirs which are partially reproduced in this book. Though brimming with information on high politics, the particular quality of the information lies in the authors' keen attention to the frequently mundane and therefore often highly representative and symbolic aspects of daily life in what was then, by all estimates, the most 'revolutionary' city on European soil. Combined with a refreshing frankness on matters of interpersonal relationships, partially due to the epistolary nature of most of these texts, the resulting anthology of observations on the Catalan Revolution furnish a unique insight into the reality of this important world political event and, even more so, into the milieu of foreign radicals in Barcelona.

For what also emerges crystal-clear from these unique primary sources is the inevitable fact that Lois (and Charles) Orr, though living in the midst of Catalans and Spanish, spent most of their time engaged in activity and conversation with fellow revolutionaries from outside Spain. It is this rare combination – attention to Far-Left politics, proto-feminist observations on the personal and the political in the middle of revolution and civil war, the outsiders' insights into everyday life in 'the strangest city in the world today' (the words of the then-American Consul General in Barcelona), and the no-holds-barred description of this cluster of foreign activists who had flocked to Spain to fight a battle they had often lost at home – which gives substance and body to this edition, which has no parallel in the literature to date. The occasionally disarming naiveté of the main observer, which the reader shall notice in small portions of this text, adds to the authenticity of the described situations and moods.

The inclusion of all letters in their entirety would have exceeded the desired length of this anthology. Apart from the exclusion of unnecessary and unwarranted repetition, the selection of materials is based on three distinct but hopefully complementary criteria. As already suggested above, one unique contribution of Lois' letters lies in their – oftentimes unwitting – reconstruction of the mentality of an entire generation of revolutionaries, who had flocked to Spain and who subjectively felt called upon to contribute to what they regarded as the coming 'world revolution' in what they justifiedly perceived to be the most promising location for such a breakthrough to occur in 1936–1937: Barcelona, the capital of the Catalan province in the Spanish Republic.

As will become clear from any reading of Lois' copious letters, the young couple and virtually all of their friends – who represented a cross section of the kaleidoscope of actually existing Left socialist, dissident communist and libertarian anarchist political tendencies amongst the European Far Left in the 1930s – were primarily interested in the development of revolutionary ideas and practices which could be transferred to any other place and time – and only secondarily in the concrete circumstances of life and society in Barcelona, Catalonia and Spain. The Orrs' persistent disinterest in their host culture and their corresponding inability to learn the language spoken by the vast majority of residents in Barcelona, Catalan, is vivid testimony to their primary interests and their state of mind – especially when taking into account their generally well-developed linguistic skills. Consequently, some of the greatest insights readers may derive from the letters pertain precisely to the living conditions and reality constructions by the Orrs' cohort of foreign revolutionaries on Spanish soil.

At the same time, of course, the two protagonists did not entirely live in a cocoon disconnected from the turbulent goings-on around them. Yet in part because of their linguistic handicap, in turn perpetually reinforced by their primary orientation towards the community of radical foreigners resident in Barcelona, the Orrs and most of their colorful circle of friends relied above all on non-traditional ways of learning about their immediate environment – non-traditional compared to the practices and learning patterns of the native Catalan. It was primarily the sights and sounds and smells of revolution which Lois recorded in her steady stream-of-consciousness letters she sent home. Deprived of more conventional tools of analysis in their understanding of their temporary home, the resulting record of impressions thus furnishes a highly unusual and stimulating complement to other, more conventional observations of life and politics in Barcelona in the first year of the Spanish Civil War. To emphasize the Orrs' reliance on the symbolic markers of communication, rather than language itself, I reprint the unchanged text of an article I first published in the Spring 1990 issue of the *History Workshop Journal* as Chapter 3 of this collection.

It would, however, be unfair and ahistorical to omit all references to politics as such. After all, the newly-wed couple had travelled to Barcelona because of politics, and they perceived their role as that of supporters of an ongoing social revolution. Consequently, I have included significant and representative sections of Lois' comments on Spanish and Catalan politics. While they do not necessarily add important new factual dimensions to the existing array of published observation by others in this cohort of foreign revolutionaries in Spain, they do furnish an interesting running commentary on Iberian and world politics from the perspective of the militantly anti-fascist but equally anti-Stalinist European and North American Far Left. After all, as Lois never tired to repeat in her letters, 'The revolution is practically life here....' In order to familiarize readers with the socio-political context of these letters, a brief chapter on the history and contours of the Catalan Revolution and its key players follows these introductory comments. These pages may simultaneously provide a quick reference guide to the various organizations, individual names of key politicians and acronyms strewn throughout the primary sources at the heart of this book.

Lois' letters showcase not only her socialization in the heady days of sit-down strikes and other forms of labour and/or socialist agitation in the American heartland after 1934, but they likewise suggest the influence of the feminist critique. While the glory days of first-wave feminism, strongest in the run-up to the First World War, lay more than two decades in the past, Lois appears nonetheless to have been influenced by its ongoing legacy in American society and culture, resulting in a curious and stimulating melange of feminism and the socialist idea. Chapter 2 therefore places Lois' writings in a context articulated by the more recent second wave of feminist observations and theorizations: the category of 'women's autobiography', a category of analysis applied to various forms of 'women's literature' into which a number of features of Lois' letters appear to fit in near-perfect fashion.

Some pertinent and fascinating observations by Charles Orr follow the series of lengthy excerpts from Lois' letters which form the centrepiece of this collection. Charles' reminiscences include previously unknown reflections on the personalities and activities of George Orwell and, especially, Orwell's wife, Eileen O'Shaughnessy; the latter worked for the POUM as Charles' assistant while her husband fought in the trenches of Aragón. Last but not least follows a series of documents pertaining to the arrest and brief imprisonment of the young American couple in the cells of the Stalinist secret police then operating with increasing impunity in inverse proportion to the withering of the social-revolutionary dynamic of the Spanish and Catalan Revolution.

This last set of documents are important for any comprehensive understanding of the Catalan Revolution and, indeed, the Spanish Civil War. For they vividly demonstrate the consequences of the policies pursued by the moderate forces on the Republican side in the context of the mid-to-late 1930s. At a time when Moscow, the main supplier of military material for the anti-Franco side, engaged in a series of kafkaesque show trials in order to eliminate the threat of any serious opposition arising from the ranks of critics of the Stalinist regime back home, it only stood to reason that Republican Spain would have to tolerate similar repressive moves to stave off and to snuff out all real and potential opposition to the moderate and anti-revolutionary Republican forces on the part of precisely these Left socialist, dissident communist and libertarian anarchist upholders of a non-repressive, liberatory road to socialism.

With the crushing of the Catalan Revolution, the hopes and illusions of an entire generation of activists – symbolically represented by the cohort of foreign revolutionaries surrounding Lois and Charles Orr – were laid to rest. It came as little surprise to them that the defeat of the Catalan Revolution also set the stage for the subsequent defeat of the Republican side in the Spanish Civil War. Six months after Franco's final victory, German troops forced their way across the Polish border, and the world was set ablaze again in what Arno Mayer has aptly described as the 'Second Thirty Years War'.

* * *

Finally, here is a note on editorial policies with regard to the copious letters at the heart of this book. I have endeavoured to retain Lois' particular writing style, including her frequent recourse to dashes rather than commas or full stops. Likewise, most abbreviations have been retained as well – for example 'tho', 'govt', and so on – as have certain idiosyncratic expressions, such as her repeated references to 'milicians', that is members of the grass-roots militias set up in the wake of the revolutionary response to Franco's revolt.

1
The Catalan Revolution

When Lois and Charles Orr arrived in Barcelona in the last days of the summer of 1936, the city was showing all the signs of a most unusual development. The exterior of the cityscape was dominated by the banners, posters, parades and demonstrations of the revolutionary Left, especially the anarchists. In a remarkable process, in the space of two months the political and cultural ambience of Barcelona – a city which had always been in flux[1] – had been profoundly transformed into a showcase of the libertarian anarchist collectivist spirit. The presence of the National Labor Confederation/Iberian Anarchist Federation (CNT/FAI), the most visible force amongst the anarchist Left, was impossible to miss.

> CNT/FAI armbands were worn, and CNT/FAI signs and banners were painted or plastered on every available wall on buses, cars, and trains as well, usually courtesy of the painters' syndicate. Anarchist headquarters on Vía Layetana (later changed to Vía Durruti) had a mural several stories high, and so did the telephone building. Hundreds of open-air rallies and demonstrations were held in the parks, and the Barcelona bullring was a favored place for big meetings of the two organisations.[2]

What had happened to bring about this profound interior and exterior transformation of the Catalan port city on the Mediterranean?

The Second Republic (from April 1931 to July 1936)

Almost from its beginning, the short-lived Second Spanish Republic (1931–1939) was a hotbed of political activism and intrigue used and abused by the entire spectrum of political opinion, from the far Left to the far Right.[3] The first major political and military altercation occurred in October 1934, when a social-democratic-led armed rebellion broke out to stave off a perceived threat from the radical Right. The armed clashes were most pronounced in the mining region of Asturias, where the anarchist CNT joined with social democracy in a militant, working class–based, united front.[4] In Catalonia the revolt took on more the character of a nationalist revolt.[5] Both uprisings failed, yet the ensuing repression only served further to fuel the pent-up aspirations of the socialist, anarchist and nationalist ranks, paving the way for the successful election of a Popular Front government in February 1936.[6]

The election of a government supported by social democracy, communism and the bourgeois Left opened the floodgates to rank-and-file spontaneous initiative. Political prisoners were freed by the insurgent masses; a strike wave broke out throughout the cities of Spain; and in the countryside land occupations and the settling of old scores became commonplace. If there ever was a case where class struggles in the most basic sense of that term were not only advocated but practised on a daily basis and in the most remote stretches of a country, this was true for Spain in the 1930s.[7] What perhaps most frightened the Spanish rural and urban elite was the fact that they had lost the initiative. From October 1934 to February 1936, in the *bienio negro* (dark two years), landlords and the urban rich had been in the control seat of economic and political violence. Now the tables were turned, and the urban and rural poor responded in kind. But by July 1936 the stage was ready for a counter-revolutionary coup to put an end to this experiment in creeping social revolution.

On 17 July 1936 General Franco stepped in to stop the tide of 'red anarchy'. From a military aspect, his coup d'état was relatively well organized and should have succeeded had the urban and rural poor followed the advice of their Popular Front leaders. But what Franco had not counted on was yet another, even more powerful, spontaneous self-expression of the Spanish masses who refused to capitulate before the apparent superior military might of the counter-revolutionary rebels. Whereas the parties of the Popular Front counselled caution and strict adherence to the rules of bourgeois parliamentary politics, strongly urging trust in the supposedly democratic spirit of the various forces of law and order, rank-and-file initiative resulted in the spontaneous creation of armed workers' militias, heroic and often poorly armed assaults on strongholds of the putschists and a general flowering of self-organization to crush the Francoist Right. In the end Franco's forces, the

Movimiento, wound up initially controlling only Morocco, small parts of Andalusia and a stretch of territory in the north reaching from Navarre, a royalist stronghold, to Galicia, excluding most of Asturias and the Basque Country.

> In effect, each time that the workers' organisations allowed themselves to be paralyzed by their anxiety to respect Republican legality and each time that their leaders were satisfied with what was said by the officers, the latter prevailed. On the other hand, the *Movimiento* was repulsed whenever the workers had time to arm and whenever they set about the destruction of the Army as such, independently of their leaders' positions or the attitudes of "legitimate" public authorities.[8]

A bloody civil war ensued, lasting almost three years.

As could be predicted, the partial victory of the (mostly) working-class Left only served further to heat up the social and political atmosphere throughout Republican Spain. With the notable exception of the Basque Country, spontaneous land occupations and urban expropriations became less the exception than the norm. Within Spain, Catalonia led the way in the largely unplanned fashioning of a post-capitalist society and culture – and within Catalonia, Barcelona. Yet neither Republican Spain nor Catalonia in particular were nominally governed by forces sanctioning this social revolutionary trend. In the year after July 1936 Republican Spain therefore witnessed a classic case of dual power, two models of political, economic and cultural paradigms vying for supremacy – only, in this instance, the process was forcefully co-determined by the exigencies of an anti-fascist civil war, fought jointly by both Republican camps against the conservative Right. It was a situation unlike any other in the history of revolutionary movements in the twentieth century.

Franco's coup, masterminded from the Canary Islands, began in Melilla on North African soil on 17 July. On 18 July Franco's forces controlled Spanish Morocco and spread to the mainland. Serious fighting did not break out in Barcelona before 19 July and lasted two days.[9] When the dust settled on the barricades, the city was effectively controlled by the working-class Left. The Catalan Revolution, simultaneously the most profound and least recognized social revolution in modern history, had begun.[10]

The trend towards self-organization

The elementary process of social revolution took on many forms, though a common trait everywhere was the formation of organs of self-government by the forces of the working-class Left. In the words of Burnett Bolloten, the foremost American authority on the Spanish Civil War, 'The courts of law were supplanted by revolutionary tribunals, which dispensed justice in their own way. (...) The banks were raided and their safe deposit boxes emptied. Penitentiaries and jails were invaded, their records destroyed, their inmates liberated.'[11] 'Motion-picture theaters and legitimate theaters, newspapers and printing shops, department stores and hotels, deluxe restaurants and bars were likewise sequestered or controlled, as were the headquarters of business and professional associations and thousands of dwellings owned by the upper classes.'[12] Most importantly, Bolloten contends that political and military power 'was split into countless fragments and scattered in a thousand towns and villages among the revolutionary committees that had instituted control over post and telegraph offices, radio stations, and telephone exchanges, organized police squads and tribunals, highway and frontier patrols, transport and supply services, and created militia units for the battlefronts'.[13]

Apart from the distant, national, Popular Front government initially headed by the liberal José Giral, for many months after 20 July political power in Barcelona was effectively contested by three competing authorities: the regional government, the Generalitat, controlled by the Catalan nationalist, bourgeois Left; the Antifascist Militia Committee, the central body representing the ubiquitous local revolutionary committees; and the grassroots revolutionary committees themselves, charged with various tasks depending on location and circumstance. In the first two and a half months of the Catalan Revolution, the Antifascist Militia Committee was far more powerful than the Generalitat, though neighbourhood revolutionary committees frequently acted in an uncoordinated and autonomous fashion, disregarding both the Generalitat and the Antifascist Militia Committee.[14]

A central element of this trend towards workers' control and self-management was the rush towards collectivizations. Esenwein and Shubert contend that, in all of Spain, 1 million urban and 750,000 agricultural collectives sprang up literally overnight, 'although it was in Catalonia, the centre of Spain's manufacturing industries, that industrial or urban collectivisations went the deepest'.[15] 'The collectivisations, whether violently denounced by their adversaries, ... in practice ignored for many years by the historical profession, or idealized by the majority of anarchist commentators, constituted a contradictory reality',[16] frightening beyond measure the fragile forces of the Catalan bourgeoisie. According to one source, 50% of the Barcelonan bourgeoisie fled outright; 40% were 'eliminated from the social sphere'; and only 10% remained at the site of production.[17] Few enterprises escaped collectivization, although firms owned by foreign investors were subject to relatively mild forms of expropriation, experiencing variants of workers' control rather than outright workers' self-management.[18] The working class appeared firmly in control of a major industrial zone in the Spanish state.

Collectivization was equally widespread in much of Republican Spain's countryside.[19] Indeed, it was in portions of the Catalan and Aragonese hinterland that the self-organization of social, political and cultural affairs was most fully developed, as the traditional authorities had literally disappeared, contrary to Barcelona, where, even in the summer of 1936, the bourgeois nationalist government never gave up its claim to represent the sole legitimate authority.[20]

The third and perhaps most crucial area of social life where revolutionary committees held undisputed sway at least for some months was the military.

> Because the [Republican] government lacked the necessary forces with which to combat the military insurrection, the weight of the struggle at the fronts fell upon the labor unions and proletarian parties that organised militia forces under commanders appointed or elected from amongst the most resolute and respected of their men. These militia units, or "columns," as they were generally called, to which army officers were attached under the watchful eye of party or union representatives, were controlled exclusively by the organisation that had created them, the officers assigned by the war minister possessing little or no authority.[21]

This description of the origins of the Spanish militias depicts the proletarian military forces as they existed throughout Spain in the aftermath of Franco's mid-July coup. For several months, there was little that the central government could do to counteract this trend towards the self-organization of military forces in Republican Spain, powerfully undergirding the more general trend towards self-management in all walks of life.[22]

The slow waning of the Catalan Revolution

Yet a number of countervailing influences were at work that, in the end, resulted in a gradual process of 'normalization' of the Spanish Republican military. Apart from the desire of more conservative forces for a return to 'normalcy', the militias suffered from a number of debilitating flaws. They generally distrusted professional advisors, despite the lack of trained officers within the militias' ranks. Volunteer militia units frequently disintegrated under the onslaught of superior enemy firepower. There existed 'no central general staff in the proper sense of that word'. And individual militia units frequently operated with minimal concern for other columns, even neighbouring ones, leading to tragic misunderstandings sapping militia morale.[23] None of these drawbacks were necessarily inherent to a democratic system of military affairs, but, given that they occurred in the context of a vicious civil war, such flaws eventually permitted the advocates of a traditional, hierarchically organized military to regain the upper hand. It did not help matters that the primary source of arms for Republican Spain was the Soviet government, itself frontally opposed to any experience in self-management or workers' control, be it in industry, agriculture or the military.[24]

Much has been made of Soviet conservatism as a key reason for the eventual demise of the Spanish and Catalan Revolution. Far more important than the very real Soviet complicity were two key political developments taking place in the month of September 1936. On 4 September 1936, a new Popular Front government was announced. The previous cabinet, headed by Giral, was exclusively composed of Left bourgeois Republicans. The new government was headed by the Left-wing socialist Francisco Largo Caballero, and included radical and moderate socialists and communists side by side with the three remaining Republicans.[25] In late September the Catalan President Lluís Companys announced a similar shake-up in the composition of the Generalitat. The new Catalan government included not only the Left bourgeois nationalists, but, for the first time, also members of the anarchist CNT, the communist Unified Socialist Party of Catalonia (PSUC) and the dissident communist Workers Party of Marxist Unification (POUM).[26]

Both measures led to the incorporation of working-class forces into the structures of traditional governments. The Left wing of the social democratic Socialist Workers Party of Spain (PSOE), the CNT and POUM had hitherto been key supporters of the self-management structures, the ubiquitous 'revolutionary committees', in Catalonia and throughout Spain. With their entry into traditional cabinet politics they immediately began to de-emphasize the necessity and utility of such alternative forms of government. On 30 September 1936 a series of decrees were passed 'formally militarizing the militias'.[27] More importantly perhaps, on 1 October 1936 the Catalan Antifascist Militia Committee dissolved itself, a move followed up on 9 October with a Generalitat decree, supported by CNT and POUM representatives, to liquidate all local revolutionary committees.[28]

The general trend towards dissolution of elements of self-management in Spanish and Catalan society is perhaps best exemplified by a seemingly supportive decree issued by the Generalitat on 24 October 1936. On that date, the coalition cabinet announced a measure legalizing the collectivization of Catalan industry, but at a price. In a significant restrictive clause, only enterprises with more than 100 employees were to be covered by this decree, and, most crucially, the individual factories were to be strictly subsumed under the authority of a centralized planning and decision-making body.[29] While it is clear that some form of supra-factory control would have been beneficial to the shaky health of the Catalan economy, the main gist of this decree was far less benevolent. According to Carlos Semprún-Maura, 'the state took charge of the collectivisations primarily to reign them in but also, and above all else, to spread its own influence and control to the detriment of workers' autonomy'.[30]

October 1936, then, constitutes a decisive turning point towards the reflux of social revolution in Catalonia and Spain. Yet the passing of a decree does not always immediately translate into reality, particularly under circumstances of revolution and civil war. In effect, Spain, and Catalonia in particular saw many more months in which the spirit of self-management could be unmistakably felt. Resistance to 'normalisation' was widespread, both in the economic and in the military domains.[31] Thus, when Lois Orr arrived in Barcelona, she stepped into the middle of a revolutionary situation that was only beginning to be curtailed by hostile forces as well as by the self-limiting strategy of CNT and POUM in upcoming months. Lois' letters bear witness to the continued extraordinary presence of the revolutionary spirit in the streets and neighbourhoods of Barcelona for at least eight more months after September 1936. The Catalan Revolution did not end with the wave of dissolutions and decrees that spelled the nominal end of the period when 'revolutionary committees' held sway.

The Barcelona May Events

Lois Orr's letters break off with the outbreak of openly counter-revolutionary terror in the streets of the very centre of revolutionary activities, the so-called 'Barcelona May Events'. Lois and Charles were eyewitnesses to this remarkable episode as well as victims of the ensuing repression of the dissident communist Left. The May Events therefore constitute a real and symbolic end point to this narrative as they exemplify the definite conclusion of meaningful dual power in Catalonia and the final stage of Lois' and Charles' Catalan experience.

On the afternoon of 3 May 1937, the communist police commissioner, with probable backing by the Generalitat, sent a truckload of Assault Guards to retake the central telephone exchange in the Plaça de Catalunya, a centrally located and highly visible symbol of dual power in the very heart of Barcelona. The CNT had sequestered and administered the Telefónica ever since the July battles nearly one year earlier. Confronted by the sudden appearance of the forces of the state, the anarchists defended their building, solidarity strikes broke out throughout the city and barricades went up in and around Barcelona. The fighting raged for nearly three days, about 200–500 lives were lost, and the Generalitat in the end mediated a ceasefire, leaving the military stand-off inconclusive.[32] Yet within very few days it became readily apparent that the May Events, for all practical purposes, spelled the end of the period of meaningful dual power in Barcelona and therefore in Spain.[33]

The reason behind this was that the bloody fighting provoked a national governmental crisis as Largo Caballero decisively refused to support the Generalitat and to rein in the anarchists and POUM. Ever since 1933 Largo Caballero had been the figurehead of the radical Left-wing faction within Spanish social democracy. In the aftermath of the May Events, more conservative forces within his own party used this opportunity to join forces with the openly counter-revolutionary communists and the bourgeois Left to remove Largo from the posts of minister of war and prime minister, which he held simultaneously. On 17 May the moderate socialist Juan Negrín took over the premiership.[34] From now on the various levels of official government in Catalonia and Spain exhibited few compunctions in the marginalization and repression of the revolutionary Left. As Lois' and Charles' experience proves, even the Stalinist secret police could now operate with virtual impunity throughout Spain. The Catalan Revolution had come to an end.

Political parties on the Barcelonan Left

The fall of Largo Caballero symbolized the relative decline of the Left-wing faction within the PSOE from the formerly dominant position it had occupied since 1933. For almost four years the violent social conflicts within Spanish society had catapulted Largo Caballero, in prior years a moderate force in Spanish socialist politics, to the position of charismatic spokesperson for the radical Left. While refusing to join the camp of Marxist revolutionaries, composed of members of the dissident communist and Left socialist splinter groups, Largo Caballero gave expression to the hopes of those disaffected and radicalized members of Spanish society who had not adopted anarchism as their preferred ideology. The PSOE's Centrist wing included Indalecio Prieto as undisputed intellectual leader for much of the 1930s. Prieto was a principal architect of the Spanish Popular Front. By the late spring of 1937, however, much of the PSOE's following had begun to move into the orbit of Spanish communism, the latter a distinctly moderate force in the Republican camp. Consequently, it only stood to reason that a colourless sympathizer of Soviet communism, Juan Negrín, took over from Largo Caballero in May 1937 – and not the more independent-minded, though equally moderate, Prieto.[35]

Spanish anarchism was solidly organized into the CNT, an anarcho-syndicalist trade–union-cum-political-party founded in 1910. By 1927 a clandestinely operating cadre organization, the FAI, began to operate as the virtual control centre behind the mass-based CNT, pushing the latter towards repeated attempts at localized military rebellions, refusing to permit CNT engagement in electoral politics and thus remaining in splendid isolation from other forces of the Left. By early 1936, after the *bienio negro*, CNT and FAI had grown sufficiently savvy indirectly to encourage anarchist voters to cast their ballots for the Popular Front. The CNT–FAI furthermore, as we have seen, proved itself pragmatic enough in the course of 1936 to join traditional coalition cabinets – first in Catalonia and then, in early November 1936, at the national level. Still, the forces of the CNT–FAI were by far the most powerful force on the revolutionary Left in Republican Spain, and it was largely due to CNT–FAI pressure that the Spanish and Catalan Revolutions managed to take hold and survive for almost one year, despite the best efforts of more moderate forces to roll back its gains.[36]

Within Catalonia, the dissident communist POUM was the sole other numerically at least somewhat significant portion of the revolutionary Left. Founded in September 1935, most of its members came from the Catalonia-based Workers' and Peasants' Bloc (BOC), originally a constituent part of the Right Opposition within the Communist International. The second, numerically insignificant but theoretically astute component part of the POUM originated in the Left Opposition within the Communist International. The POUM was highly critical of the relatively moderate Popular Front, but joined in its electoral association in February 1936 in order to retain a link with the masses. For similar reasons, the POUM agreed to join the Generalitat in late September 1936. The POUM incorporated the spirit of workers' control and self-management no less than the CNT–FAI, and it became the central target for repression after the Barcelona May Events. Charles Orr became a member of the POUM; Lois stood close to the Trotskyist tendency within and outside the POUM.[37]

The Moscow-oriented Spanish Communist Party (PCE) was a marginal force in Spanish politics till 1936. A strong advocate of a Popular Front since the late spring of 1935, towards the end of 1935, in part by dint of the existence of the Soviet example as an alternative to the crisis of capitalism in the 1930s, the PCE had acquired sufficient prestige to exert significant intellectual influence over important elements within the social democratic leadership and ranks. A first organizational success could be recorded in April 1936 when the social democratic youth organization merged with the communist youth group. Within days of Franco's coup, the Catalan branch of the PSOE, together with small splinter groups, likewise carried out a merger with the Catalan branch of the PCE to form the PSUC. Always under strict Soviet control, the PCE and PSUC became the most forceful advocates of moderation in the Republican camp.[38]

Catalan nationalism

Catalonia's rise to prominence as an economic, political and linguistic entity can be traced back to the rise of a Catalan commercial empire in the High to Late Middle Ages. In the eyes of Pierre Vilar, the foremost historian of Catalonia, 'thirteenth- and fourteenth century Catalonia [was] the most precocious nation-state of Europe: language, territory, economic life, political institutions, and cultural community were present at this early date'.[39] By the fifteenth century, however, the Castilian court was beginning to encroach on Catalan autonomy, which was formally abolished in 1716. By various direct and indirect means the central government promoted Castilian over the Catalan vernacular, though Catalan remained the language of ordinary communication throughout the modern age. Meaningful autonomy, however, did not re-emerge until the advent of the Second Republic.[40]

By 1932 an official statute of autonomy was issued to Catalonia and, throughout the lifespan of the Republic, the Left bourgeois *Esquerra Republicana* was the dominant political force of Catalan nationalism in the Catalan government, the Generalitat. Though nominally in power till the end of the civil war, the Generalitat fell victim to the consequences of the May Events as well. In effect, the national government used the excuse of the Barcelonan fighting to revoke the Generalitat's authority over the Catalan army and police forces, thus terminating the brief experiment in meaningful Catalan autonomy.[41] Catalan autonomy in the interwar years thus rose and fell with the forceful emergence and eventual decline of social conflicts in Catalan and Spanish civil society. This, however, did not mean, as Lois' letters show, that social revolutionaries and Catalan nationalists operated in complementary fashion or even understood each other. Still, a strong populist streak in *Esquerra* nationalism permitted, for the most part, a relatively peaceful coexistence with the social revolutionary anarchist camp, unless the latter resorted to arms.

Foreign revolutionaries in Barcelona

By the summer of 1936, most European countries had abandoned the path of political democracy. With the notable exception of Czechoslovakia, by the mid-1930s most Eastern, Central and Southern European states had adopted one of several forms of political dictatorship.[42] One of the consequences of these developments in the political sphere was a flood of refugees across the continent, most of them political activists trying to escape persecution, imprisonment, torture and the possibility of death. Yet for such exiles, the menu of available political safe havens narrowed as the decade progressed. It did not help matters that many refugees were located somewhere on the political far Left.

Therefore, when the Spanish Revolution erupted in the summer of 1936, Spain immediately became a beacon of hope. Spain incorporated simultaneously the possibility that the drift towards dictatorships could be stopped and that social revolution was a practical option. Within Spain, Catalonia saw the most concentrated expression of these hopes – and within Catalonia, Barcelona. For roughly ten months after July 1936, the Catalan port city on the Mediterranean became – for antifascists! – the freest city in the world. Local politics being dominated by anarcho-syndicalists, virtually every possible tendency or fraction of the anarchist, Marxist and libertarian Left made its presence felt. While Catalan activists served as the backbone of this experiment in proletarian democracy, foreign sympathizers added their own peculiar and particular touches to this kaleidoscope of political views and philosophies of life. Barcelona became a magnet for foreign revolutionaries. Some considered Barcelona merely a stopover on their frequently torturous journey to join the International Brigades. Of those who stayed, many came to test out their political theories; most came because they sensed a home away from home; virtually all of them flocked to Barcelona because they sensed a strong affinity for the free-wheeling political atmosphere prevailing along the main boulevards of downtown Barcelona, the Ramblas. With few exceptions, they came to help the process of social revolution – though few agreed on what this process really meant.[43]

Lois and Charles Orr fit in exceedingly well into this cauldron of radical political beliefs. Though relatively safe because of their American citizenship, enabling them to return to their home country at will, a privilege beyond the reach of most foreign revolutionaries in their circle of friends, they shared most trials and tribulations of these foreign comrades, including their eventual imprisonment in a communist prison. The intervention by the American Consul General appears to have been decisive in securing Lois' and Charles' ultimate release. In that not unimportant sense, but in that sense only, the story of Lois Orr differs from that of most other foreigners in Barcelona. In virtually all other respects, her personal and political itinerary may stand for that of many of her friends and comrades.

Notes

1. The Olympic year 1992 saw the publication in English of three stimulating monographs on the political, social and cultural history of Barcelona which, though of varying quality, may serve as useful introductions: Robert Hughes, *Barcelona* (New York: Knopf, 1992); Manuel Vázquez Montalbán, *Barcelonas* (London: Verso, 1992); and Temma Kaplan, *Red City Blue Period: Social Movements in Picasso's Barcelona* (Berkeley: University of California Press, 1992). For a more recent collection of stimulating articles on aspects of Barcelona's social, cultural and political history, see Angel Smith (ed.), *Red Barcelona: Social Protest and Labor Mobilisation in the Twentieth Century* (London: Routledge, 2002).
2. Robert W. Kern, *Red Years/Black Years: A Political History of Spanish Anarchism, 1911–1937* (Philadelphia: ISHI, 1978), p. 164.
3. The most insightful analysis of the Second Republic remains Gabriel Jackson, *The Spanish Republic and the Civil War, 1931–1939* (Princeton: Princeton University Press, 1965). The meticulous, though conservative, Stanley

G. Payne authored the most comprehensive survey of Second Republic politics up to the outbreak of the civil war, *Spain's First Democracy: The Second Republic, 1931–1936* (Madison: University of Wisconsin Press, 1993). The most thorough empirical study of the Second Republic in the years of the civil war is now Helen Graham, *The Spanish Republic at War, 1936–1939* (Cambridge: Cambridge University Press, 2002). Pierre Broué and Émile Témime, *The Revolution and Civil War in Spain* (Cambridge, MA: MIT Press, 1972), remains unsurpassed in its analytical precision and understanding of the various political and social actors on the Republican side, although George Esenwein and Adrian Shubert, *Spain at War: The Spanish Civil War in Context, 1931–1939* (London: Longman, 1995), is a necessary complement and update of Broué and Témime's 1961 modern classic.
4. On the 'Asturian Commune' see, above all, Paco Ignacio Taibo II, *Asturias 1934*, 2 vols (Madrid: Júcar, 1980), and David Ruiz, *Insurrección defensiva y revolución obrera* (Barcelona: Labor, 1988). A concise English-language survey is presented by Adrian Shubert, 'The Epic Failure: The Asturian Revolution of October 1934', in Paul Preston (ed.), *Revolution and War in Spain, 1931–1939* (London: Methuen, 1984), pp. 113–136.
5. For an accessible English-language survey of October 1934 in Catalonia, see Norman Jones, 'Regionalism and Revolution in Catalonia', in Preston (ed.), *Revolution and War*, pp. 85–112. A solid political history of Catalonia under the Second Republic can be found in Victor Alba, *Catalonia: A Profile* (New York: Praeger, 1975), pp. 110–178.
6. The political and social background to the genesis of a Popular Front is masterfully demonstrated for Catalonia by Ricard Vinyes i Ribes, *La Catalunya internacional* (Barcelona: Curial, 1983).
7. Broué and Témime, *Revolution and Civil War*, pp. 80–81, provide a brief but evocative description of this elementary and largely spontaneous process. For a statistical table demonstrating the unique level of militancy in Spanish society up to 1934, see Gerd-Rainer Horn, *European Socialists Respond to Fascism: Ideology, Activism and Contingency in the 1930s* (New York: Oxford University Press, 1996), p. 55.
8. Broué and Témime, *Revolution and Civil War*, p. 104.
9. Evocative descriptions of the barricade fighting in Barcelona are perhaps most easily accessible to an English-speaking audience in Ronald Fraser, *Blood of Spain: An Oral History of the Spanish Civil War* (New York: Pantheon, 1979), pp. 62–73, 110–113.
10. The first scholar to have drawn attention to this peculiar historiographical fate of the Catalan Revolution was Noam Chomsky in a 1967 article which has recently been reissued as a monograph, *Objectivity and Liberal Scholarship* (New York: Free Press, 2003). Emphasizing the vanguard role of Catalonia, George Esenwein and Adrian Shubert more recently also pointed to the internationally unique role of the Catalan and, more generally, the Spanish Revolution: 'When compared to the Russian example, it is patent that in Spain the degree of workers' control was far more penetrating and of greater magnitude'; see their *Spain at War*, p. 134. Perhaps the most thorough depiction of Catalan political culture under the Second Republic as a whole is Enric Ucelay da Cal, *La Catalunya populista: Imatge, cultura i política en l'etapa republicana (1931–1939)* (Barcelona: La Magrana, 1982).

11. Burnett Bolloten, *The Spanish Civil War: Revolution and Counterrevolution* (Chapel Hill: University of North Carolina Press, 1991), p. 50.
12. Bolloten, *Spanish Civil War*, p. 55.
13. Ibid., p. 53.
14. See Walther L. Bernecker, *Anarchismus und Bürgerkrieg: Zur Geschichte der Sozialen Revolution in Spanien 1936–1939* (Hamburg: Hoffman und Campe, 1978), p. 220, for a concise analysis of the initial relationship of forces in revolutionary Barcelona. In general, Bernecker provides the most comprehensive and scholarly analysis of social revolution for the entire Republican-dominated areas of Spain. For excellent surveys of the dynamic of social revolution in specific locations in Catalonia, see Jordi Piqué i Padró, *La crisi de la reraguarda. Revolució i guerra civil a Tarragona (1936–1939)* (Barcelona: Publicacions de l'Abadia de Montserrat, 1998); Xavier Pujadas i Martí, *Tortosa, 1936–1939: Mentalitats, revolució i guerra civil* (Tortosa: Dertosa, 1988); Miquel Térmens i Graells, *Revolució i guerra civil a Igualada (1936–1939)* (Barcelona: Publicacions de l'Abadia de Montserrat, 1991); and Joan Sagués San José, *Una ciutat en guerra: Lleida en la guerra civil espanyola (1936–1939)* (Barcelona: Publicacions de l'Abadia de Montserrat, 2003). Pelai Pagès, 'Les transformacions revolucionàries i la vida política. Catalunya 1936–1939', in Francesc Roca et al., *La guerra i la revolució a Catalunya* (Barcelona: Promociones y Publicaciones Universitarias, 1990), is a brief but pithy overview. An informative perspective from the conservative point of view can be had in Claudi Ametlla, *Catalunya. Paradís perdut (la guerra civil i la revolució anarco-comunista)* (Barcelona: Selecta, 1984), particularly pp. 39–187. For insightful perspectives on the new forms of local political power, see, for instance, Pujadas i Martí, *Tortosa*, pp. 135–146, 179–196; Piqué i Padró, *Tarragona*, pp. 39–56; Térmens i Graells, *Igualada*, pp. 61–128; and Sagués San José, *Lleida*, pp. 71–91.
15. Esenwein and Shubert, *Spain at War*, p. 133. The heady, festive atmosphere of Barcelona in the summer of 1936 is particularly well captured in Fraser, *Blood of Spain*, pp. 137–154.
16. Carlos Semprún-Maura, *Revolución y contrarrevolución en Cataluña (1936–1939)* (Barcelona: Tusquets, 1977), p. 179.
17. Reported in Michael Seidman, *Workers Against Work: Labor in Paris and Barcelona During the Popular Fronts* (Berkeley: University of California Press, 1991), pp. 82–83, citation on p. 82.
18. See Bernecker, *Anarchismus und Bürgerkrieg*, pp. 146–147, for the Catalan revolutionaries' relatively cautious treatment of foreign investments. A useful five-point typology of collectivizations, ranging from control via nationalization (primarily of war industries) to outright collective ownership, can be gauged in Bernecker, *Anarchismus und Bürgerkrieg*, p. 207. For the most convincing overall view of the collectivization process in Catalonia as a whole, see Antoni Castells i Duran, *Desarrollo y significado del proceso estatizador en la experiencia colectivista catalana (1936–1939)* (Madrid: Nossa y Jara, 1996). An earlier detailed overall description and analysis of the Catalan political economy in the years of the civil war is Josep Maria Bricall, *Política Econòmica de la Generalitat (1936–1939)*, 2 vols (Barcelona: Edicions 62, 1978). A memoir by a former anarchist and administrator within the Generalitat's Department of Labor in the years under consideration – Albert

Pérez Baró, *Trenta Mesos de Col.lectivisme a Catalunya (1936–1939)* (Esplugues de Llobregat: Ariel, 1970) – is an additional indispensable source for the comprehension of this turbulent period. The brief survey by Francesc Roca, 'Economia i revolució a Catalunya, al 1936–1939', in Roca et al., *La guerra i la revolució*, pp. 13–22, can be of interest despite its brevity. For the local dimension, see, above all, Antoni Castells Durán, *Les Col.lectivitzacions a Barcelona 1936–1937* (Barcelona: Hacer, 1993), and also Piqué i Padró, *Tarragona*, pp. 331–378, and Sagués San José, *Lleida*, pp. 177–261. An interesting, little-known survey of collectivization in urban Catalonia is Jacques J. Giele, *Arbeiderszelfbestuur in Spanje* (Amsterdam: Anarchistiese Uitgaven, 1975).
19. For the most succinct survey and analysis of rural collectivization in Spain, see Bernecker, *Anarchismus und Bürgerkrieg*, pp. 45–136. For an English-language anthology of sympathetic descriptions of rural anarchist collectives, see Sam Dolgoff (ed.), *The Anarchist Collectives: Workers' Self-Management in the Spanish Revolution, 1936–1939* (New York: Free Life, 1974), pp. 129–164. For an important study of a key region, see Julián Casanova, *Anarquismo y revolución en la sociedad aragonesa, 1936–1938* (Barcelona: Critica, 2006 [1985]). Indispensable local studies of rural collectivization in Catalonia include, above all, Marciano Cárdaba, *Campesinos y revolución en Cataluña: Colectividades agrarias en las comarcas de Girona, 1936–1939* (Madrid: Anselmo Lorenzo, 2002), but see also Pujadas i Martí, *Tortosa*, pp. 161–178.
20. On the comparatively unfettered presence of 'direct democracy' in rural Catalonia and Aragon, see Semprún-Maura, *Revolución*, p. 179, and the studies mentioned in the preceding note.
21. Bolloten, *Spanish Civil War*, p. 250.
22. For surveys of the role and function of militias on the Republican side in the Spanish Civil War, see Bolloten, *Spanish Civil War*, pp. 249–265, and Michael Alpert, *El ejército republicano en la guerra civil* (Paris: Ruede ibérico, 1977), pp. 37–70. Local studies of revolutionary militias include Piqué i Padró, *Tarragona*, pp. 81–107. I cannot address more than in passing the role of the International Brigades, the close to 60,000 international volunteers for the military defence of the Spanish Republic who found their way to Spain at various times and often under the most harrowing circumstances, frequently experiencing the revolutionary atmosphere in Barcelona on their way to their deployment at various fronts. In this context it is, however, worth highlighting the source of the very first foreign volunteers to join the Spanish militias after 17 July, when some of the athletes who had arrived in Barcelona from more than 20 countries to participate in the Popular Olympiad, set up to protest the holding of the official 1936 Olympics in Nazi Germany, opted for military engagement instead of demonstrating their athletic skills. The *Olimpíada Popular* had been scheduled to be held in Barcelona from 22 to 26 July 1936. On this counter-Olympiad of Barcelona, which was ultimately pre-empted by Franco's coup, see Carles Santacana and Xavier Pujadas, *L'altra Olimpíada: Barcelona '36* (Barcelona: Llibres de l'Index, 2006 [1990]).
23. The development of the Republican military units, featuring the gradual absorption of 'irregular' militias into the far more traditional command

structures of the rapidly developing Republican forces, can be studied, from varying perspectives, in Bolloten, *Spanish Civil War*, particularly pp. 249–279, citation on p. 258; Graham, *Republic at War*, pp. 131–214; and Semprún-Maura, *Revolución*, pp. 187–236.

24. A solid survey of communist involvement on the moderate side within the Republican camp is, once again, provided by Bolloten, *Spanish Civil War*, pp. 381–480. A trenchant analysis of the international context within which the Soviet Union supported Republican Spain is E.H. Carr, *The Comintern & the Spanish Civil War* (New York: Pantheon, 1984). Furthermore, Gerald Howson, *Arms for Spain: The Untold Story of the Spanish Civil War* (London: J. Murray, 1998), and Ronald Radosh, Mary R. Habeck and Grigory Sevostianov (eds), *Spain Betrayed: The Soviet Union in the Spanish Civil War* (New Haven: Yale University Press, 2001), are more recent indispensable reference works on this host of issues.
25. The respective cabinet compositions are listed in Bolloten, *Spanish Civil War*, pp. 46–47, 118.
26. The new cabinet composition of the Generalitat can be studied in Bolloten, *Spanish Civil War*, pp. 402–403. Broué and Témime, *Revolution and Civil War*, p. 202, give 26 September as the date when the new cabinet was announced; Semprún-Maura, *Revolución*, p. 195, points out 27 September as the date; and Bolloten, *Spanish Civil War*, p. 402, suggests 28 September, as does Graham, *Republic at War*, p. 229. I will survey the party political spectrum in a separate section later in this chapter.
27. On the machinations behind this new 'Popular Army', see Bolloten, *Spanish Civil War*, pp. 272–279. The citation is taken from Graham, *Republic at War*, p. 148.
28. On these decisive steps in Catalonia, see Broué and Témime, *Revolution and Civil War*, p. 204. Semprún-Maura dates the Antifascist Militia Committee's autodissolution to 3 October; see his *Revolución*, p. 195. Helen Graham rightfully points to the close connection between the CNT's agreement to dissolve the Antifascist Militia Committee and the CNT's entry into the Generalitat; see Graham, *Republic at War*, p. 227.
29. See especially Bernecker, *Anarchismus und Bürgerkrieg*, pp. 175–188, for a detailed analysis of the collectivization decree of 24 October 1936.
30. Semprún-Maura, *Revolución*, p. 122.
31. On the delaying tactics of the (mostly) anarchist rank and file committed to self-management, see Semprún-Maura, *Revolución*, pp. 134–137, 206–220.
32. The literature on the May Events is plentiful and extremely partisan. The most famous literary rendition of this episode is George Orwell, *Homage to Catalonia* (New York: Harcourt, Brace & World, 1952), pp. 121–179. Orwell fought in the ranks of the POUM militias on the Aragonese front and happened to be on leave in Barcelona when the May Events erupted. For a recent and likewise well-balanced English-language summary, see Esenwein and Shubert, *Spain at War*, pp. 220–224. See also Frank Mintz and Miguel Peciña, *Los Amigos de Durruti, los trotsquistas y los sucesos de Mayo* (Madrid: Campo Abierto, 1978). Most recently, on the occasion of the seventieth 'anniversary' of the Barcelona May Days, two new publications have updated the story behind the event from differing perspectives: Ferran Gallego, *Barcelona,*

mayo de 1937 (Barcelona: Debate, 2007); and Ferran Aisa, *Contrarevolució: Els Fets de Maig de 1937* (Barcelona: Edicions de 1984, 2007).

33. The end of dual power was accompanied by severe repression of the revolutionary forces in all of Spain. For Catalonia, the discussion and the detailed listings of Josep M. Solé i Sabaté and Joan Villarroya i Font, *La repressió a la reraguarda de Catalunya (1936–1939)*, 2 vols (Barcelona: Publicacions de l'Abadia de Montserrat, 1989/1990), accounting for victims of all factions on the Republican side for the entire duration of the civil war, are a good place to start. For the specific repression of revolutionary factions in Tarragona, see Piqué i Padró, *Tarragona*, pp. 193–222. The chapter on repression in Manuel Gimeno, *Revolució, guerra i repressió al Pallars (1936–1939)* (Barcelona: Publicacions de l'Abadia de Montserrat, 1989), pp. 54–90, covers all types of repression, but including the reverberations of the *fets de maig*. The May Events and their repercussion in Tortosa and Lleida are covered in Pujadas i Martí, *Tortosa*, pp. 197–212, and Sagués San José, *Lleida*, pp. 130–151.
34. See Bolloten, *Spanish Civil War*, pp. 462–473, for a detailed narrative of the fall of Largo Caballero from power.
35. On the political itinerary of Spanish socialism in the 1930s, see, amongst many other works, Paul Preston, *The Coming of the Spanish Civil War* (London: Methuen, 1983), particularly chapters 3, 5 and 7. For Spanish social democracy in the civil war years, see, above all, Helen Graham, *Socialism and War: The Spanish Socialist Party in Power and Crisis, 1936–1939* (Cambridge: Cambridge University Press, 1991).
36. The literature on Spanish anarchism in the 1930s is no longer just the exclusive domain of former CNT activists. Perhaps the most solid overall survey of Spanish anarchosyndicalism in this turbulent decade was, for a long time, John Brademas's slightly reworked 1953 dissertation, *Anarcosindicalismo y revolución en España (1930–1937)* (Esplugues de Llobregat: Ariel, 1974). But see now, above all else, Julián Casanova, *Anarchism, the Republic and the Spanish Civil War, 1931–1939* (London: Routledge, 2005), and Heleno Saña, *Die libertäre Revolution: Die Anarchisten im spanischen Bürgerkrieg* (Hamburg: Nautilus, 2001). Amongst the plethora of anarchist reminiscences, see most notably José Peirats, *La CNT en la revolución española*, 3 vols (Paris: Ruedo Ibérico, 1971), now available in English as *The CNT in the Spanish Revolution*, 3 vols (Hastings: Christie Books, 2001–2005).
37. On the POUM, see, above all, Reiner Tosstorff, *Die POUM im spanischen Bürgerkrieg* (Frankfurt: ISP-Verlag, 1987), the abridged and updated new edition of the former work; Reiner Tosstorff, *Die POUM in der spanischen Revolution* (Karlsruhe: ISP, 2006); and Victor Alba and Stephen Schwartz, *Spanish Marxism vs. Soviet Communism* (New Brunswick: Transaction, 1988). On the BOC, see Andrew Durgan, 'Dissident Communism in Catalonia 1930–1936', Diss. (Queen Mary College: University of London, 1988), and Andrew Durgan, *BOC 1930–1936: el Bloque Obrero y Campesino* (Barcelona: Laertes, 1996).
38. By far the outstanding work on Second Republic Spanish communism is Rafael Cruz, *El Partido Comunista de España en la II República* (Madrid: Alianza, 1987). On the PSUC, see Josep Lluís Martín i Ramos, *Els orígens del Partit Socialista Unificat de Catalunya (1930–1936)* (Barcelona: Curial, 1977). On Spanish socialist/communist youth politics in the 1930s, see Ramón Casterás

Archidona, *Las JSUC: ante la guerra y la revolución (1936–1939)* (Barcelona: Nova Terra, 1977).
39. Paraphrased by Kathryn A. Woolard, *Double-Talk: Bilingualism and the Politics of Ethnicity in Catalonia* (Stanford: Stanford University Press, 1989), p. 17.
40. Apart from Woolard, *Double-Talk*, pp. 12–28, see also Hank Johnston, *Tales of Nationalism: Catalonia, 1939–1979* (New Brunswick: Rutgers University Press, 1991), pp. 29–38, and Juan Díez Medrano, *Divided Nations: Class, Politics, and Nationalism in the Basque Country and Catalonia* (Ithaca: Cornell University Press, 1995), pp. 90–106, for brief English-language overviews of the history of Catalan nationhood and nationalism.
41. On the end of Catalan autonomy in 1937, see Esenwein and Shubert, *Spain at War*, p. 224.
42. On this continental tilt towards dictatorships, see Horn, *European Socialists*, pp. 5–6.
43. On the presence of these foreign revolutionaries in Barcelona, see my 'The Language of Symbols and the Barriers of Language: Foreigners' Perceptions of Social Revolution (Barcelona 1936–1937)', *History Workshop Journal*, 29 (Spring 1990), 42–64, reprinted in this book as Chapter 3. There exists, of course, a plethora of memoirs of varying quality on this phenomenon of 'revolutionary tourism' in Barcelona. On some of the attendant sociopsychological consequences of these foreign revolutionaries' projection of their desire for social revolution, often by then decisively crushed in their native lands, onto Catalonian and Spanish politics, see Gerd-Rainer Horn, 'Mentalität und Revolution. Lebensbedingungen und Realitätskonstruktionen ausländischer Sympathisanten der katalanischen Revolution', in Andreas Graf (ed.), *Anarchisten gegen Hitler: Anarchisten, Anarcho-Syndikalisten, Rätekommunisten in Widerstand und Exil* (Berlin: Lukas, 2001), pp. 156–188.

2
Women's Autobiographies: History and Meaning

In the course of the 1980s, a new genre of literary studies emerged. The study of women's autobiographies has become an interdisciplinary area of scholarly pursuit in its own right, with anthologies and conferences devoted solely to this subject. Such a novel object of investigation has naturally called forth a number of theorizations of varying qualities. But, before addressing the historiography of women's autobiography, it may be useful to first briefly survey the history of autobiography.

The history of autobiography

One of the difficulties of writings on autobiography consists in the precise definition and identification of an 'autobiography.' According to James Olney, a key authority on this subject matter, the very first books published with that noun as part of their title were printed and sold in 1834. But, Olney justifiedly contends, it would be preposterous to deny the autobiographical value of such earlier writings as Jean-Jacques Rousseau's *Confessions*, Michel de Montaigne's *Essays*, St Augustine's *Confessions*, or, indeed, Plato's *Seventh Epistle*.[1] The real discussion on the nature of autobiographies concerns in part matters of format and style. Can a diary be considered an autobiography? Are journals or letters part of the autobiographical genre? The debate remains inconclusive and continues today.

While the definition of an autobiography remains subject to dispute, even amongst today's generation of feminist scholars of women's autobiographies, by contrast the scholarship on men's and women's autobiographies appears uncharacteristically united in their attribution of such literary products to the tradition of Western Civilization. Sidonie Smith, the most widely published feminist authority on women's autobiography, for instance, claims that 'autobiography consolidated its status as one of the West's master discourses, a discourse that has served to power and define centers, margins, boundaries, and grounds of action in the West'.[2] In this assessment she merely echoes the point of view of Georges Gusdorf, generally regarded as the leading traditionalist scholar of autobiographical writings, who claims

> that autobiography is not to be found outside of our cultural area; one would say that it expresses a concern peculiar to Western man, a concern that has been of good use in his systematic conquest of the universe and that he has communicated to men of other cultures; but those men will thereby have been annexed by a sort of intellectual colonizing to a mentality that was not their own.[3]

Yet the claim of autobiography as an innate product of androcentric Western Civilization rests on shaky grounds. To fully address the flawed vision of such theorizings goes beyond the limits of this introduction. It may suffice to draw attention to the recognition by some feminist and some traditionalist critics, who happen to work on non-Western cultural productions, of at least several strains of autobiographical writing – by women, but not only by women – originating in cultural contexts that disprove their supposed Eurocentric nature. In a fascinating study of Japanese women's literature in the ninth to twelfth centuries, Richard Bowring draws attention to 'a distinguished group of female introspective writings' which he regards as 'among the earliest examples of the attempt by women living in a male-dominated society to define the self in textual terms'.[4] The post-classical Arab world provides yet another case of autobiographical writings unencumbered by the halo of Western Civilization.[5] And, indeed, even such an ardent defender of the occidental origin and nature of the autobiographic genre as Roy Pascal cannot avoid an occasional glance at non-Western autobiographies, such as the memoirs of Babur, founder of the Mughal dynasty in India, a work which, Pascal regretfully concedes, 'would occupy a significant place in the history of autobiography had it belonged to Europe...'.[6]

The essentialist stage

Regardless of the empirical awareness of non-European autobiographical writing, serious scholarship of this genre is barely a century old. Furthermore, until the 1980s at best only cursory attention was bestowed upon the more specific subcategory of women's autobiographies. It was not until 1980, as a direct consequence of the second wave of feminism, that the first serious secondary works on specifically women's autobiographies saw the light of day.[7] In 1980 Mary G. Mason published an article on the subject in the same anthology which, for the first time, made available in English Gusdorf's path-breaking analysis of autobiographical work.[8] More importantly, in that very same year, Estelle C. Jelinek edited the first anthology of writings on women's autobiography.[9]

Whereas Mason's article, though empirically of great interest at that time, posed few theoretical insights or challenges, Jelinek's introduction for the first time theorized specific characteristics and contributions of women's autobiographies as separate and distinct from more traditional men's autobiographies. Jelinek first highlighted the then-prevalent scholarly consensus 'that a good autobiography not only focusses on its author but also reveals his connectedness to the rest of society; it is representative of his times, a mirror of his era'.[10] By contrast, Jelinek contends,

> women's autobiographies rarely mirror the establishment history of their times. They emphasize to a much lesser extent the public aspects of their lives, the affairs of the world, or even their careers, and concentrate instead on their personal lives – domestic details, family difficulties, close friends, and especially people who influenced them.[11]

This is especially salient, Jelinek adds, in the case of autobiographies by women who were indeed public personas in every traditional sense of this expression.

Six years later, Jelinek expanded on this theme in a major monograph. The author noted a pervasive sense of alterity in women's autobiographies, a trait noticeably absent from most men's writings in this genre. But this relative sense of alienation is perhaps more than balanced by 'the positive delineation of a female culture, a women's world'.[12] Most notably, Jelinek describes the impact of women's consciousness on matters of style and representation within their work. 'Rather than progressive, linear, unidimensional works that men wrote – chronicles, res gestae, intellectual histories – most women's self-portraits are cast in discontinuous forms and disjunctive narratives.' Addressing women's prose in the nineteenth century, Jelinek continues, 'Diaries, letters, and journals... are accessible forms for women whose emotional, intellectual and practical lives are fragmented by domestic responsibilities that leave them little leisure time to contemplate or integrate their experiences. Even in more shaped narratives and autobiographies proper, a disjunctiveness persists.'[13]

Yet as liberating as this new feminist critique certainly was at the time, like anything else it came with strings attached. Similar to other contributions of early second wave feminism, the new feminist critique lapsed into an ultimately self-defeating essentialism, counterposing male and female, public and private, Western and 'other'.[14] In a most revealing and insightful passage, Nancy K. Miller recaps the significance of this stage in the evolution of feminist thought. She writes,

> To be sure, by the end of the decade [of the 1970s] feminist anthropologists were doing cross-cultural work, and decrying the abuses of Feminist Woman. But their appeal for a discourse articulating the diversity of situated, delineated, unevenly developed female subjects was not to find an echo in mainstream feminist literary studies for a while.[15]

Only towards the very end of the 1980s, says Miller, did the feminist critique suspend its increasingly anachronistic essentialist belief in 'woman' as a generic, unified category of analysis.[16]

From 'Woman' to 'Women'

In the most recent period a new consensus appears to emerge, stressing the multiplicity of voices expressed by women's autobiographies. Women's autobiographies, observers say, are far more difficult to categorize than men's self-reflections. Indeed, even within a single woman's autobiography several distinct voices may be heard. Whereas traditional men's autobiographies are said to reflect the Enlightenment belief in a consistently rational and democratic self which is, almost by definition, universal, autonomous and free, by contrast women authors highlight the 'exotic, unruly, irrational, uncivilized, regional, or paradoxically unnatural'.[17] An imaginative analysis of women's autobiographies from a feminist perspective, then, results in the celebration of the 'contingent, chaotic, tangential'[18] and stimulating engagements 'with the cacophonous voices of cultural discourses'[19] hitherto suppressed by the dominant Enlightenment paradigm in traditionalist Eurocentric cultural studies. A feminist critique no longer regards women's autobiographical writings as deviations from a supposedly universal norm mandated by the standards of Western Civilization. Women's autobiographies are still judged to be different from men's autobiographical writing, but only in the sense of including a far greater diversity of voices, not as literary productions conforming to a uniform standard, even if radically divergent from men's preoccupations.

The most innovative strands of the feminist critique of women's autobiographies have moved on from a celebration of 'woman' as 'other' towards the celebration/anticipation of elements of a non-hierarchical, egalitarian, androgynous society of the future. Gaining strength from the relative de-emphasis of individualism and the corresponding relative stress on collective solidarities in women's autobiographical narratives,[20] the cutting edge of today's feminist literary criticism sees women's autobiographical writing as the most promising manifestation of what the German Marxist philosopher Ernst Bloch regarded as 'the principle of hope' or 'the anticipation or prefiguration of utopia'.[21] Sidonie Smith's chapter on 'Autobiographical Manifestos' may stand as one of the most developed feminist literary contributions to emancipatory politics, with Donna Haraway's 'A Cyborg Manifesto' perhaps the most well known revolutionary anticipation of utopia.[22]

By the early 1990s, Sidonie Smith could proclaim that 'it is a wonderful time of autobiographical experimentation as well as autobiographical traditionalism'. 'There seems an endless variety to personal writings, autobiographical novels, personal essays, journals, diaries, collections of letters, travel literature, oral histories, ethnographies, testimonials, and prison narratives. Autobiographical subjects are everywhere.' Yet precisely this 'cacophony of autobiographical voices'[23] reintroduces the contentious issue of what precisely constitutes autobiography, as alluded to earlier in this chapter. Smith herself, in her earlier work, *A Poetics of Women's Autobiography*, restricts her analysis 'of the relationship of gender to genre to formal autobiography as it emerged in the West over the last five hundred years';[24] but Smith certainly has no difficulties including other forms of writing under the same label. Other scholars are less all-inclusive. Estelle C. Jelinek, for instance, explicitly states that 'diaries, letters, and journals' go virtually unmentioned in her work 'because I do not consider them autobiographies'.[25] Perhaps a reasonable compromise would be the inclusion of such 'informal autobiographies' under the same heading but to be aware of the specificities of each subcategory. To quote Sidonie Smith one last time, 'Each of those forms urges the critic to ask different kinds of questions in addition to the common ones.'[26]

Testimonios

As Lois Orr's narrative appears in the form of letters, I would like to devote the remainder of this chapter to a brief description of the problematics and the benefits of analysing women's autobiographies in the epistolary form. Yet, because her letters reflect in part the cultural influence of the north-eastern portion of Spain, Catalonia, where she then lived, I shall first briefly address a subgenre of women's autobiographies that has emerged most forcefully in the Hispanic portion of the world: *testimonios*. *Testimonios* are book-length life stories told by frequently illiterate or semi-literate individuals in narrative form to a recorder. The narrator is usually at the centre of the plot itself, though the significance of the story line is the collectivity being described. The spotlight is never on the main protagonist. At best the protagonist's fate exemplifies the larger picture, leading two key literary critics of *testimonios* to question whether *testimonios* should be subsumed under the category of autobiography.[27]

Perhaps the most theoretically astute book-length study on *testimonios* as a category of literary production in its own right is Rosaura Sánchez's study of nineteenth-century *testimonios* in the Californian context. Incorporating theoretical insights gained by both Marxist and postmodern cultural theorists, Sánchez stresses the multiplicity of voices recognized by others as inherent to women's autobiographies, but then adds a new twist: the double presence of narrator and transcriber. 'In its very production the mediated testimonial introduces a disjuncture, a doubling, a split voice, an overlay of subaltern and hegemonic narrative spaces, perceptible in its dual modality: oral and written.'[28] Shirley Mangini has recently pioneered the application of such insights to the understanding of what Mangini terms 'memory texts of the women from the Spanish civil war'.[29] Yet Mangini is exclusively concerned with Spanish women's writings. Lois Orr, by contrast, was an American, and her literary output was in the form of letters, a category of writings Mangini leaves unaddressed. It is therefore incumbent to address the specific insights gained from studying women's letters.[30]

The significance of women's letters

In a stimulating article on an epistolary autobiography by a German noblewoman written around the year 1800, Katherine R. Goodman draws attention to the fact that, to the best of Goodman's knowledge, autobiographies written by one author in the form of a letter exchange between two individuals is a form of autobiography 'unique to women'.[31] In this specific instance Elisabeth von Stägemann wrote all letters 'from Elisabeth to Meta' by herself and 'in large measure retrospectively'.[32] What this enabled von Stägemann to do was to give free play to social convention, which demanded rational description and discussion of von Stägemann's life's twists and turns in an autobiography, the voice of 'Meta', at the same time that, through the voice of 'Elisabeth', the author was able to express the introspective and reflective side. 'Only by explicitly positing both a voice of social reason (Meta) and a voice of personal experience (Elisabeth) – imagination, emotion, and intuition – was she able to give a fair representation of her personal history and struggle.'[33] Katherine R. Goodman refers to similar instances of women's epistolary autobiographies and concludes, referring to the traditional androcentric function of autobiography, that 'all [women's autobiographies] implicitly question the Goethean notion of a self-identical and autonomous self fulfilling its telos in harmony with the external world. Such an apotheosis was an impossibility for a woman. Epistolary autobiography permitted formal expression of that fundamental lack of harmonious identity.'[34]

Elisabeth von Stägemann's letters were fictive letters. Lois Orr, by contrast, wrote her extant letters in the heat of the battle to real-life individuals, mostly members of her family in the United States. Can actual letters fulfil a function equally or even more revealing than fictive ones? Here Deborah Kaplan's fascinating analysis of Jane Austen's private letters indeed strongly suggests that actual correspondence can give even greater insights into the (auto)biography of a woman than more customary and acceptable forms of literary production. Indeed, Kaplan's comparison of Austen's letters and novels underscores that the former are far more reflective accounts of the contradictory nature of women's experience in nineteenth-century British gentry culture than the latter.

Austen's letters reflect the existence of two oftentimes clashing cultures, one being 'the male-dominated gentry society in general and her brothers in particular' and the other being 'a women's culture, which generated, out of a subordination based on gender, an acute consciousness of women's "situation," an awareness of women's conscious bonds, and a set of positive, specifically female values'.[35] This fundamental disjuncture undergoes a significant transformation within her novels. Her fictive writings 'present worlds in which the two cultural experiences are wholly conflated. Thus, they depict a single gentry culture, but one which is feminized.'[36] While this may have been a reflection of Austen's utopian longings, it also constitutes a significant distortion of her own life's experiences. But what do Jane Austen's letters have to say about Lois Orr's epistolary output?

Apart from highlighting the difference between Austen's prose and Austen's letters, Deborah Kaplan draws attention to a number of elements in Austen's letters that bear an uncanny resemblance to the output of Orr. For instance, Kaplan underscores the more intimate quality of letters making it easier to voice 'cultural identifications shared by letter writer and reader. (...) If the letters express multiple, indeed even opposing, cultural values, they do so because this private genre has no intrinsic censoring feature which would suppress or resolve cultural contradictions.'[37] Kaplan stresses the particularly intimate communication between Austen and her female correspondents. And, indeed, Lois Orr's letters permit not only important insights about American cultural assumptions and (mis)conceptions about life in Catalonia, but her letters to her sister in particular are vivid testimony to the simultaneous existence of at least two worlds within which Lois Orr lived: the political world of Barcelona in the midst of revolution and civil war – and the gendered experience of what it meant to live and work in such a fascinating, though male-dominated world. Lois Orr's letters reflect her understanding of the contradictory and sometimes complementary dual worlds of Barcelona in an exemplary fashion. Considering herself a socialist feminist at a time when the two concepts were rarely joined, let alone experienced, was a continuously fascinating though frequently frustrating lesson for Lois Orr, and her letters are living testimony to this state of affairs.[38]

Yet there is more to a comparison between Austen's and Orr's letters than the relatively unsurprising more intimate character of epistolary communication. In a passage on Austen's epistolary form, Kaplan describes the novelist's writing style in a manner that could equally well describe Orr's letters. Kaplan states that concrete information in Austen's letters is conveyed

> not by extended narratives, by stories, but by short, informative bursts of prose. News is demarcated by sudden and rapid changes of direction, usually without preparatory transitions. Although not every letter employs them, the majority use dashes frequently to take the place of descriptions and transitions. They enforce the bulletinlike quality of the discourse and enable sudden shifts that obey no principles of ordering except, occasionally, chronological sequencing.[39]

As any reader of Orr's letters will conclude, the description of Austen's epistolary style fully describes Orr's method of writing letters as well.

Conclusion

In conclusion, I do not intend to postulate a specific women's epistolary style based on the indeed astounding parallels between Austen's and Orr's letters. My reluctance to have recourse to essentialisms, in addition to the lack of significant comparative data, cautions against any such undertaking. But what I want to suggest is that Lois Orr's letters are not only excellent insights into the gendered experience of the Catalan Revolution, but that they fall squarely into the category of women's autobiographies, if in the broader sense of that term. As such, Lois Orr's letters give expression simultaneously to her personal struggle to give meaning to her experience of revolution and civil war and to the collective efforts by a group of individuals to help shape the contours of those events. Only, in this case, the community she represented was the enclave of foreigners that had chosen Barcelona as their domicile, and not the Catalan themselves. Moreover, within this community Orr's letters reflect simultaneously the culture of foreigners in general and the culture of women foreigners in particular. This multi-layered experience of revolution and civil war as seen through the eyes of a young American socialist feminist will hopefully take its place as a somewhat unusual contribution to the burgeoning literature on women's autobiographies. Last but not least, in its celebration of a socialist feminist future, Lois Orr's epistolary autobiography also fully conforms to the most recent wave of feminist productions in the realm of literary self-portraits, anticipating and celebrating the possibility of a different kind of world.

Notes

1. James Olney, 'Autobiography and the Cultural Moment: A Thematic, Historical, and Bibliographical Introduction', in James Olney (ed.), *Autobiography: Essays Theoretical and Critical* (Princeton: Princeton University Press, 1980), pp. 5–6.
2. Sidonie Smith, *Subjectivity, Identity, and the Body: Women's Autobiographical Practices in the Twentieth Century* (Bloomington: Indiana University Press, 1993), p. 18.
3. Georges Gusdorf, 'Conditions and Limits of Autobiography', in Olney (ed.), *Autobiography*, p. 29.

4. Richard Bowring, 'The Female Hand in Heian Japan: A First Reading', in Domna C. Stanton (ed.), *The Female Autograph: Theory and Practice of Autobiography From the Tenth to the Twentieth Century* (Chicago: University of Chicago Press, 1987), p. 50. For an English translation of one such piece of writing, see Richard Bowring (ed.), *Murasaki Shikibu: Her Diary and Poetic Memoirs* (Princeton: Princeton University Press, 1982). A thoughtful cultural analysis of Murasaki Shikibu's major literary work is available in Richard Bowring, *Murasaki Shikibu: The Tale of Genji* (Cambridge, MA: Cambridge University Press, 1988).
5. Leila Ahmed, 'Between Two Worlds: The Formation of a Turn-of-the Century Egyptian Feminist', in Bella Brodzki and Celeste Schenk (eds), *Life/Lines: Theorizing Women's Autobiography* (Ithaca: Cornell University Press, 1988), p. 154.
6. Roy Pascal, *Design and Truth in Autobiography* (New York: Garland, 1985), p. 22. For Babur's memoirs, see Annette Susannah Beveridge, *The Babur-nama in English*, 2 vols (London: Luzac & Co., 1922).
7. For another recent survey of the literature on women's autobiographies, see Sidonie Smith and Julia Watson, 'Introduction: Situating Subjectivity in Women's Autobiographical Practices', in Sidonie Smith and Julia Watson (eds), *Women, Autobiography, Theory: A Reader* (Madison: University of Wisconsin Press, 1998), pp. 3–52.
8. Mary G. Mason, 'The Other Voice: Autobiographies of Women Writers', in Olney (ed.), *Autobiography*, pp. 207–235.
9. Estelle C. Jelinek (ed.), *Women's Autobiography: Essays in Criticism* (Bloomington: Indiana University Press, 1980).
10. Estelle C. Jelinek, 'Introduction: Women's Autobiography and the Male Tradition', in Jelinek (ed.), *Women's Autobiography*, p. 7.
11. Jelinek, 'Introduction', pp. 7–8.
12. Estelle C. Jelinek, *The Tradition of Women's Autobiography: From Antiquity to the Present* (Boston: Twayne, 1986), p. 187.
13. Jelinek, *Tradition*, p. 104.
14. A concise reference to these limitations of the first feminist analysis of women's autobiographies can be found in Sidonie Smith, *A Poetics of Women's Autobiography* (Bloomington: Indiana University Press, 1987), p. 17, with a related though guarded critique of the so-called 'French feminists' on p. 58.
15. Nancy K. Miller, *Getting Personal: Feminist Occasions and Other Autobiographical Acts* (New York: Routledge, 1991), p. 125.
16. Two studies that reflect the struggle to overcome both then-available discourses on autobiographies in the latter half of the 1980s – the androcentric traditionalist version and the essentialist feminist variant – are Nancy K. Miller, 'Changing the Subject: Authorship, Writing, and the Reader', in Teresa de Lauretis (ed.), *Feminist Studies/Critical Studies* (Bloomington: Indiana University Press, 1986), particularly pp. 114–117, and Domna C. Stanton, 'Autogynography: Is the Subject Different?' in Stanton (ed.), *Female Autograph*, pp. 3–20.
17. Smith, *Subjectivity*, pp. 9–10. 'With their entry there is mess and clutter all around' (p. 20).
18. Smith, *Subjectivity*, p. 8.

19. Ibid., p. 21.
20. The emphasis on the 'awareness of group identity as it intersects with individual identity' is the signal contribution by Susan Stanford Friedman in her 'Women's Autobiographical Selves: Theory and Practice', in Shari Benstock (ed.), *The Private Self: Theory and Practice of Women's Autobiographical Writings* (Chapel Hill: University of North Carolina Press, 1988), see particularly pp. 34-44.
21. See, for instance, Ernst Bloch, *The Utopian Function of Art and Literature* (Cambridge, MA.: MIT Press, 1988). The relevance of Ernst Bloch to the feminist literature of the 1990s was first brought to my attention by Tim Dayton, 'Reclaiming Utopia: The Legacy of Ernst Bloch', *Against the Current*, 62 (May/June 1996), 37-41, a timely article which sent me back to my German-language pocketbook edition of Bloch's writings I laboured through more than 30 years ago. Obviously, another key figure of interest in this latest turn of feminist cultural studies is the Russian Marxist Mikhail Bakhtin, who, contrary to Bloch, is at times explicitly recognized as an inspiration by late-twentieth-century feminist critics.
22. Smith's chapter (in *Subjectivity*, pp. 154-182) ends with an analysis of Donna Haraway's essay, which is perhaps most easily accessible, entitled 'A Cyborg Manifesto: Science, Technology, and Socialist-Feminism in the Late Twentieth Century', in Donna Haraway, *Simians, Cyborgs, and Women* (New York: Routledge, 1991), pp. 149-181. Though, to end on a slightly critical note, I cannot help but notice that, in some respects, Smith and Haraway belabour in a language heavily suffused with fuzzy postmodern idiom the identical points raised in much more straightforward and accessible English by Sheila Rowbotham in her chapter, 'Through the Looking-Glass', in her *Woman's Consciousness, Men's World* (Harmondsworth: Penguin, 1973), citation on p. 29. Sheila Rowbotham has, of course, since then produced one of the most remarkable autobiographies of anyone active in the 1960s, *Promise of a Dream: Remembering the Sixties* (London: Allen Lane, 2000). In style and substance, unsurprisingly, *Promise of a Dream* conforms to all the standards of women's autobiographies discussed in this chapter.
23. Smith, *Subjectivity*, p. 62.
24. Smith, *Poetics*, p. 19.
25. Jelinek, *Tradition*, p. xii.
26. Smith, *Poetics*, p. 19.
27. See John Beverley, 'The Margin at the Center: On Testimonios (Testimonial Narratives)', in Sidonie Smith and Julia Watson (eds), *De/Colonizing the Subject: The Politics of Gender in Women's Autobiography* (Minneapolis: University of Minnesota Press, 1992), p. 118, and, for greater detail on this issue, Doris Sommer, ' "Not Just a Personal Story": Women's Testimonios and the Plural Self', in Brodzki and Schenk (eds), *Life/Lines*, pp. 107-130.
28. Rosaura Sánchez, *Telling Identities: The California Testimonios* (Minneapolis: University of Minnesota Press, 1995), p. 8. I thank Maureen Dolan for the initial reference to this book. For additional important theorizations of *testimonios*, see Hugo Achugar, 'Historias Paralelas/Historias Ejemplares: La Historia y la Voz del Otro', *Revista de crítica literaria latinoamericana*, 36 (September 1992), 49-71, and John Beverley, ' "Through All Things Modern": Second Thoughts on Testimonio', *Boundary*, 18/2 (Summer 1991), 1-21.

29. Shirley Mangini, *Memories of Resistance: Women's Voices from the Spanish Civil War* (New Haven: Yale University Press, 1995), citation on p. 56. Besides linking Spanish women's narratives to the ongoing theoretical debates on women's autobiographies, Mangini's fourth chapter, 'Towards a Theory of Memory Texts', is a useful introduction to the promise and perils of women's autobiographical writings about the civil war and its aftermath.
30. For a recent anthology devoted precisely to this topic, see Rebecca Earle (ed.), *Epistolary Selves: Letters and Letter-Writers, 1600–1945* (Aldershot: Ashgate, 1999).
31. Katherine R. Goodman, 'Elisabeth to Meta: Epistolary Autobiography and the Postulation of the Self', in Brodzki and Schenk (eds), *Life/Lines*, p. 317.
32. Goodman, 'Elisabeth to Meta', p. 311.
33. Ibid., p. 317.
34. Ibid., p. 318.
35. Deborah Kaplan, 'Representing Two Cultures: Jane Austen's Letters', in Benstock (ed.), *Private Self*, p. 215.
36. Kaplan, 'Two Cultures', p. 225.
37. Ibid., p. 212.
38. A further parallel emerges between Kaplan's comparative analysis of Austen's fiction and letters and Orr's literary output when contrasting Orr's letters with her three manuscripts on the Catalan Revolution. Orr's manuscripts include neither any significant references to the androcentric nature of the Catalan revolt nor any of her proto-feminist reflections that suffuse her letters.
39. Kaplan, 'Two Cultures', p. 216.

3
The Language of Symbols and the Barriers of Language: Foreigners' Perceptions of Social Revolution (Barcelona 1936–1937)

> *That summer of 1936, as in the tenth and eleventh centuries, the roads of southern France were alive with dissident artists, intellectuals, poets and dreamers moving towards the Pyrenees in search of the Holy Grail. We did not seek it at Mont Salvat as the Cathars did, but beneath Barcelona's Mont Tibidabo and in the foothills of Madrid's Guadarrama Mountains, where The Revolution was to bring the Kingdom of Heaven on earth.*
>
> Lois Orr (1979)

* * *

Revolutions have always exerted a certain fascination on contemporaries beyond the frontiers of the states in which they occurred. Thus, the stream of 'tourists' into Portugal became so steady in the course of the 1974–1976 'revolution of the carnations' that Portuguese border guards turned away many would-be visitors who were suspected to be more interested in the vagaries of far-Left politics than the beaches of the Algarve. Depending on the degree of the insurgents' success, the host nation was not always equally averse to the influx of foreign observers. And not all strangers were, by any means, sympathetic to the processes of radical social change they came to observe. Yet, whether out of a desire for fulfilment, learning experience or, perhaps, simply adventure, revolutions have consistently been focal points of foreigners' attention.

The literary by-product of that phenomenon is a vast body of writings by such foreigners who recorded their impressions of the respective significant events. As a result, they frequently played a crucial, though necessarily limited, role in shaping world public opinion.[1] In this regard, the investigation of the ways in which such individuals formed their own opinion of the turbulent world around them remains of crucial interest to more than just biographers.

The study of the shaping of opinions and beliefs is, of course, notoriously difficult and elusive. And while there are several potentially fruitful ways of attempting this project, none of them are completely satisfactory. One could, for instance, focus on the breadth of knowledge about the given situation which the respective future authors possessed or lacked. Yet this approach immediately calls forth additional queries. How does one measure breadth of knowledge? Is knowledge derived from books necessarily inferior to lived experience? How many pages of learned tomes equal one day under the Paris Commune? And, of course, how realistic is it to expect to be able to amass comparable data for all surveyed authors?

Meaningful sociological analysis of the writers in question will thus at best be reduced to the interpretation of such data as language proficiency, the identity of key informants and the like. Yet as helpful as these bits of information may turn out to be – and the second part of this chapter relies on such data to some extent – they cannot furnish a comprehensive answer. For the phenomenon of cognition and perception, especially in a strange and new environment, is never a coldly calculable one, as any anthropologist will readily concede.

Anthropologists, more than any other social scientists perhaps, have been keenly aware of the pitfalls and shortcomings of studying 'foreign societies'. In an essay on anthropological understanding, Clifford Geertz underscores that an ethnographer does not and 'largely cannot perceive what his informants perceive. What he perceives, and that uncertainly enough, is what they perceive "with" – or "by means of," or "through"...or whatever the word should be.' For observers of social revolution this view suggests that the comprehension of such momentous events is greatly facilitated by the symbolism prevalent in the specific historical context, whether consciously recognized or not. And one does not have to advocate an almost exclusive reliance on the power of symbols in order to see the value of 'searching out and analyzing the symbolic forms – words, images, institutions, behaviors – in terms of which, in each place, people actually represented themselves to themselves and to one another'.[2]

In the following pages I will thus attempt to reconstruct one major pattern of understanding of several dozen authors who lived through a specific social revolution in the twentieth century and who oftentimes had very little in common except for the fact that they were confronted with the same historical phenomenon. And, to anticipate one of the tentative conclusions, it is the congruency of their respective observations – despite their heterogeneous political persuasions – which confirms the importance of symbolic representations in the shaping of foreigners' views of social revolution.

In the subsequent part of this chapter I will then 'flesh out' the study of foreigners' perceptions of social revolution by focusing on one particular individual's experience and learning process in that same historical context. Here I will also utilize other data besides the impact of symbols, for I do not believe that symbolism alone can be any more a universal guide to understanding than the study of party platforms or raw statistical data. In this segment I will try to recreate some of the living conditions and the general atmosphere in which this particular individual formed her opinion of the world around her. Finally, I will close with a few very tentative conclusions to be drawn from this study of foreigners' perceptions of social revolution.

Before engaging in the analysis of foreigners' memoirs, however, it is necessary to say a few words about the concrete historical setting which engendered this literature in the first place: the social revolution in Catalonia and Aragon. It was triggered by the Francoist uprising in July 1936, which called forth a vigorous counteroffensive in most parts of Spain oftentimes leading to spontaneous expropriations wherever the rebels failed to gain the upper hand. But only in Catalonia and Aragon did the process of radical change develop into a major phenomenon with a momentum quite distinct and separate from the Spanish Civil War as such. This revolution became one of the most deepseated attempts at social transformation in twentieth-century Europe, affecting not just patterns of ownership of the means of production in industry and agriculture, but also going far beyond to include, for example, aspects of cultural and educational policy most frequently shaped by visions of 'libertarian communism' characterizing the main tendencies of the Left in the north-eastern portion of the Spanish state: anarcho-syndicalism, Caballerist socialism and the dissident communist POUM.[3]

Given the importance of this social experiment, one cannot help but notice the relative absence of serious scholarly attention devoted to this question. Noam Chomsky, in his important article 'Objectivity and Liberal Scholarship', was one of the first scholars in the English-speaking world to draw attention to this state of affairs.[4] Yet the answers he provides – particularly his emphasis on the 'counterrevolutionary subordination' of liberal scholarship – are by no means fully convincing. Without wanting to engage in undue speculation, I believe that the solution to this riddle may also be found in the national and international conjuncture of the Catalan and Aragonese revolution: that is, this event was and remains overshadowed by the simultaneous Spanish Civil War, the continental preoccupation with the fight of 'democracy' against fascism (especially in hindsight) and the ongoing mystique of the Popular Front. The combination of these factors, and not just the shortcomings of the relevant historians, has contributed to the persistent lack of substantive evaluations of this major episode of interwar European history.

This all-too-brief allusion to the pertinent historiographical debates (or lack of them) may serve to elucidate one of the key characteristics of the memoir literature to which I shall now turn: its highly partisan nature and the persistence of gross distortions of actual events even in the most recently published volumes.[5] Yet, as mentioned before, it is precisely their omnipresent references to identical forms of symbolic representation, despite deep political disagreements of the respective observers, which also characterize the literature of reminiscences of the Spanish Revolution and which make it thus a particularly valuable and challenging terrain for the understanding of the power of symbols.

I should add that, for the purposes of this study, the geographic focus will be restricted to Barcelona. This Mediterranean port city was the only location affected by this social upheaval which was visited by virtually all foreigners in Republican Spain, thus providing a sufficiently representative sample of foreigners' impressions.

* * *

In his remarkable study of the German Left in the Spanish Civil War, Patrik von zur Mühlen underscores the extent to which the Spain of 1936 must have seemed like a strange and exotic place for the foreigners who flocked to Republican Spain, incomparably more difficult to comprehend and to adjust to than may seem natural for the more cosmopolitan tourist or political observer of the late twentieth century.[6] This handicap, combined with the inability of many foreigners to communicate in Spanish, not to speak of Catalan, significantly narrowed the range of possible sources of understanding for these foreign observers and participants.

It is thus crucial to address a potential concern which may arise when trying to analyse such foreign observations of social revolution: the validity of these accounts. In responding to such justified queries,

I would like to draw attention to an illuminating passage from a work of recent feminist scholarship which is extremely pertinent in this context:

> It is commonly argued that the lack of objective validity in subjective experience arises from an individual propensity to twist and turn, reinterpret and falsify, forget and repress events, pursuing what is in fact no more than an ideological construction of individuality, giving oneself an identity for the present to which the contents of the past are subordinated. It is therefore assumed that the individuals' accounts of themselves and their analyses of the world are not to be trusted; they are coloured by subjectivity. *In our research, by contrast, we were concerned precisely with the ways in which individuals construct their identity, the things that become subjectively significant to them.*[7]

When faced with the task of analysing the process of cognition and, more concretely in this instance, the importance of symbols for the comprehension of a given social context, the literature of foreigners' memoirs constitutes one of the best possible media for this particular problematic. For, most frequently unable to read the literature or engage in conversation with the local population, these observers were forced to pay inordinate attention to other forms of communication.

Naturally, the more time elapses between the actual event and the recording thereof, the more additional objective and subjective distortions and modifications may enter the picture. Thus, one may doubt whether Willy Brandt's first significant observation after crossing the border from France into Spain was really the desecration of church property and, if so, whether it really caused the moral discomfort he records in his autobiography.[8] But, again, the object of this chapter is not the reconstruction of the reality of the Catalan Revolution, an undertaking which would do well to utilize the literature of foreign observations, but which would also have to proceed with great caution in this field. Instead, I am concerned with the sources of understanding and, in the ensuing pages, the impact of – most frequently visible – symbols on the powers of perception.

How, then, did these foreigners, who came to observe the revolution, or – more frequently – who came to observe, participate in and report on the Spanish Civil War, realize that there was a social upheaval of great magnitude in progress? What convinced them that 'business was not quite as usual', apart from the already unusual enough circumstances of a civil war between Republicans and Nationalists?

The exposure to the power of symbols began quite frequently at the point of entry into Republican Spain. Under ordinary circumstances a border crossing was a fairly trivial occurrence. John Langdon-Davies, for whom this was by no means the first trip to Spain, recalls his August 1936 attempt to enter Spain at Puigcerda:

> Everybody knows the sort of thing that happens; you produce your passport; somebody stamps it, and on you go. But now it was different. I opened the document; there, large as life were the magic words: "We, James Ramsay MacDonald, a member of his Britannic Majesty's Most Honourable Privy Council... request and require... all those whom it may concern to allow the bearer to pass freely without let or hindrance...." But by passing out of the world of democratic compromise into one of cruder realities and more real crudities I had outstepped the limits of James Ramsay MacDonald's magical efficacy. The official looked at my passport and shook his head.... All the officials, the carabineros, the anti-fascist militiamen shook their heads. It was true that I seemed to be *muy bien documentado* [very well documented], but all this *no vale nada*, wasn't worth the paper it was written on, unless I got a pass from the local Committee.[9]

The crucial test was to prove one's anti-fascist leanings and, if possible, produce appropriate credentials.

Emma Goldman was first denied entry near Port Bou in September 1936: 'I presented my British passport which was scorned by the border guards. I then took out my CNT–FAI credentials, and the stern faces lit up with enthusiasm and friendliness.'[10] For Paul and Clara Thalmann the major key to entry into Spain was a copy of a recent edition of the Swiss *Arbeiterzeitung* which happened to include a travelogue with some anarchist border control stamps reproduced somewhere within its pages.[11] John McNair was permitted to cross the border only after producing 'a letter from the I.L.P. stating that he was taking greetings of solidarity and a gift of money to the Spanish workers'. And before entering Spain he received a 'workers' passport' adorned with the various stamps of the Catalan workers' organizations. According to Fenner Brockway, McNair showed this 'workers' passport' to all roadway patrols who demanded to see documentation: 'Often the militia-man could not read, but when, among the stamps at the bottom of McNair's authorization, he saw the symbol of his own organization, he waved the car on with a friendly "Salud", and with clenched fist raised.'[12]

After the enactment of the Non-Intervention Pact, the situation changed considerably. Now the French border guards made it extremely difficult for foreigners to enter Spain, forcing many potential volunteers for the international brigades and other visitors to Spain to hike the remote pathways of the Pyrenees in order to reach their destination. Some, like the Social Democrat Rolf Reventlow, entered Spain by plane. But for most of them the first exposure to Spain was nonetheless a significant event. Reventlow remembers handing over his Czecho-Slovakian refugee passport to the official at Barcelona airport. The man glanced at the entries, noticed the inscription 'German Emigrant' and shook Reventlow's hand. Reventlow writes, 'It was the first time that I was greeted in such a manner at a border crossing since I had crossed the Riesengebirge, and thereby the German border, in the early morning hours of March 1933.'[13]

The trip from the border to Barcelona, the almost inevitable first leg of a trip for foreigners entering Spain, usually turned out to be a further memorable experience. The Thalmanns, after being wined and dined by the border guards, were allotted a space on a dilapidated truck full of *milicianos* on its way to Barcelona.[14] Most foreigners, however, managed to go by train. And here the new arrivals were amazed to see locomotives and railroad cars neatly painted with anti-fascist motifs and slogans. The Austrian Franz Haiderer, for instance, arrived at the Figueras railway station in November 1936: 'The locomotive was all trimmed up, everything in red/black and red, by the UGT/CNT. Then we rode on to Barcelona. At the various stops the population greeted us with oranges and tangerines.'[15]

This reception must have been particularly impressive after a long and tortuous journey from their respective native lands. Another Austrian, Josef Schneeweiss, had hitch-hiked from Vienna to escape his fate as a soldier under a dictatorship. His train to Barcelona was likewise painted with uplifting slogans. 'Everywhere peasants greeted the train with a raised fist. We greeted them back and shouted: "Salud".'[16] Finally, the travellers reached Barcelona. And while many of them went on to join the brigades or to report on the war, virtually everyone was deeply moved by what they saw: 'What a city! It was just like a volcano, erupting in all directions at the same time. A breathtaking, awe-inspiring and heartwarming spectacle of noise, bustle, enthusiasm and gaiety. A revolutionary city in the full flood of revolutionary zest and zeal; an unforgettable sight.'[17] 'Barcelona is always a fascinating and wonderful city but under the present circumstances I found it deliriously exciting.'[18] 'We walked about in a feeling of air and light.'[19] 'All this was queer and moving. There was much in it that I did not understand, in some ways I did not even like it, but I recognized it immediately as a state of affairs worth fighting for.'[20]

> And, then, as we turned round the corner of the Ramblas (the chief artery of Barcelona) came a tremendous surprise: before our eyes, in a flash, unfolded itself the revolution. It was overwhelming. It was as if we had been landed on a continent different from anything I had seen before.[21]

What caused this outburst of metaphoric language? What made these foreign observers almost instantly aware of the importance of what they saw in 'the strangest city in the world to-day?'[22] Here are some representative descriptions: 'The first impression: armed workers, rifles on their shoulders, but wearing their civilian clothes.'[23] 'We arrived in Barcelona in the course of the evening. Everywhere signs of tremendous enthusiasm, everywhere fluttered the flags of the Anarcho-Syndicalists.'[24] 'On our arrival at Barcelona station we were met by a huge reception. Bands were playing on the platform, there were red flags and banners, and the chanting of revolutionary slogans.'[25]

> It seemed as though people from miles around had left their houses, shops, offices and factories to greet us. Every building was festooned with the red flag of the Communists, the red and black of the Anarchists and the colours of the Catalan Nationalists. Every available wall was covered with posters exhorting the people to come to the defence of the Republic and to enter the fight to smash the Fascist insurrectionists. This was a city which belonged to its people, who had taken it into custody in a series of bloody street skirmishes.[26]

These examples, which could be multiplied at will, suggest that at least the initial impressions of Barcelona were heavily determined by visual representations, symbols of workers' power, enhanced by the militant but festive atmosphere of the Barcelona railway station 'welcoming committee' for those foreigners who came as volunteers to join the Republican army. Not everyone, of course, was equally overwhelmed by these outward signs of radical change. And it must be stressed that it would obviously be preposterous and misleading to affix sole explanatory powers to the influence of symbols in this process of instilling an awareness of deep-going social transformation in the hearts and minds of these, usually sympathetic, foreigners. Those who stayed for a while inevitably came to rely on additional sources of information. And some may have been more 'cerebral' personalities to begin with. Yet in reading account after account of the Year One of the Catalan Revolution, there emerge certain distinct patterns of cognition, and the role of symbols stands out as a prime factor in this process of political acculturation.

Some key categories of such tokens of social change are the ubiquitous flags, posters, badges and party emblems, and also, no less significant, habits of dress, the ever-presence of armed detachments in civilian garb throughout the cityscape and the visible remains of anti-clerical actions. In the remainder of this section I will give some additional examples of the impact of visual images which profoundly affected the judgement of foreign observers.

A sea of multi-coloured posters was one picture which awaited the unsuspecting foreigner: 'The revolutionary posters were everywhere, flaming from the walls in clean reds and blues that made the few remaining advertisements look like daubs of mud.'[27] For the pro-Republican Catholic Prince Hubertus Friedrich of Loewenstein 'posters in many colours were the first indications of the new kind of life into which I was about to plunge'.[28] And the description of life in Barcelona by H. Edward Knoblaugh, the correspondent for the Associated Press, is a good example of how staunch conservatives were likewise stirred by the images unfolding before their very eyes:

> The red and black flag of the Anarchists was everywhere – hung from balconies, suspended from cords strung across the thoroughfares and fastened to sticks wired to the fronts of commandeered automobiles. No attempt was being made to police the city. Scowling through their week-old beards, the militia, dressed in blue overalls or simply in denim trousers and dirty shirts, with red and black neckerchiefs about their throats, were as thick as flies. Lounging here and there or speeding through the streets in their requisitioned private cars with the black snouts of submachine guns protruding over the window sills, these Catalonian Anarchists looked fierce enough to startle even the directors of a Hollywood mob scene.[29]

Of course what was interpreted by Knoblaugh as lawlessness and chaos was seen in different ways by less prejudiced observers. Thus Paul Thalmann describes a similar scene, but he concludes, '*Alles sah schrecklich martialisch und doch irgendwie gemütlich aus.* (Everything looked terribly combative yet at the same time somehow easy-going.)'[30]

Walking up and down the Ramblas, the Australian Mary Low noticed the multitude of stands selling party badges:

> There were all kinds and shapes, made out in the initials of the various parties. Some were very attractive – big silver shields, with the sickle and hammer in red, or else in white on a background like a red star, and then squares divided diagonally into black and red, the Anarchist colours. It was astonishing how many different sorts there were, and how many people selling them. I looked round me on the Ramblas. Nearly everybody wore a badge of some kind pinned to his shirt.[31]

Of course, the mere combination of red and black on flags, walls or shoeshine boxes signalled party-political persuasions, and a badge was merely one additional means of expression.[32] Franz Haiderer, for instance, makes a simple equation: 'The streetcars and trucks were all painted red and black. *Alles war anarchistisch, ganz Katalonien.* (Everything was anarchist, all of Catalonia.)'[33] And Rolf Reventlow remembers that 'even the mechanical brooms of the city sanitation department were devoted to the teachings of Michail Bakhunin'.[34]

In his fascinating analysis of clothing styles and social change in the transition from Jacobin Radicalism to Chartism in England, Paul Pickering recently drew the attention of labour historians to the importance of sartorial symbols in the process of working-class radicalization.[35] Similar observations have been made in Barcelona.

George Orwell's recollections are, of course, famous for the description of the prevalence of 'rough working-class clothes, or blue overalls or some variant of the militia uniform',[36] but he was not the only one recording this state of affairs. Jason Gurney, for instance, refers to the popularity of 'the *mono* – a blue denim boiler-suit, a khaki forage cap and a red and black neckerchief'. He goes on to state that 'collars and ties disappeared and everyone considered it wise to adopt a proletarian form of dress. Hats, other than the militia forage cap, had disappeared.'[37] Borkenau's observations were very similar:

> No more well-dressed young women and fashionable senoritos on the Ramblas! Only working men and working women; no hats even! The Generalitat, by wireless, had advised people not to wear them, because it might look "bourgeois" and make a bad impression. The Ramblas are not less colourful than before, because there is the infinite variety of blue, red, black, of the party badges, the neckties, the

fancy uniforms of the militia. But what a contrast with the pretty shining colours of the Catalan upper-class girls of former days![38]

And even a hostile observer, who railed against the anarchists' disinterest in military uniforms, goes on to admit, 'Of course you could tell an anarchist anywhere, because all anarchists dressed the same way.... You could spot an anarchist from miles off.'[39]

The results of anti-clerical actions were one of the favourite examples cited by conservative observers in order to draw attention to the 'immorality' of this social experiment. H. Edward Knoblaugh 'made a tour of the Barcelona churches and Rightist centres which the Left extremists had pillaged and burned' since his previous visit:

> The statues and paintings had been destroyed or moved, the altars ripped out, the stained-glass windows broken. The burial vaults in the floors of some of the churches had been forced open and the century-old mummified bodies of nuns and priests had been removed from their mouldy resting-places. On the steps of the Carmelite church were arrayed a dozen or more of the skeletons of nuns in standing and reclining postures.[40]

Cedric Salter, the correspondent for the *London Daily Telegraph*, also focuses on the 'sacrilegious' destruction of artistic treasures in a burning church he happened to pass by, and he adds, 'From the high carved stone pulpit an elderly priest swung very slowly to and fro by his sickeningly elongated neck.'[41]

The same situation was interpreted in a very different manner by other eyewitnesses, though without necessarily condoning all aspects of the violence. Thus, Augustin Souchy observed the tendency to transform churches into cooperative workshops, and he reasons, 'Where mass was read, now the love of fellow human beings prevails. What was formerly mysticism is now concrete wellbeing. A work of profound interior and exterior transformation.'[42] But, regardless of what meaning these foreign observers read into what they saw, the focus of their observations was identical. Where conservatives saw destruction, revolutionaries celebrated liberation; hostile observers focused on demolition, supporters of anti-clerical actions on construction. Both paid equal attention to the 'desecrated' place of worship.

One could go on at length citing additional examples of the impact of these and other symbolic acts or representations. Yet the most convincing argument for their strength and their exemplary reflection of events lies in the virtually universal recourse to such imagery on the part of foreign observers describing the return of Barcelona's political and economic life 'to normal abnormality', to use the words of the American Consul General;[43] that is the reflux of social revolution, the waning of the influence of the anarchists, the destruction of the POUM, the gradual dismantling of the 'libertarian infrastructure' and the increasing domination of the Stalinist PSUC.

George Orwell had this to say upon seeing Barcelona in April 1937, five months after his first visit to that city: 'The change in the aspect of the crowd was startling. The militia uniform and the blue overalls had almost disappeared; everyone seemed to be wearing the smart summer suits in which Spanish tailors specialize. Fat prosperous men, elegant women, and sleek cars were everywhere.'[44] Franz Borkenau, when returning to Barcelona in January 1937 after a prolonged visit to the rest of Republican Spain, likewise noticed the absence of

> barricades in the streets; no more cars covered with revolutionary initials and filled with men in red neckties rushing through the town; no more workers in civilian clothes, but rifles on their shoulders; as a matter of fact, very few armed men at all, and those mostly asaltos and guardias in brilliant uniforms; no more seething life around the party centres and no large car-parks before their entries; and the red banners and inscriptions, so shining in August, had faded.[45]

The dispatches to the State Department by the American Consulate in Barcelona constitute the conservative counterpart to Orwell, Borkenau and others. Thus the Consul General expressed relief when he was able to report the presence of 'fewer groups of armed irresponsibles wandering about the streets' and that (in a mass demonstration on 28 February 1937) 'the national Republican flag was more in evidence than it has been for several months'.[46] But the Surrealist and POUM activist Mary Low's description captures the contradictory meaning of these symbolic changes better than others:

> The Catalan flag was [now] carried automatically with the red banners and the black, there were less women mingled among the men going to the front, there were no longer dogs and cats following on the end of a string, or perched on kit-bags. It was all as it should be, and we stood more of a chance of winning the war perhaps,

but meanwhile the chance of winning the revolution was growing gradually fainter.[47]

* * *

For two American newly-weds, Charles and Lois Orr, this experience of the Catalan Revolution came to be a major turning point in their lives. Both had been active in Socialist politics prior to the summer of 1936, and Charles in particular was no newcomer to Leftist activism, having been involved in Socialist Party work in Michigan and Kentucky. Thus their honeymoon, which began sometime in the summer of 1936 and was originally meant to include extensive stays in Europe and India, promised to be no ordinary holiday from the outset. As it happened, however, they never made it to Asia. Their projected short visit to Barcelona turned into a ten-month long adventure, which was only ended by their arrest at the hands of the Stalinist secret police in the wake of the 1937 Barcelona 'May Days', their eventual release and their subsequent departure to France.

The Orrs learned of the outbreak of the civil war in Spain while travelling in Germany. According to one account the couple immediately decided to go to Spain.[48] This is highly unlikely, for it took almost another two months before they hitch-hiked to Perpignan, the major gateway to Catalonia. As they soon found out, however, this was only the beginning of their problems which were not unlike that of many other foreigners flocking to Spain. Their experiences may stand for those of many, if not most, of the foreign observers fascinated by the unfolding of events in the Catalan port city in 1936 and 1937.

Years later Lois Orr recounted their efforts to procure entry into Spain:

> When I learned that my American passport was not enough to get me into Spain I was ready to give up. Later that beautiful Sunday morning I watched the Perpignan People's Front parade under the plane trees. On impulse, I followed the parade to their headquarters, and soon found a kind French socialist to listen to my problems. He very obligingly wrote out a document saying I was a genuine antifascist, signed it and stamped it.

Then, she added, 'I learned that all the border patrols were anarchists who didn't care a hoot about the People's Front.'[49]

As expected the border crossing was not easy. They were first taken to the Figueras Anti-Fascist Committee's Control Committee, where, with the aid of a translator, they convinced the officials in charge to permit entry to Spain. Yet the obligatory border ritual was not over yet. That evening they went drinking with their translator, who became rather talkative and apparently explained too much. The next day the young couple was arrested and hauled before the police on suspicion of being spies. After a further 24 hours, the *Investigació Social* was in the end 'more convinced than ever that we were all right, and we were given an additional stamp to pass to Barcelona'.[50] Forty-three years later Lois Orr writes,

> Once the printed words had jumped from the stamp onto the paper, it was like the working of the Good Forces for the peasants and workers of the revolutionary committees. (...) After the barricades went up July 19, 1936, revolutionaries at village checkpoints and city barrios soon learned the magic anarchist letters CNT-FAI-AIT, the magic socialist letters UGT-PSOE or POUM, and the omnipresent words of power, *El Comité de Control*.[51]

In Barcelona the Orrs rapidly developed contacts with the foreign-language representatives of the anarchists and the POUM. Soon they volunteered their services for the POUM's English-language bulletin and radio broadcasts, and they were allotted a room in the Hotel Falcon, the headquarters of the dissident communist organization in Spain. Finally, in early November Lois Orr received a paying job in the Propaganda Department of the Catalan Regional Government, the Generalitat.

The role of symbolic representations in the process of comprehending an alien environment has already been extensively explored in the preceding pages. It would be redundant to spend much additional time on this particular subject in the description of the experiences of Lois and her husband. A few examples will suffice to prove that her perceptions were not significantly different from those of the other foreign observers.

In mid-November 1936 she made the following statement in a letter to her parents:

> Since we first came here this town has become extremely bourgeois. All these women roaming around in the streets in their fur coats and men in big expensive overcoats and shoes. Where, oh where are the overalls of yesterday? At last our money came, and I was all prepared to buy myself a lovely pair of overalls and a lumberjack, when I suddenly realized that no women were wearing them anymore, and

besides that I have a job in the Generality, where people vie with each other dressing more elaborately, especially the women. Brea made Mary quit wearing her overalls and trouser suits three weeks ago.[52]

Soon thereafter she added a postscript to a letter in hurried writing, underscoring the symbolic significance of military formations in civilian clothes and the atmosphere associated with their presence: 'Just a few minutes ago a column of about 300 French volunteers marched down the Ramblas. Their band was playing the "Internationale", *and was I glad to hear them.*'[53]

In general, Lois Orr had a keen eye for the symbolic language of her Catalan hosts, as in the following description of seemingly insignificant details:

There are, of course, lots of things going on around here that would astonish any 100% American. One is the free way in which the Anarchist trade unions have adopted Popeye as their own pet mascot. In the little stands on the Ramblas everywhere they sell pins, scarves and statues of Popeye waving an anarchist flag of black and red. Betty Boop is also much in favor among the Anarchists, but Mickey Mouse, who is the idol of the people, is so popular that [it] is necessary that he be non-partisan. The anarchists all wear tiny silk triangles instead of neckties, printed red and black with various designs – a victory wreath, pictures of dead comrades, a clenched fist, and, most popular of all, a nude woman.[54]

This passage raises several interesting questions. Why the choice of American cartoon characters as symbols of Leftist empowerment? And what does the apparent ubiquity of symbols degrading to women suggest for the relationship between the sexes in the Catalan Revolution? These issues, however, can be satisfactorily answered only in a full-scale study of the Catalan events themselves, and they will therefore have to go unanswered in the present text.[55]

The real value of Lois' letters[56] lies above all in their richness of detail which permits the reader to capture a larger range of influences on her process of cognition, in addition to the mere perception of visual – and other – symbols. From the study of Lois Orr's letters it becomes quite apparent that, besides the manifold and multi-coloured symbols of the rise and demise of social revolution, the other major determining factor in the shaping of her beliefs was the body of people with whom she shared her everyday life. And in her case, as in that of the great majority of foreigners in Barcelona, it is clear that this key group of individuals was essentially composed of other foreigners like herself, rather than natives of the country and city she was living in at the time.

Thus, in one of her first letters to her family, Lois writes, 'I'm having the time of my life here', and she refers to the stimulating personalities she has recently encountered. Virtually none of her contacts, however, were Spanish or Catalan. Instead, she admiringly describes her acquaintances as 'the cream of the intellectual crop of Germany, and the French and English comrades are all intensely interesting'.[57] More than a month later Charles concurred, 'We like it here, and [we] are building up lots of friends among the foreigners here. But our Spanish & Catalan don't progress.'[58] And so it may very well have been more than an inadvertent expression when Lois mentioned at the beginning of March: 'There have been some nice people around here – English, I mean.'[59]

And, indeed, it would have been utterly surprising had the two American socialists not taken advantage of the extraordinary internationalist vibrancy of Barcelona in the heady days of 1936 and 1937. Immediately upon their arrival in Barcelona, they were fortunate enough to literally run into the president of the American Young People's Socialist League, Ernest Erber, who introduced them to Helmut Ruediger, a leading anarchist theoretician with many useful and interesting connections to Spanish and non-Spanish personalities on the Left.[60] Soon they became acquainted with the German Trotskyist Hans Freund, better known as 'Moulin', who was a key individual in the colourful spectrum of the far-Left political organizations operating in Spain and who was probably responsible for the early disenchantment with Popular Front politics by Lois Orr in particular.[61] Other close friends included a former stage manager for the 'Berliner Stadt-Theater', the anarchist Willi Marckwald and the American Russell Blackwell, who had already accumulated revolutionary credentials during his years in the Mexican Communist Party.

The Orrs likewise used every opportunity to participate in political and cultural events, particularly when they featured famous foreign sympathizers with the Spanish cause. Thus the very day that Moulin was introduced to Lois, 'he took me to a CNT mass meeting at the Olympia Theater to hear Emma Goldman'.[62] They went to hear Erwin Piscator, the German writer and theatre director. And in April 1937 Lois casually mentions that 'Charlie was busy last night introducing John Dos Passos to Nin and Andrade',[63] two key POUM leaders, the former having been Minister of Justice in the Catalan Government for three months in the fall of 1936.

But this extensive reliance on other foreigners as a political and social support group had several severe drawbacks. In December 1936, for instance, Lois described the way opinions were formed amongst foreigners in the teeming Hotel Falcon in the following manner:

> In our hotel, there is a general ignorance as to what is going on, most of the learned comrades can't read Spanish and have great difficulty keeping up on affairs. Each has, usually, one trusted source of information, his "contact" in the POUM, Spanish contact. So we learn by long discussions when each expounds his line, his sources of information, and what he has learned. *Primitive, but effective.*[64]

But the soundness of her conclusion is rather doubtful, particularly since Lois also repeatedly refers to an inherent tendency towards sectarianism on the part of her co-tenants and others in her circle of friends:

> Most of the foreigners here come from little fraction groups that have the whole course of the revolution mapped out according to pp. 293, 277, 231, of CAPITAL, other pages of Engels and Lenin. But, as far as the peculiarities of this revolutionary situation are concerned, that is another question, which doesn't alter the prescribed line.[65]

The very same letter carrying the description of the 'primitive but effective' means of information also alludes to 'life in Hotel Falcon among the most intellectual of the intellectuals – each of whom belongs to some one or two-member fraction – who all have a particular line which they are trying to influence the POUM exec committee to adopt as the only way to save the revolution'.[66] But even without the heavy dose of factional competition which appears to have characterized the foreigners in Hotel Falcon, such a 'system of communication' is severely limited and restricting. The resulting flow of information leaves much room for chance and creates the perfect conditions for unsubstantiated rumours. It is bound to result in inevitable distortions of reality.

The rational kernel of this seemingly bizarre system of communication is, of course, the lack of other more appropriate means of communication, above all the ability to speak, read or write in the language of their host country. And, to take up the case of the Orrs again, this would have meant a certain degree of proficiency in Catalan or, at the very least, Spanish. Awareness of this deficiency is present in many of their letters from the very beginning until the very end of their stay. Thus Lois mentions in October that they would like to make money by engaging in journalism: 'But, you know, it is very hard to find out what is going on here if you cannot speak the language.'[67] In early January she reported that 'I am beginning to pick up a little Spanish, but still very little.'[68] Charles complained in November that he 'can not learn to talk Spanish here. They only speak this funny Catalan stuff.'[69] And his record of progress was slower than one might expect for someone who was able to communicate in French and German (as was Lois, one should add). In mid-March he was finally able 'to talk a little Spanish now – but it is mixed so with Catalan that it makes a funny melange'.[70] One month later Lois still made plans to spend some time by herself in a village 'to learn Catalan, and [to] get to know a little more about the people'.[71]

The linguistic and cultural barrier between foreigner and native is readily apparent in Lois' treatment of Catalan nationalism. Catalonia had for several centuries been the economically most advanced part of the Spanish state and had continuously demanded, if not always retained, a measure of regional autonomy. Less than two years prior to the Orrs' arrival in Barcelona, this Mediterranean industrial centre had seen an emotional and sporadically violent defence of Catalan regionalism, which coincided with the Asturian miners' revolt of 6 October 1934.

But, oblivious to these and other facts of local and regional politics, on 4 February 1937 Lois Orr informed her mother, 'It just occurs to me that if I were a loyal Catalan, I would say Barcelona, Catalonia, and not Spain. However, let it go. These people here are fiends on this subject of Catalanism.' She added, 'This spirit of nationalism has no place in a workers' world, of course.'[72] And in early March she berated her mother who enquired about local habits and customs. Lois noted that 'Catalan culture is only Spanish culture under a different flag' and proudly proclaimed that 'the most important thing about the Catalan workers at this particular moment is not that they wear red hats and drink wine from such funny bottles, but the fact that they are the vanguard of the world working class'.[73]

Apparently, Lois was at this stage quite taken in by the reductionist fervour of her foreign friends and comrades despite her occasional statements to the contrary. Her belief in the universal applicability of 'time-tested' models of how to bring about radical social change outweighed considerations of local political culture and the peculiarities of the Catalan Left. It was only towards the very end of her stay that she began to consider taking an interest in the intricacies of the world around her. On 11 April 1937 she wrote, 'You know, mother, you are right about getting to know the Catalan people. I don't really know them or understand them.' And it was at this point that Lois professed the desire to spend 'a week or more' in the Catalan countryside. But the limited vision and the real dilemma of Lois Orr – and that of others like her–is expressed in the immediately succeeding sentence: 'Of course, it isn't as if I had been spending my time here in a vacuum, because I have learned a tremendous lot about the hearts and lives of the foreigners who travel around – refugees, journalists, these sophisticated people of the Parisian culture, and lots of things.'[74]

For Lois Orr, the Catalan Revolution was still an enigma yet to be fully comprehended by the time she was forced to leave Barcelona ten months after she had arrived. Nevertheless, it was a time of profound politicization for the young American socialist,[75] and not all of this occurred within the vibrant but volatile community of foreign revolutionaries resident in Barcelona. But, as the preceding pages have hopefully made clear, her understanding of social revolution in a foreign land at the time of her residence in Barcelona was limited by several important constraints. In the end, Lois' on-the-spot interpretation of the Catalan Revolution was a curious mixture of first-hand impressions mediated by symbolic acts or representations and second-hand knowledge gained primarily from equally handicapped foreigners.[76]

* * *

While adducing a fair number of examples from published works of foreign observers in the description of the impact of symbols, I have relied on the experience of one particular individual for the study of the role of the social milieu affecting the opinions of foreigners in revolutionary Barcelona. Thus the conclusions to be drawn from the latter section must be even more circumspect than those from the discussion of symbolic communication and social revolution. Not all foreign authors were as linguistically disadvantaged as the Orrs. Few foreign observers were familiar with that particular group of rebels in the Hotel Falcon. And virtually none of them were as young as Lois Orr.

Nonetheless, a close reading of the relevant texts suggests that the case of the Orrs was by no means unusual.[77] Only one of the surveyed authors appears to have mastered Catalan at the time: John Langdon-Davies, the correspondent for the *News Chronicle*. Their individual social and informational support network rarely coincided with that of any of their colleagues, but virtually all of these writers sought out the company of other foreign observers or participants, regardless of the degree of familiarity with the customs of Iberia. And, indeed, it would have been astonishing had they done differently under the circumstances. Thus, the adventures of Lois Orr can be seen as a suitable example of a foreigner's odyssey in a foreign city in turmoil.

What becomes clear, then, in conclusion, is the degree to which the observations by foreigners in Barcelona were shaped by two key determining factors: the language of symbols and the milieu of linguistically isolated foreigners, with the latter further subdivided into numerous subgroups, depending on their political preferences and social contacts. The implications of this involuntary 'choice' of sources are disturbing.

In the previous section I have alluded to the limitations arising from reliance on the views of other outsiders. The unsatisfactory and restricting role of symbols is evidenced by the simple juxtaposition of varying interpretations of similar images; for instance, the descriptions of the anarchist militia by H. Edward Knoblaugh and Paul Thalmann referred to above, or the divergent views of anti-clerical actions. For there is no necessary link between the perception of identical symbols and the ensuing interpretation of the corresponding reality which gave rise to these symbols in the first place.

Symbols and foreigners' enclaves, the two most common sources of understanding of an alien environment, play a key role in the political acculturation of foreign observers. This constitutes the central finding of this chapter. But these factors do not necessarily bring about a uniform understanding of events. The image of unshaven, mono-clad, gun-wielding individuals in red and black vehicles inevitably impresses upon even the least suspecting foreigner that something profoundly different and extraordinary is under way. Yet this awareness of the unusual does not automatically translate into a matching perception of reality. Symbols and debates among foreigners are the key sources of understanding; without them most foreigners would be hopelessly adrift. But they can only aid in the scratching of the surface. They may, perhaps, even reinforce prior prejudices and foregone conclusions.

The Barcelona of 1936 and 1937, of course, constitutes only one example of social revolution. Thus it would be extremely helpful to carry out similar analyses of other circumstances. The Russian and French revolutions are only two of the most well known and well documented cases of social upheaval witnessed by scores of foreign observers.[78] Only by the extension of the survey to other cases will it be possible to substantiate or relativize the above conclusions.

An important subject matter, which I have so far consciously neglected to address, is the reason for the prominence of *some* symbols, given the multitude of visual images which, perhaps, could have served a similar function. In some cases one need not search very far or analyse very deep. But in general, it would take a much greater familiarity with the customs and the habits of daily life in Catalonia than I can lay claim to in order to venture forth more than semi-educated guesses.

After all, this study has not been concerned with illuminating how the native population formed its opinion, and the role of neighbourhoods, friendship networks or visual images in this process. This would undoubtedly be a work of great interest, yet it is a topic beyond the scope of this chapter. One of the main concerns has been, instead, to suggest the particular appropriateness of studying the political acculturation process of foreign observers, when trying to gauge the role of visual symbols in the process of cognition. For, as has been repeatedly stated, these individuals are more likely to rely on texts other than written or spoken words in their efforts to understand their immediate environment.

The importance of unspoken and unwritten texts suggests one further message. The trend towards 'discourse analysis' within history will undoubtedly result in a further upgrading of the status of 'texts' in works to come. In and of itself this development is highly welcome and long overdue. Yet, if the current crop of writings on history and language is any indication, there looms the inherent danger that historians will give preference to only one, or perhaps two, particular species of texts: the written version, which, conveniently, is also the most familiar one; and the spoken form. Gareth Stedman Jones' *Languages of Class*[79] remains the most prominent early indication of such a trend. Peter Schoettler's recent article 'Historians and Discourse Analysis'[80] constitutes one of the most theoretically astute but equally unidimensional attempts to place exclusive emphasis on written texts as the privileged pathways to new insights.

Of course, when pressed for more exact definitions, discourse analysis advocates may proclaim innocence from this charge and underscore, as do Ernesto Laclau and Chantal Mouffe, 'that by discourse we do not mean a combination of speech and writing, but rather that speech and writing are themselves but internal components of discursive totalities'.[81] And a number of authors, such as Lynn Hunt,[82] have successfully integrated a great variety of 'texts' into their analysis of crucial political conjunctures.

But the future will tell which categories of texts will become the preferred focus of attention by discourse analysts within the discipline of history. This study of visual images in revolutionary Barcelona, however, has hopefully shown that the necessary concern over texts must go beyond the mere preoccupation with one or two subcategories, or it will lose in depth what it may gain in technical sophistication. It would, indeed, be a major loss if the new dimension of textual analysis within history would become a limited and limiting experience similar to the passing vogue for psychohistory.

Notes

1. I include the qualifying caveat because it is clear that the mass media are vastly more influential policy shapers than memoirs and political travelogues. But what follows holds true, to a large extent, for the mass media as well, since several authors surveyed in this study were either part-time or full-time correspondents for foreign newspapers or tried to use journalism as an occasional source of income during their stay in Spain.
2. Clifford Geertz, *Local Knowledge* (New York: Basic Books, 1983), p. 58.
3. Apart from the openly partisan and somewhat uncritical accounts by Frank Mintz, *L'Autogestion dans l'Espagne révolutionnaire* (Paris: La Découverte, 1976), and Gaston Leval, *Collectives in the Spanish Revolution* (London: Freedom Press, 1975), the best works on the Catalan and Aragonese revolution are Walther Bernecker, *Anarchismus und Bürgerkrieg: Zur Geschichte der Sozialen Revolution in Spanien 1936–1939* (Hamburg: Hoffmann & Campe, 1978); Burnett Bolloten, *The Spanish Revolution* (Chapel Hill: University of North Carolina Press, 1979), who is particularly lucid on the implication of the revolutionaries' military policy; and Pierre Broué and Emile Témime, *The Revolution and the Civil War in Spain* (Cambridge: MIT Press, 1972). The latter volume is the best introduction to this topic from the overall perspective of social upheaval in the midst of civil war. A recent, more specialized study of one particular aspect is Julián Casanova, *Anarquismo y revolución en la sociedad rural aragonesa, 1936–1938* (Madrid: Siglo XXI, 1985).
4. Noam Chomsky, 'Objectivity and Liberal Scholarship', in *American Power and the New Mandarins* (New York: Pantheon, 1967), pp. 23–158.
5. But this is symptomatic of virtually all writings on Spain under the Popular Front. Thus, even the historian Hywel Francis commits the 'error' of categorizing the Barcelona 'May Days' of 1937 as a 'POUM rising', 47 years after this myth was first propounded and exposed; see Hywel Francis, *Miners Against Fascism: Wales and the Spanish Civil War* (London: Lawrence and Wishart, 1984), p. 229.
6. Patrik von zur Mühlen, *Spanien war ihre Hoffnung: Die deutsche Linke im spanischen Bürgerkrieg 1936 bis 1939* (Berlin: Dietz, 1985), p. 15 and passim.
7. Frigga Haug, 'Memory Work', in Frigga Haug et al. (eds), *Female Sexualization: A Collective Work of Memory* (London: Verso, 1987), p. 40; emphasis added.
8. Willy Brandt, *Links und frei: Mein Weg 1930–1950* (Hamburg: Hoffmann & Campe, 1982), pp. 217–218.
9. John Langdon-Davies, *Behind the Spanish Barricades* (New York: McBride, 1936), p. 90. All but the last ellipses are in the original text.

10. University of Michigan Library, Labadie Collection, Emma Goldman Collection of Papers – Emma Goldman, 'My Second Visit to Spain: September 16th–November 6th, 1937', typescript (4 March 1938), p. 1. In the quotation Goldman reminisces about her first visit to Republican Spain.
11. Paul Thalmann, *Wo die Freiheit stirbt* (Olten: Walter, 1974), p. 133.
12. Fenner Brockway, *Workers' Front* (London: Secker and Warburg, 1938), pp. 91–92.
13. Rolf Reventlow, *Spanien in diesem Jahrhundert: Bürgerkrieg, Vorgeschichte und Auswirkungen* (Vienna: Europa, 1968), p. 141.
14. Thalmann, *Freiheit*, pp. 133–134.
15. 'Interview mit Franz Haiderer', in Dokumentationsarchiv des österreichischen Widerstands (ed.), *Für Spaniens Freiheit: Österreicher an der Seite der Spanischen Republik* (Vienna: Österreichischer Bundesverlag, 1986), p. 122.
16. 'Bericht von Josef Schneeweiss über seine Fahrt nach Spanien', in Dokumentationsarchiv, *Spaniens Freiheit*, p. 52.
17. Walter Gregory, *The Shallow Grave* (London: Gollancz, 1986), pp. 26–27.
18. Jason Gurney, *Crusade in Spain* (London: Faber and Faber, 1974), p. 52.
19. Mary Low and Juan Breá, *Red Spanish Notebook: The First Six Months of the Revolution and the Civil War* (San Francisco: City Lights, 1979), p. 20.
20. George Orwell, *Homage to Catalonia* (New York: Harcourt, Brace, 1952), p. 5.
21. Frank Borkenau, *The Spanish Cockpit* (Ann Arbor: University of Michigan Press, 1963), p. 69.
22. Langdon-Davies, *Spanish Barricades*, p. 116.
23. Borkenau, *Cockpit*, p. 70.
24. 'Bericht von Josef Schneeweiss', p. 53.
25. Gurney, *Crusade*, p. 47.
26. Gregory, *Shallow Grave*, p. 27.
27. Orwell, *Homage*, p. 5.
28. Prince Hubertus Friedrich of Loewenstein, *A Catholic in Republican Spain* (London: Victor Gollancz, 1937), p. 20.
29. H. Edward Knoblaugh, *Correspondent in Spain* (London: Sheed & Ward, 1937), p. 33.
30. Thalmann, *Freiheit*, p. 135.
31. Low and Breá, *Notebook*, pp. 21–22.
32. However, the Englishman Sir Peter Chalmers Mitchell learned the value of a badge and other symbolic means of communication when briefly arrested by the anarchist militia in Malaga. He was told to wear a British badge on his coat and was taught 'the various salutes, so that all would be well with persons who did not recognise the British badge'. He added, 'It is true that I procured a small Union Jack, and, as often as I remembered, wore it on my jacket when I was on the streets of Malaga, but from that day on I got more friendly greetings than sour looks, and felt quite safe personally, until the Rebels [the Francoist troops] entered'; see Sir Peter Chalmers Mitchell, *My House in Málaga* (London: Faber and Faber, 1938), pp. 118–120.
33. 'Interview mit Franz Haiderer', p. 122.
34. Reventlow, *Spanien*, p. 142.
35. Paul A. Pickering, 'Class Without Words: Symbolic Communication in the Chartist Movement', *Past and Present*, 122 (August 1986), 144–162.
36. Orwell, *Homage*, p. 5.

37. Gurney, *Crusade*, pp. 48–49.
38. Borkenau, *Cockpit*, p. 70.
39. Carl Marzani, in John Gerassi (ed.), *The Premature Antifascists: North American Volunteers in the Spanish Civil War, 1936–39: An Oral History* (New York: Praeger, 1986), p. 146.
40. Knoblaugh, *Correspondent*, p. 32.
41. Cedric Salter, *Try-Out in Spain* (New York: Harper, 1943), p. 20.
42. Augustin Souchy, *With the Peasants of Aragon* (Minneapolis: Soil of Liberty, 1982), p. 97.
43. Cited in James Cortada (ed.), *A City in War: American Views On Barcelona and the Spanish Civil War, 1936–39* (Wilmington: Scholarly Resources, 1985), p. 120. This book with a promising subtitle is essentially composed of nothing but United States Foreign Service communications to the Department of State. As a documentation of official American attitudes to the issues of revolution and civil war, however, they are rather useful, and indicate the hostile stance of Roosevelt's administration.
44. Orwell, *Homage*, pp. 109–110.
45. Borkenau, *Cockpit*, p. 175.
46. Cited in Cortada, *City in War*, pp. 40, 95.
47. Low and Breá, *Notebook*, p. 214.
48. University of Michigan Library, Labadie Collection, Lois and Charles Orr papers (UML LC ORR), Frank L. Denby, 'An Interview with Charles Orr', Paris, 15 July 1937. Typescript in folder: Orr, Charles, Writings 1937 July.
49. UML LC ORR – Lois Orr, *Spain 1936–1939: A Short History of the Spanish Revolution*, unpublished manuscript, 1961, p. 1a.
50. UML LC ORR – Lois Orr to 'Dear Family', 23 September 1936, p. 5. All letters and postcards can be found in various folders labelled 'Correspondence' unless indicated otherwise.
51. UML LC ORR – Lois Orr, *The Anarchist Millenium*, unpublished manuscript, 1979, p. 3.
52. UML LC ORR – Lois Orr to 'Dear Family', 12 November 1936. The reference to 'Brea' and 'Mary' allude to Mary Low and Juan Breá, authors of the *Red Spanish Notebook*, repeatedly quoted above. Mary Low was a close friend of Lois Orr, who worked together with her in the offices of the POUM and the Generality.
53. UML LC ORR – Lois Orr to 'Family', 30 November 1936, p. 10; emphasis added.
54. UML LC ORR – Lois Orr, unaddressed letter fragment, in file: Outgoing Correspondence, September–October 1936.
55. On the gender issue, see also Lois' reference to the abundance of pornographic material: 'Oh, these pamphlets tho! Nude nuns and dreadfully lewd looking priests, and everyone you see on a street car or in a park, men, women and children are reading the tripe.' UML LC ORR – Lois Orr to 'Dear daddy', 2 November 1936, p. 3. For some stimulating comments on a matter which may, perhaps, throw some light on the seemingly paradoxical role of American cartoon characters in Catalan politics, see chapter 8 on 'The Dialectics of Symbolic Inversion' in Bruce Lincoln, *Discourse and the Construction of Society* (New York: Oxford University Press, 1989), particularly pp. 142–148.

56. The vast bulk of the Orr papers in the University of Michigan Library's Labadie Collection are letters which Lois wrote to friends and family. As she stated later, 'at nineteen I was a prodigious letter writer, and my victims preserved innumerable pages of stream-of-consciousness writing, more than enough to make up for the equally numerous pages lost when the Russians confiscated my journals and diaries in 1937'. UML LC ORR – p. 9 of unpaginated 'Preface' to Lois Orr, *Spain 1936–1939*.
57. UML LC ORR – Lois Orr to her family, 30 September 1936, p. 6.
58. UML LC ORR – Charles Orr to 'Dear Folks', 8 December 1936, p. 1.
59. UML LC ORR – Lois Orr to 'Dear Family', 4 March 1937, p. 1. One of these 'nice people' was Eileen Blair, George Orwell's wife, who worked under Charles Orr in the English-language department of the POUM. The nominal head of this bureau was John McNair of the British Independent Labour Party.
60. UML LC ORR – Lois Orr, *Anarchist Millenium*, p. 14. On the significance of Helmut Ruediger as an incisive critic of anarchist theory and practice from within the ranks of the anarchist movement, see Mühlen, *Spanien war ihre Hoffnung*, pp. 110–111 and passim.
61. See the countless references to Moulin throughout her letters and her 1961 comment: 'Without saying much, Moulin really took my political education in hand'; UML LC ORR – Lois Orr, *Spain 1936–1939*, p. 17. Moulin became one of the victims of GPU liquidationism after the Barcelona 'May Days'.
62. UML LC ORR – Lois Orr, *Spain 1936–1939*, p. 17.
63. UML LC ORR – Lois Orr to her family, 29 April 1937, p. 15.
64. UML LC ORR – Lois Orr to 'Dear Orrs', 14 December 1936, p. 1; emphasis added.
65. UML LC ORR – Lois Orr to 'Dear Family', 4 February 1937, p. 2.
66. UML LC ORR – Lois Orr to 'Dear Orrs', 14 December 1936, p. 1.
67. UML LC ORR – Lois Orr to 'Dear Family', 7 October 1936, p. 8.
68. Ibid., 4 January 1937, p. 3.
69. UML LC ORR – Charles Orr to 'Dear Culters', 10 November 1936, pp. 10–11.
70. UML LC ORR – Charles Orr to 'Dear Mother', 10 March 1937, postcard.
71. UML LC ORR – Lois Orr to 'Dear Mother and Daddy', 11 April 1937, p. 2.
72. UML LC ORR – Lois Orr to 'Dear Family', 4 February 1937, p. 1.
73. UML LC ORR – Lois Orr to her mother, 7 March 1937, pp. 2–3.
74. UML LC ORR – Lois Orr to 'Dear Mother and Daddy', 11 April 1937, p. 2.
75. Charles, who was about ten years older than the 19-year-old Lois, at one point gave this somewhat paternalistic glimpse of her political maturation in Barcelona: 'She has a tendency to go to extremes when she gets a new interest or theory – it sometimes seems to conservative old me. But she learns quickly. You should hear her worry about the world political situation! The role of the Anarchists in the revolution, marriage theory, dress, beards, sur-realism and a hundred things I never thought about before'; UML LC ORR – Charles Orr to 'Dear Culters', 10 November 1936, p. 12.
76. In the following years and decades, Lois Orr continued her engagement with politics and with Spain. She improved her Catalan and Spanish, worked on behalf of Spanish political prisoners and, finally, wrote an extremely

thoughtful (yet still unpublished) study of the Spanish Revolution. Three versions of her manuscript are extant in the Orr papers, two of which I have quoted repeatedly in the preceding chapters.
77. And lest it be feared that Lois Orr, in 1936, was only a young, naive and bungling American in search of simple adventure – and, therefore, unrepresentative of other foreigners – here is a recent judgement by the then-POUM activist and co-author of the *Red Spanish Notebook*, Mary Low: 'Lois Orr was certainly a good friend of mine, and a far better-prepared Marxist and revolutionary than I could ever hope to be' – Letter from Mary Low Machado to author, 8 October 1988. For another assessment of Lois (and Charles), see Ernest Erber's impression of the couple as 'extraordinarily honest persons'. But, whereas Charles appeared more mature, 'Lois might have been the more talented and intelligent of the two.' However, Ernest Erber also recalls an incident early in Lois' period of residence in Barcelona when she showed him an article she had written for her college paper, which Erber found 'embarrassingly naïve'. Letter from Ernest Erber to author, 23 June 1989.
78. And, indeed, it appears that some key architects of the French Revolution were acutely aware of the impact of symbols on foreign perceptions of social revolution, for one of the considerations for the design of major representative structures was their potential impact on visitors from abroad; see Mona Ozouf, *La fête révolutionnaire, 1789–1799* (Paris: Gallimard, 1976), p. 159.
79. Gareth Stedman Jones, *Languages of Class* (Cambridge: Cambridge University Press, 1983).
80. Peter Schoettler, 'Historians and Discourse Analysis', *History Workshop Journal*, 27 (Spring 1989), 37–65.
81. Ernesto Laclau and Chantal Mouffe, 'Post-Marxism without Apologies', *New Left Review*, 166 (1987), 82.
82. Lynn Hunt, *Politics, Culture, and Class in the French Revolution* (Berkeley: University of California Press, 1984).

Illustration 1 Large excerpt from *Barcelona*

Illustration 2 Large excerpt from *Barricades*

Illustration 3 Large excerpt from *The Defense of the Faith*

Illustration 4   Large excerpt from *To the Front*

Illustration 5   Large excerpt from *Trade Unions*

Illustration 6 Live Forces (Fuerzas Vivas)

Illustration 7 The League of Nations

Illustration 8 Large excerpt from *Arrival of Soviet Smoke* (*Llegada del humo soviético*), or *Up in Soviet Smoke*

Illustration 9 The Trade Union Leader and His Wife

Illustration 10 Large excerpt from *May '37*, or *The Barcelona May Days*

Illustration 11   Passage to France

Illustration 12   'Celebrating Franco' – Excerpt from *L'Uruguay*

4
Letters from Barcelona (Autumn)

This first section of letter excerpts covers the period ranging from 21 September to 14 December 1936. This autumn season may well be regarded as the heroic and optimistic period of the Catalan Revolution, although signs of reflux of the revolutionary fervour characteristic of these months were plentiful – and are duly noted in Lois' letters. Shortly after the arrival of the Orrs in Barcelona, the Catalan government underwent a reorganization, broadening the ruling coalition to include for the first time the dissident communist POUM and the anarchist CNT. Lois' letters are brimming with enthusiasm as the future appeared promising for the cause of revolutionary change which was uppermost in the young woman's mind. Adding to the dizzying circumstances of Catalan politics were a series of often chance encounters with other foreign revolutionaries visiting Barcelona for varying lengths of time.

A number of wonderfully evocative passages in Lois' letters convey the exalting spirit of those days. Everything seemed possible at the time, and the free-flowing accounts tell the story of a social revolution in the making, which the young couple are in perfect position to observe from the vantage point of their room in the headquarters of the POUM on the Ramblas in the heart of Barcelona. Yet, as the autumn months proceed, the observant sympathizers of radical politics have increasing recourse to cautionary remarks. Soon after their arrival, Lois considered purchasing the informal 'uniform' of the mono, a dark blue overall suit worn by supporters of the revolution. But on 12 November 1936 Lois lamented, 'Where, oh where are the overalls of yesterday?' Translating this symbolic marker into straightforwardly political terms, Lois observed on 14 December, 'The situation here is somewhat confusing now. The war drags on but the revolution doesn't make much progress.' And it was not only revolutionary politics which appeared to be cooling down. As autumn turned into winter, given the absence of proper heating in most

Barcelona houses at that time, Lois quipped that 'the only only place you can be really comfortable, all good revolutionaries agree, is in bed'.

1. Postcard written by Charles Orr to his mother, Emma Orr, on 21 September 1936

We are here almost a week now – the most interesting experience we ever had.[1] Through Ernest Erber,[2] President of the Young People's Socialist League,[3] we have been able to make all contacts – the envy of the journalists here! I may get a job here doing statistics for the Catalonian Government. But do not be concerned for our safety, as all is perfectly orderly. We wander about at 2 am with no danger. And France is not far away.

These cards[4] designed by a French woman are sold for the *Milicias Antifascistas*, who are the de facto government. We just heard Emma Goldman[5] speak.

2. Letter written by Lois (and Charles) to her family on 23 September 1936

I guess it's about time you got a letter. The last time I wrote was from Marseilles. Then we didn't know exactly what we were going to do – At least we weren't at all sure that we would be able to do it – We hitchhiked up through – rather down through – the southern part of France. Provence. It is quite a lovely country. The roads are lined for miles with plane trees and all they grow in that country is grapes. For wine, of course. The towns, on the whole, are a barren lot – yellow blank house fronts on a narrow street – and quite uninteresting as a whole. Aix was nice though.

We came up to Perpignan – where we made contacts with the local popular front, trying to get papers going into Spain. We had, of course, no identification cards as members of the Socialist Party because in Germany, Italy or British India they wouldn't be any help at all. We needed a pass or identification-as-a-friend card of some sort to get past the militia *comités* on the border and everywhere else. We finally found a secretary of the popular front who gave us a [illegible] to a border officer in Spain. So on a rainy Tuesday[6] we crossed into Spain. Because we didn't have many documents on us, we were sped in an official car – all automobiles have been confiscated – to Figueras where we were taken into the *Control Guerra*[7] of the local Anti-Fascist Committee.

I might explain to you that all over Catalonia Anti-Fascist Committees have been set up. These consist of representatives from all the workers' organisations in proportion to their strength: CNT... FAI... UGT... also the Socialist Party and Communist Party and Left Republican bourgeois parties are represented. These committees work, as far as I can discover, in conjunction with the ordinary government. There exist various branches of the Anti-Fascist Committees – police, transportation, passes, propaganda, sanitation, industry, control. The workers have taken over and reorganized transportation and other big industries. The stores, cafes, etc., remain still mostly in private hands. The public buildings, hotels, theaters and movie houses have been put under social control. Here in Barcelona, since July 17, a war industry has been established.

Oh, to get back. In Figueras Tuesday night we went to a play put on by the local entertainment department for the benefit of the militias at the front. The *milicià* who had translated (Spanish–French) for us at the *Control Guerra* took us. Unfortunately the dialogue was in Catalan which we could of course not understand. It was a 3-act drama of motherlove and fascism. This *milicià* began to explain to us all about his various gun permits, trade union cards, etc., and on the whole was too informative – the next day observers reported the whole thing and we were taken before the police – *Investigació Social*. We soon convinced them that we had not learned anything important and that we were good comrades. However it was necessary to remain an additional 24 hours in Figueras to have our journals, letters, etc., translated. After that they were more convinced than ever that we were all right and we were given an additional stamp to pass to Barcelona. [...]

We got to Barcelona on the train Thursday. We established connections with the press dept. of the *Generalitat* and got press cards – through a German woman refugee, of whom there are many there, helping with the war – Communists, Socialists and Anarchists. Luckily, we stumbled upon Ernest Erber (there in the press and propaganda bureau), president of the Young People's Socialist League of America. He had been to the Youth Congress at Geneva[8] – with which he was thoroughly disgusted – where he had met some anarchist youth. They brought him back with them. He helped us establish our identity. He has a lot of good contacts with the various organisations here, which he passed on to us – [...]

We have a room in a little pension down near the harbor for 7 pesetas a day each – We are going to get another one tho. The food is grand and our room is nice and clean with a big window – balcony. But it lacks running water, bathroom and other American conveniences that we rather demand. Our regular meals consist of soup – spaghetti, or

Boston beans or cabbage – the last [illegible] of which you eat with olive oil and which are grand – sometimes the beans are in a tomato sauce and sometimes just cooked in butter – or fried patties of potatoes which are creamed somehow and cooked in bread crumbs – then after that (our second course) – we get beef cooked in tomato sauce or with peppers – or else meat and potatoes – and salad of tomatoes and green stuff. Then fruit and of course wine. Incidentally – tell daddy I don't smoke at all – I didn't anyhow, you know, pop.

All that stuff you read about night violence in Barcelona is the bunk. The hours here are late – breakfast is served from 9–10 – lunch from 2–3 and dinner from 8–9 – so that puts C. and me out late whenever we go – as we did Saturday to hear Emma Goldman at an Anarchist meeting – but we've never seen or heard a thing out of the ordinary.

Keep on writing us to AmexCo, Marseilles, as they have complete instructions how to keep in touch with us. Incidentally, it was originally my idea to come to Spain, and don't you all worry about us because we are perfectly safe. Everything is orderly and normal here and well-controlled. [. . .]

Well, this is a terrible country to bring Lois to – she got all mosquito bites here![9] But otherwise all is orderly enough, and now we have bought and sewed together some mosquito netting, so that danger is about over [addendum in Lois' handwriting: 'They were flea bits, we discovered, not mosquitoes.'] The fact is, we never were in a more interesting situation, where one can see tremendous social change at a visible pace. The spirit of the people is at a high pitch – so that one can scarcely see how they can be beat. In some parts, as here in Catalonia, the social revolution has already advanced a step – but nothing very complete as yet. The abolition of clerical schools is perhaps the most important step, aside from the assumption of government in fact by the (United Front) Anti-fascist committees.

We are studying the structure and extent of the movement with a view to writing magazine articles on it. We can write them up on board ship, since we sail from Marseilles Oct. 10. We will be here till about Oct. 5. [. . .] [M]ost of the summer we sat along either muddy or dusty roads wishing a car would come along. Now we run around trying to interview and meet big shots in the revolution here – [. . .] [H]ere every party has its [radio] station. We were up in the Anarchist one – in the new Chamber of Commerce Building – which they have seized. They got the most and best here – cars, trucks, hotels + buildings. They send one series of harangues over the air – people gather in the street down in front to listen. Our friend Erber speaks in English over them. [. . .]

3. Letter written by Lois to her family, begun on 27 September and ended on 30 September 1936

I have a lot to tell you. Here in Barcelona, I think I already explained something to you about the political situation. After the days of street fighting in July, there was a Comité of anti-fascist militias set up because the Anarchists refused to participate in any bourgeois government. So there was dual power between the Generalitat and the Comités. Just the last couple of days the anarchists have agreed to enter a cabinet which of course is much against this principle. The POUM, which is against the idea of fighting or working for a bourgeois democracy – it is revolutionary marxist and believes that the workers should fight fascism at the front and the other forms of bourgeois domination at the rear – has also refused hitherto to participate in any cabinets of the bourgeois Generality. Just the other day tho, the cabinet of the Generality was reorganized and the anarchists and POUM entered it with the Socialists, Communists and left bourgeois parties. The program of the cabinet is a socialist one, but some of us are still wondering about this. The PSUC is not revolutionary; it is fighting for a bourgeois democracy because, if a Socialist State is established in Spain, it will have repercussions in Europe which may upset the status quo and seriously harm Soviet Russia – forcing her to fight, etc. So the followers of Marx & Lenin here are sacrificing the revolution to Soviet Russia; in other words, in the common parlance around here, they are dirty Stalinists. The PSUC, however, does not have a mass following in Catalonia. It is the anarchists who are the key as to whether the revolution will succeed here or not. They are of course revolutionaries, but they refuse to work within the forms of the bourgeois government here, and also so far have refused to establish new forms of their own. [...]

Meanwhile Charlie and I have a room in the Hotel Falcón which has been taken over by the POUM to house its militia and other retainers. We are working for the POUM English press and radio department. The only other person in it is Mary Breá[10] – an English girl who is married to a Cuban. But I am sleepy now and am going to bed.

We eat our meals at POUM free – all is free.[11] In the once elegant dining room of the hotel. Now there are two servings of each meal – 200 or so people at each. The table is set with fork – some are wooden – spoon if there is soup – bread and wine glasses. The meal itself consists of two dishes and fruit for desert, and wine. [...]

All the mail going out and coming into Spain is opened – but we can send ours out uncensored by the POUM post, which sends a car over into France twice a week to mail letters. POUM does not believe in censorship. [...]

Oh, I started to tell you – we have meat and fish every meal and one other vegetable or soup. It's a very substantial diet, needless to say – and the food is quite good. As Mary says, the manager of our hotel is quite a genius at requisitioning and if, as is very likely, there is a food shortage in Barcelona this winter, we won't have to worry. Of course the militias and political organisations come first in matters of food etc. And that means us.

Our job here consists of translating articles from *La Batalla*, POUM's paper, to be read in English over the radio, and preparing and sending out POUM's English Bulletin – which will soon be printed instead of mimeographed as it is now. Charlie is looking for a more serious job – this one keeps us busy from 10 am till 8 pm. The whole of Catalan industry is being reorganised on a socialist basis and there is a great need for anybody who knows statistics or methods of questionnaires etc etc. But CNT, which is running the business, doesn't want to use C, because a) he is a socialist and b) he is an American. But – we just learned that Toledo has fallen and –

I'm having the time of my life here – the people, of course, are the cream of the intellectual crop of Germany, and the French and English comrades are all intensely interesting.[12] Last night we met by accident an American from N.Y. who has been at the front ever since the war broke out. He was studying medicine in Switzerland then, as he could not get into an American university. We went – with him and Mary and Erber to see *Chapaiev*, a swell Russian movie,[13] for 3 cents a seat. There was also a French dramatisation of one of the books of Zola's series. The one before *Nana*, about her mother. It was quite sordid, naturally, but well produced and acted – Especially the part where Nana's stepfather has D.T.[14] and dies in a padded cell. (!!!)

Charlie and I just wrote (yes, today) to our ship company, asking for our tickets to be changed from Oct. 10 to December – as we want to stay here in Barcelona and work. POUM has just requisitioned an office for its foreign propaganda staff – an architect's office, with suboffices etc etc. Very well with wooden panelling on the walls, big carved desks etc etc. That, incidentally, is where this paper came from.[15] The people are scared to come back and get their papers and stuff – tho they are supposed to take everything away but the essential office equipment. They were subdivision creators etc. It really is a lot of fun being a revolutionary when your side is on top.

Of course, the govt, the Communist Party & Soc. Party here are trying to make out that this is a war to save democracy, but all the milicians who are going to the front to get their arms legs heads etc shot off don't have any illusions. They are fighting for a social revolution and not to save some bourgeois republican govt which would give right back to the capitalists the factories, railroads, buildings that they have claimed as their own.

Please for goodness sake don't worry about us. This is a gloriously exciting place to be – the morale and spirit are high and of course it is the most interesting spot in the world at this particular moment. And quite safe. I have a notion that the gov't is going to be [illegible], but if anything bad happens, C. and I plan to go to France and wait our lot. We can live there quite cheaply since the devaluation.

Annie, you would be tremendously interested in the posters being done here. Some, especially the CNT ones are very artistic. C. is making a collection and having them sent back to America. Why don't you write me a letter yourself? Haven't you gotten the dress I sent you from Germany yet? I'm wondering if anything happened to it. Love to you all, and I'll write again soon.

4. *Letter written by Lois to her family on 7 October 1936*

So just this afternoon we found out that we are going to stay a couple of months more in Spain. We wrote to our boat company three times, asking them to transfer our sailing to a later date, but had no answer from them. This morning I went over to the P.O. to send a telegram; I was directed to go to the Cable Bilboa Co. on the 2nd floor to see if I had received any answer to the letters. There I found a couple of English conservatives fuming because they had to work in Spain. I didn't tell them any of my politics of course, and they were very nice to me. Sent a long cable to the [illegible] Co. free, sent the answer back to here, and then another cable giving our instructions to the Co. – all gratis of course, all cables are supposed to be sent thro the gov't office, but as this private co. owns the lines & equipment, it is still allowed to function. And of course their wires are open to the executives and their friends. The ship co. had received instructions from London that we were not sailing and are holding our tickets for us.

Of course, we want to stay here a while now. Free room and board and we are right in the middle of making history. I s'pose, daddy, you never [illegible] that I'd really be helping to remake the world. Tho of course this is only a small part of the world, and, besides, what we are making may eventually be torn down. We don't know.

Incidentally, Moulin[16] (I don't remember if I told you of him or not – he is a German refugee journalist friend of Erber's, a POUM man) is now in Madrid and wants us to come there to work on POUM's English broadcasts which he has to do, and he can hardly speak English. We are not going tho, because we have a job here, and because we think that Madrid will be cut and besieged before long. We don't know, of course. It's hard to get news here; when anything bad happens for the government they stop foreign newspapers from coming in. When Toledo fell it wasn't in our papers and foreign newspapers were prohibited for a week – [...]

My new stationery is from our new office. Our typewriters there are very bad, tho. Did I tell you about Erber's German refugee friend who is now an officer of CNT and who broke up a big Nazi spy ring here in Barcelona after the rebellion? He got a lot of new typewriters among other equipment incl. Nazi uniforms from them. (This is not general knowledge as it would probably frighten the population into a German scare.)

The official milicians' uniform around here is a very dark blue overall suit. All the women at POUM have them too, but I understand that they have quit issuing them now. I guess I'll buy myself one of them, because we only brought my little suitcase and a raincoat bundle of things in here with us. [...]

They have evidently run out of requisitioning wine here, because we only get one glass once a day, and sometimes none at all. But otherwise the food is very good and we get quite too much. Charlie makes a habit of getting seconds of whatever soup or vegetable we get. Incidentally, you might tell your wonderful Willie B. to try cooking potatoes (peeled) and cauliflower together in olive oil. It is very delicious as done here. They also have some little pinkish yellow beans this shape and size [a drawing accompanies these lines], which they serve in olive oil and which are also quite delicious.

Of course there is talk of giving everybody working for the POUM a milician's wage of 10 pesetas a day (80 cents) which would be very swell – as C. & I can have a good Pension for 7.50 pesetas a day for everything (2 bottles of wine each meal, but not coffee afterwards. That is 3 cents extra a meal) included – apiece, which would leave us a little for extras – not much.

Yesterday was the anniversary of the October revolt[17] – you remember – it only held out in the Asturias – and we had parades all morning long – from 9–2:30. CNT and the anarchists were not there as they did not participate in this revolt – (probably) believing it an insincere one.[18] Now are they sorry. Our office has a balcony right above that of the POUM exec. committee – on the Ramblas, and were we much political!

POUM's delegations from Valencia carried the banner 'War on the Front and Revolution behind the Lines.'

All of which must seem very far off and strange to you. You seem very far off to me, but when I read your letters about the familiar places and people, I don't feel so far away. Daddy, your letters are swell. I get homesick invariably after I read them, which may or may not be a sign they're 'good' – but anyhow I love 'em. [...]

Mother, C. and I are working hard on magazine articles and are trying to make a little money that way. I did one rather superficial thing for the *Cardinal*.[19] But you know, it is very hard to find out what is going on here if you cannot speak the language. The most important changes, of course, are the economic, and that is why I am trying to get us jobs in the Economic Council, which is directing the economic reorganisation of Catalonian industry. I don't know what we'll be able to do tho.

Barcelona is an old, dirty, picturesque city.

We just this minute got up from dinner; we were talking to a Frenchman who was asking us – rather telling us – about America.[20] He said he had a friend who was there and he said the food was very poor, and besides every time he went into a hotel they must know if he and his companion are married etc etc which he considered very uncivilised. In France, all you have to do is fill out a typewritten page of questions in every hotel for the police – ages, place of birth, mother's name. [...]

Note for the ladies only: There are practically the same modern conveniences here (in the way of Kotex etc) as in America. There are always local versions of 'ladies bands' as they are called which are the same as we use in America. Only here in Spain they happen to be made of cotton. I get the curse ok and you would have died to see – when we were being investigated in Figueras – the milician nosing into our contraceptives. He couldn't make head or tails out of it. Love to everybody and write soon.

P.S. Billy, are you going to play in the Thanksgiving game? Over here they call football 'rugby' and soccer 'football.'

5. *Letter written by Lois to her sister Anne on 14 and 15 October 1936*

Of course if I were with you all the time I wouldn't be so affectionate, but since I'm not, I am.

There are two sisters in the Hotel Falcón that make me think of us. Why, I don't exactly know, because they don't resemble us in the least except for the fact that they are sisters. They are Germans; their father[21] leads a group in the International Lenin Column, which is now, I think, at the Madrid Front. It is the column of POUM men which took Mount Aragon – mostly foreigners and A-1 soldiers. Their mother is a tall short-haired pretty, but quite plain looking woman and she works with her daughters in the German section of the POUM foreign press. The girls are 15 and 16, I think, or maybe younger. But they look about our age and are of course mature. They speak, as all these educated continentals do, German, English, French and Spanish. The elder one has yellow hair, blue eyes and is quite pretty. They are both rather quiet and reserved – shy, I suppose, and a little out of place among so many adults. She wears the best looking shirts and [illegible] blouses and has quite a figure. The younger one is even more quiet, if possible, has light brown hair and eyes, and wears rather undistinctive clothes. They do the mimeographing of the Bulletins – German, Italian, Dutch.

Because our Bulletin is now printed!! The first issue hasn't come back from the printer yet – the proofs – but as the linotyper is a Spaniard, I can imagine that we are going to have an interesting time of it.

Our room in the Hotel Falcón is clean, has red plush chairs, running water and is quite modern, but not at all homey. The nicest thing about it is that we have a balcony of our own, that we can take our chairs out on at night when we want to look at the sky, or in the day when we want to sit in the sunshine. It is also a very convenient place to hang out clothes etc. Etc means my white shoes which I wash with the greatest of ease whenever necessary.

Our office is very nice, tho. And has quite an atmosphere about it. It is on the Ramblas – which I must have described to you – and whenever we hear drums or an extra amount of noise, we go running out to the balcony in front – Italians, Germans, Dutch and English – to see the parade or whatever go by. Usually, it's the PSUC – the lousy Stalinists – III International (with great fury), and when it is, there are repeated accusations that they keep their men away from the front to parade. Today I heard a tremendous noise of chants or something. It was hundreds of Anarchist women – in locked arms, groups of 10 or 8, marching down the Ramblas after an Anarchist flag, chanting and singing. This morning, a lovely sunny one, we were in our office – which has a big balconied window overlooking somebody's lovely private garden – and we heard all sorts of noises like factory whistles, boat whistles, horns and what not. Vague and quite exciting – so out we all rush to the Ramblas, all look over our balcony. But we just see people walking calmly around in the sunshine – back and forth as always. Later on we found that it was a Russian boat with potatoes *etc (!)*[22] which had been stopped by four Italian battleship outside the 3-mile limit of the harbor. Finally it (or another one maybe) went away to Cartagena – kept inside the 3mi. limit and came back to Barcelona. Anyhow, PSUC was at the harbor with many banners, people etc, taking all possible credit for the Soviet Union, the boat, everything. All of which is very exciting and I don't at all object. I only wish the Soviet Union would send us more guns, cannons, airplanes, etc. The anarchist women were parading about that, I think.

Tonight, after I spoke on the radio, I was up in my room writing – our hotel is at the end of the Ramblas near to the harbor – and I heard drums, etc. I went outside and there was PSUC with all red flags, pictures of Stalin etc. [...]

You see, the head of all the bulletins is a Dutchman.[23] And the mimeographing and printing is all done by the Germans because there are more of them. The whole place is very sedate, with high rich wooden panelling in the 2 rooms, which were formerly [illegible] for public consumption. Ours was a drawing room, as were the other 3. [...]

It's great fun here – exciting and I'm learning a lot – revolutionary theory and practice especially. [...]

This is before we go to the office.[24] C. is washing his hair. Then we will go out and get a café au lait (which is 95% hot milk & 5% coffee and very good coffee) and some bread or a roll. Then I will take a tram – painted red & black – anarchist colors – to the P.O. and see if any letters have come and mail this. The stamp you see on there costs about 3 cents because of an agreement between Spain and the USA.

The other day – Sunday we have free completely – we visited a German Jewish friend of ours – who is yellow haired, blue eyed and very Aryan looking.[25] He lives with his sister and her husband (she has straight black hair & is Jewish looking) on one of the hills of the city. He has some very fine first editions of poetry books. He was formerly stage manager for a Berlin theater (*Stadttheater*) and is a very artistic and interesting chap. He showed us a little book he has of old medieval illustrations to songs of minnesingers – a gorgeous old thing.

I told you about our hours, didn't I? – we eat breakfast from 10 to 10:30. We work from 10:30 or 11:00 to 1:30. Then at 2:00 we eat lunch. At 3:30 or 4:00 we go back to work and at about 7:00 (or later if there is extra work to do) quit. At 9:00 or 9:30 we have dinner. After dinner I lie down on the bed a minute to rest and for the last week, I just go right to sleep – at 10:15 or 10:30. Last night tho, Charlie read me several of a series of short articles he is doing for *La Batalla* (POUM's paper) on the Economics of Social Revolution. They are surprisingly good.

We are having more money in bills sent over from the Amexco in Marseilles and as soon as it comes we are (1) going to make a picnic with our German friends on one of the mountains here and (2) going to buy underclothes with the greatest of joy. How long we stay here depends on how soon it turns into an international war and which side starts out by taking Barcelona. If the wrong side does, we lodge ourselves in the Am. Consulate and take the next boat to India. If the right side does, I don't know what we will do.

6. *Letter written by Lois to her family on 27 October 1936*

Boy, boy, life in Barcelona is really exciting.[26] It's generally known or accepted that Russia is going to start eventually to send arms over here, intervening for the 'bourgeois republic.' In fact, the PSUC have forced the anarchists into an alliance – of their trade unions and parties – by threatening to withdraw or prevent the arms from coming. All of which leaves our little POUM out in the cold. Besides that, the POUM's plan for collectivization *without* indemnity – for which the CNT & FAI promised to vote – has fallen thru, as the anarchists have thrown their support to the PSUC's plan of collectivization with indemnity, which I think is certainly selling yourself out to the bourgeoisie. If you're going to collectivize, for heaven's sake, don't pander with paying back the bourgeois. It either is a workers' state or it isn't, and if it isn't and you have to politely pay the bourgeoisie for what you take from them – you might as well give it back – especially as you don't have the wherewithal to pay 'em anyhow.

But the anarchists, ideologically, are really not with the Stalinists – as far as they are with anybody ideologically. This ideology consists mostly of the things they're *against* because they lack theories to meet all the facets of the present situation. But they are for *liberty* against *dictatorship* – as in Russia – and they are tremendous internationalists – not 'socialism in one stateists'.[27]

We have just written a protest to the POUM executive committee about our housing, as, due to some politicking, we are about to be moved from our hotel to an impossible place.[28] We are going to have it mimeographed and send copies to them every two days, knowing Spanish character as we do. The Germans (none of whom are Jewish, for Daddy's benefit) have raised so much heck that the Local Committee thinks they are quite disagreeable.

Our food continues o.k., except that we don't get grapes so often and wine only once a day. Good wine too, but Charlie always takes only half a glass and then dilutes it with water, which ruins the taste.

I am finding out more interesting things about our comrades here. The two little German sisters, whom I mentioned before, were educated before Hitler by a private tutor, and since have gone to a boarding school in Switzerland, spending their summers here in Spain, where they had a town house in Barcelona and another one in the country. They have given the Barcelona house to the POUM for a sanatorium, along with their car. And the peseta has become devaluated so that they cannot send the girls back to school. But they are good comrades and sincere radicals.

Lou Litchfield, who is the head of the foreign bulletin section, a South American from a Dutch colony who was educated in a Dutch university, is a famous writer, somewhat after the style of Ernest Hemingway, but better. He has written thirty or so novels and is quite well to do, giving his services voluntarily to the revolution. And Mary Breá and her husband are sur-realists of the most advanced type, having lived in Paris for years. Their sur-realism is not only a way of writing but a way of life. They think that G. Stein[29] was 'a little advanced' (in a condescending tone). They try of course to disassociate words from all their old – bourgeois – connotations and write with them in only the pure – proletarian – fashion in which they emerge from the subconscious. And I think you know something about the way they write, and how you are moved, not by the words themselves, but by the connections in which they appear, connections and combinations which could only be typical of the sub-conscious of one individual. Mary and Breá are in the vanguard of this group (Paris is, Mary assures me, 20 years ahead of the rest of the world), since, when one begins to try to live without any bourgeois or old and false concepts in his life, he soon finds that it is hopeless, and if he really wants to practice his philosophy of sur-realism he must throw himself into working to abolish these bourgeois conditions. Sur-realism can only exist in its pure state *after* the revolution, so the majority of these people, most of whom are in Paris of course, have put aside their pens and will write only propaganda for the revolution. So Mary and Breá are here. Some stuff, eh?

Oh, and I forgot, Freud is the only word they will hear in psychology. The latest and best.

We are being tremendously fed; I never have time to get hungry, and, as daddy guessed, I weigh more than Charlie does. (Tho I have never been sure that the scales were right as they were all public ones and, to further complicate the situation, gave results in kilos.)

We lent some money to Erber when he was here, and we just had a letter from Paris from him saying that he had sent it via the POUM representative, which we are glad to hear. We got his letter Sunday from

Androtti,[30] who is on the POUM exec committee. We were at a POUM demonstration where there were about 4.500 people. Nin, the minister of justice of the Generality, a POUM exec committee man, made a good speech – in Catalan – about his newly established courts of (proletarian) justice.[31] The PSUC and the CNT were having a united front meeting at the same time, and they had 60.000[32] (mostly anarchists, of course). Which shows just where the POUM will be if the Anarchists really sell themselves down the river to the bourgeois and the PSUC. The anarchists are really the most revolutionary of all the parties, but oh, oh, oh! How they are straying from the straight and narrow of true revolutionary action.

We think that they are still the only hope here, though, because, after the revolution is won (assuming, you understand, Russian intervention and a long and bloody war fought for 'democracy', unless the dern Russians change their line, or we – POUM and CNT – can spring a real revolution and wipe away this dern 'defend democracy' business), they will not stand for the kind of dictatorship Stalin has in Russia; they have irremovable convictions about liberty – individual responsibility etc etc, direct action – and, unless they become hopelessly hoodwinked by the Stalinists, they will continue to act on these principles. Which would mean eventually a real workers' democracy for Spain.

There are two Englishmen here – one Scotch, I beg his pardon – who are helping us temporarily with this bulletin. The Scotch lad,[33] who was three years in Glasgow Univ. doing chemistry, is going to work, we think, in a new gun cotton factory to be directed by a Belgian comrade.[34] Bob Smillie is the Scotch one's name – both ILP men – Independent Labor Party,[35] same as Jennie Lee.[36] He knows Scotch ballads, marching songs, revolutionary songs ad infinitum and is very funny. The English lad is from the Midlands – Birmingham – Ted Fletcher[37] – and speaks with a very broad accent. He is organising for the ILP an exhibit of Spanish revolutionary items – guns, shells, posters, banners, [illegible] etc etc – He has been dictating some articles to me & asked me, when he saw me typing, if he could help. Oh, he said, we'll tell them to vote for Roosevelt; it's the new Stalinist line. Which I suppose you might as well do anyhow. Now – when everything is so real and acute here – I can't imagine anything more boring than to have to listen to one of Norman Thomas' speeches.[38] In fact, the things the 'radicals' do in America seem so darn unimportant, when it's the 'revolutionaries' here who are making history.

There are two other English speaking people here – Max Fields,[39] head of League for a Revolutionary Workers' Party – (American boy) – a splinter group from the Trotskyists – and Kream[40] – a Canadian member of the same party. They are on their way to the Brussels Congress against Fascism[41] – and are here a few days studying the situation.

Our own lives would seem to be not exciting but monotonous – every morning and afternoon to the office – to bed every night after supper. Translating, typing, proof-reading for our Bulletin – you should buy a copy at SP headquarters if you don't get it – tho I did tell to send it to you. It isn't boring tho.

[…] Love to you all. I really can't think of much more to say. Contented, well-fed, warm and happy. Lois.

7. Unaddressed letter fragment, written by Lois to a distant family member or friend, undated but probably penned in late October 1936

Wouldn't you just love to be in Barcelona now? It might be enough to make you change your mind about the value of a European trip if you could have our job now. We're working for a political party in Spain – the POUM or Workers' Party of Marxist Unification. It is a 'Bolshevik-Leninist' group, with revolutionary socialists from France and Belgium in it also, and many Trotskyists. We work in the foreign propaganda (publicity for you, I suppose) section; we publish an English Bulletin and make daily broadcasts in English over the POUM short wave radio. An English girl, with an American revolutionary socialist, started the English department, and we work with her (married to an exiled Cuban revolutionary).

The political situation in Catalonia, where the revolution is further advanced than in the rest of Spain, is fascinating. Of course, if you only read the official government communiqués from Madrid, you don't know there is a revolution. The PSUC, or a fusion of II and III Internationals, a Stalinist-controlled party whose policies dominate the Madrid government, tries never to mention the word 'revolution' for fear of scaring their bourgeois allies. The POUM is continually embarrassing them by flinging back at them the slogans of Lenin and Marx, whose prestige with the workers here the PSUC is careful to monopolize, but whose ideas and theories they entirely neglect. Our pet slogan is 'War on the Front and Revolution Behind the Lines.'

The crucial organization in Catalonia, though, is the CNT or anarchist trade union body, which controls by far the greatest number of Catalonian workers. What it does will decide how revolutionary or reformist Catalonia becomes – provided we win the war of course, which is another question. We rather think that a world war is coming out of this business; because Soviet Russia, even for the most selfish, nationalistic of reasons, cannot afford to have a fascist Spain, France, Germany, Italy, Japan and Belgium to take on when Hitler starts his 'holy war' against communism.

The *esprit* here in Catalonia is a thing you couldn't possibly imagine from the run of articles in the capitalist press. The people have no doubt whatsoever that they will win; the old bourgeois epoch, as they say, seems so far from them now and so impossible to re-establish, with all its cruelty, misery and subjection. The working people absolutely run Catalonia now. But not so in Madrid, where the city, thanks to the cautious Stalinism of the Socialists and Communists, is still dominated by the bourgeois; beautifully dressed women and fastidious looking men sit in the cafes over their aperitifs or promenade on the main streets. Here in Barcelona everybody is in shirtsleeves, and, as it gets colder, crude looking sweaters. The women are all tremendously painted and curled and quite common looking; their empty heads – as a rule – don't understand exactly what this revolution means; and they still have the psychology of women enchained for so many hundreds of years.

We just met some Belgian friends of ours, who have just three minutes ago arrived back from the Huesca front. They have tremendous beards – because no man at the front ever shaves – and are quite disgusted with this war. One had a silver encrusted dagger and case taken from the fascists; he is going to sell it for the silver. They're going back to Belgium, I think, as the situation is getting hourly worse there. They are the ones who held the bridge at Irún until the last possible moment.

8. *Unaddressed letter fragment written by Lois, most likely written in late October 1936*

Meals at the Hotel Falcón are a marvel. The staff, including the cook, are of pre-revolutionary vintage and the food we get is rather good on the whole. The waiters, though, have been profoundly affected by the revolution. They go around in shirtsleeves and collarless, one in particular always with a cigarette or cigar stub hanging from his lips. The head waiter, who (we surmise) was always until now a smirking yes-man, has never been known to smile and considers himself a 'hardboiled guy' or its Spanish equivalent. (Psychology of a waiter)

There are, of course, lots of things going on around here that would astonish any 100% American. One is the free way in which the Anarchist trade unions have adopted Popeye as their own pet mascot. In the little stands on the Ramblas everywhere they sell pins, scarves and statues of Popeye waving an anarchist flag of black and red. Betty Boop is also much in favor among the Anarchists, but Mickey Mouse, who is the idol of the people, is so popular that it is necessary that he be non-partisan. The anarchists all wear tiny silk triangles instead of neckties, printed red and black with various designs – a victory wreath, pictures of dead comrades, a clenched fist, and, most popular of all, a nude woman. [...]

9. Letter written by Lois to her father on 2 November 1936

I just got your letter commenting on our coming to Spain. I must admit that I wasn't terribly surprised. You don't understand, you said, why we came here and consequently think it is pretty terrible. If you could understand, it'd be o.k. With our interests as they are, this is the only place for us to be. For any good revolutionary who wants to work with or understand the revolution and how it works, the dialectics of it, Spain is the most valuable place in the world to be. The social revolution is important to us and we want to learn and understand as much about it as is possible, because some day someone will have to make a revolution in the United States and people who know anything about it will be vitally necessary. [...]

About the danger part of it, I think we understand that better than you do. You see nothing but capitalist papers, and I have no doubt but that you are reading the most unbelievable stuff about stories of the fascists, red terror, starvation, disease and God knows what. And you don't have the elementary bias that would tend to make you discount what they say. Let me assure you that there is no red terror here;[42] the members of the workers' parties (as we are, of course) are quite safe. Life goes on here, women buy groceries at the market, children go to the new schools which have been set up in place of the church schools and utterly inadequate state schools, the old women sell flowers on the Ramblas, along with scarves and pop-eye anarchist pins, etc. etc. There are innumerable cars marked as belonging to the various trade union and worker organisations which tear unendingly about the streets.

There is a tremendous amount of activity here; there are enormous tasks to be faced – a whole new society has to be built, and besides there is a war on our hands. There is work for everybody who wants to work, in a wholesome, healthy atmosphere. Yes, this is a workers' state, but what of it? Does that make people any less human, or does it make life any less busy? When I try to understand what you mean by this danger problem it can't really seem very important. If we were at the front, where the fascists were, or if Barcelona were being bombed or if the Italians landed here – you still wouldn't have anything to worry about. The last two are possible, some time in the far future; there have been no signs of any such things yet. We are perfectly willing to take the amount of risk there is in being here, which is comparatively small; we are quite conscious that we are assuming it, and you needn't feel we are in the least irresponsible or don't know what we are doing. Anyhow, if it comes to the very worst, which no one, including us, is in the least expecting, there is always a British or American battleship in the harbor.

Anyhow, there is absolutely no reason to worry over us. We are just as safe here as we were when we were in Louisville or New York and, anyway, why should you worry? We are perfectly capable of taking care of ourselves, especially in a country where there is a' revolution going on. That place is practically our idea of heaven, and if there is any place where we would be happy and know how to manage ourselves, it would be in such a country.

So, that's off my chest, and I hope it won't worry you any more than it does us.

I think I told you in my last letter about the two English chaps who were here. They have been working with us on the bulletin, and one, who is a chemist, has almost got – knowing the Spanish character which always puts everything off till *mañana*, it is best to put it that way – a job in a new factory for making gun-cotton which is to be established at Figueras, I think. The other chap, the Englishman, is a Freudian psychologist, altho you could never tell it to hear him wail out the St. Louis Blues, or explain the tactics of setting up a proletarian dictatorship (workers' democracy is the term people use in America). He has a friend who is studying at Wisconsin State on a scholarship in history. This boy is going to have a car put at his service this summer by the people who are giving him the scholarship, and he is going to make a tour of America, and maybe a few weeks in Mexico. He wants Ted to come over there and go with him, but of course Ted is broke. Anyhow, I have given him your address in case he does manage to get there.

Charlie has two friends from the U of Michigan, who are Rhodes Scholars, one in philosophy and the other in economics. We have written them to invite them to visit us during the Christmas vacation, which would be lots of fun. Things are a little boring around here just now, there doesn't seem to be much news, so our side is probably losing somewhere. I wish the Russians would go on and declare war or not declare war. We are dickering again to get Charlie another job doing statistics for one of the trade unions which is reorganising and coordinating Catalan industry. We may have no more success than we had last time, but I hope we do. [...]

We may begin to get pay instead of room and board, some of the Germans have been raising so much heck with the executive committee. There is of course going to be a food shortage here this winter, and we will certainly be provided for at the Falcón, but we wouldn't starve anyhow – if we stay here or not.

I have been speaking on the radio a lot lately. You should try to hear me, short wave. [...]

The other day we went with Ella Smith, the Englishwoman who is a friend of Harold Laski,[43] Ramsay MacDonald[44] and other equally important English people, for a tour of the 'cultural wealth' of Barcelona. The Generalitat put it on with a big private car for her, and she asked us to come. We went to a library which was so small that it couldn't possibly hold more than fifty people, though it took up a whole building and was marvelously done. It gave me a feeling of how restricted the 'culture' was before the revolution – how few people it ever touched, and of what little importance it was. But when the Generalitat wanted to show her the 'culture' of Catalonia, such limited things were all they had to show for the old civilization. Only 50% of the people in Spain can read. What kind of 'culture' could they ever achieve? We also went over to the Department of the New Unified Schools, where we talked to the secretary, I think, of the Committee. He was full of plans and had accomplished not a few things, such as opening 75, I think he said, new schools. He took us to see a couple of church schools which had been partly burned and which were being rebuilt and remodeled to make the rooms bigger and with more sunshine. It was the only office we have found in all of Barcelona where they seemed to have any real statistics that one could trust – or any kind of efficient organization going on.

That day we also went to the famous cathedral of Barcelona, about which a guard of militias had been thrown in the first days to keep it from damage, when the workers were avenging the century-old score they had with the catholic church. Oh, how they hate it around here. And I for one can't blame them. I understand from a little bourgeois English girl that we have made friends with that the priests here were really a rascally lot and very immoral. We saw an article in a French catholic magazine which boldly declared the same thing. Oh, these pamphlets tho! Nude nuns and dreadfully lewd looking priests, and everyone you see on a street car or in a park, men, women and children are reading the tripe.

We went to see a cathedral in 'neo-Catalan' style,[45] which is absolutely fantastic. It was the creation of some one man, I understand – I wish I could think how to describe it to you. The things I have seen in it were all from concrete or stone blocks, all rounded at the edges and built into great curves and round arches, with much iron lattice work, etc. This church consisted of two tall, tall thin towers, without any ground floor buildings, it seemed. These curves of stone, one above another, made various little cave-like places into which he had put statue groups of various biblical characters, supported by, in one case, rows and rows of birds, in another by small animals, in another by grains, etc. Then about two thirds the way up the towers, he wrote in stone, many times, mounting up, up, up, as in a chant, 'sanctus, sanctus, sanctus, sanctus'. It was effective, of course, but quite crazy.

10. *Letter written by Lois (and Charles) to her family on 9–10 November 1936*

According to a letter that Bob, our Scotch comrade, got from home, Barcelona was heavily bombed last Sunday. But don't believe a word of it. Barcelona has never been bombed since the beginning of the war and won't be for some time yet. Don't believe anything you read in the capitalist press or coming from the rebel side. They tell the most tremendous lies. When we were in Germany, we heard twice that Madrid had fallen and that Barcelona was bombed and that the airdrome was completely destroyed. When we got here we found that there had not been an airplane here since the first ones were captured by our side in July. But it is so easy to tell lies that the foreign capitalist press will believe: because the fascists want so bad for the stuff they tell to be true that it's easy to tell it, and the newspapers do so much wishful thinking that it's easy for them to print it. They all want us to lose, but the Catalan proletariat will never have fascism here until there 'is not one stone left on another' – by God and by Jesus. All of which I suppose is hard on nervous people in America. Of course, I don't spend my time worrying about what you are worrying about, but my advice to you is, don't believe anything you hear until I tell you it is true.

The Generality has been reorganized and, as you know, the POUM is now participating. Mary is working in the English department for press releases and publicity of the Generality. Along with an Anarchist man and a PSUC boy who will be leaving for England. I may take the place of this boy to type the clichés and lend moral support to the revolutionary representation in the section – the POUM, in other words.

And, incidentally, to earn 12 pesetas a day – the first time in my life I ever held down a job that I earned money for. I haven't got it yet tho.
[...]

Charlie says to tell you that at last his lifelong wish to grow a beard is about to be fulfilled. Of course all the militia men who are at the front never shave, so he is not being peculiar but just conforming (like a man).

The trees are still green here, with only a hint of yellow leaves, when you go out into the hills that overlook the city. Barcelona is in a gorgeous site, as the literature of the subdivision guy who had our office used to point out.

Here they are organising a women's secretariat. One of the interesting things about it – it gives lessons in shooting, first aid, knits, and organizes food and clothes for people at the front – is the way they say always 'comrade' or 'companion' instead of the traditional words for husband and wife. That is because of the old tradition and custom of selling women into sexual slavery and of the great immorality here. They are trying to find a concept which is not legally or morally binding and which is entirely new and free from bad connotations. So they decided to say companion, which means no ties except affection, except in case there are children. We think it's a good idea. I mean I do. And besides no one ever says 'Mrs.' etc. here, only comrade, so whether you are married or not doesn't matter.

[...]

Boy, what excitement!![46] I was interrupted – it's 10:30 pm – by a low rumbling noise – We all rushed out to the harbor to see what it was, whether a signal from the fort for mobilisation or a reply to some fascist cruiser, we don't know.

A bunch of anarchists mobilized next door to us here and jumped into a truck and were off. All the short [illegible] men we've always seen carrying guns over their shoulders are now carrying them with fingers on the trigger. I love the way these anarchists don't wait for anything or anybody. But when they think they're needed, they go. It makes you feel safe to know that five minutes after you hear cannon from somewhere, hundreds of men are mobilizing with guns cocked, to find out just exactly what is going on – and ready to stop it at all costs.

But we can't find out what it is, so C. is finishing washing his underwear, and I am going to bed. Good night. *Salud.*

[...] Now Mary & Lois are working at the Publicity Office of the Generality which leaves most of the bulletin & radio translating to me.[47] Lois has a nice job – 6 or 8 hours a day – and in a nice warm room up in the richer part of town. She takes the subway up there at 9:30 am – back to lunch at 1:30 or 2 – to work at 3:30 till it is done – anywhere from 5 to 7 or 8. Is she proud to have a job! I am glad she has one and can be separate from me a few hours a day – that of course is a good thing for both of us after being together every minute all summer! One reason I wanted to come here was that we could get half settled once. The continual move is alright for a time, but to have a circle of acquaintances and a settled place to come to at night – that is necessary to real living.

So now we are six weeks or so in our same room here on the Third floor (4th or 5th in American system of counting them) rear of the Hotel Falcón. We have a nice little balcony looking over roofs and dozens of other window-door balcony combinations. If we get up early enough we have sunshine for a while on the balcony. Our office opens to the North – so in the morning, before I start translating, I walk down to the waterfront with my newspaper and sit in a little boat in the sun, reading it and deciding which articles to do. Then at 10 or 11 I go up to the office and one of the English boys takes dictation from my translating. I can go faster than he can write it – on any political article at least. But I can not learn to talk Spanish here. They only speak the funny Catalan stuff.

The food shortage is coming down and our meals here are not so much any more – mostly beans. At first we scarcely noticed it, but finally we got weak, sore throats. And so did lots of others. So now we make a systematic supplement of fruit & milk. Tomatoes, grapes, apples and milk with a little coffee in it (and syrup instead of sugar!) are all cheap. With Lois earning money, we can do right well. If it gets too thin eating, we shall have to leave, because I don't dare take any chances. Lois is prosperous enough to look at however. I think she could stand quite a famine. [...]

Lois is learning more than she did in college, I feel sure. Right now she is lying in bed reading *World Politics, 1918–1936* by R. Palme Dutt, the Hindu Communist. She has a tendency to go to extremes, when she gets a new interest or theory – it sometimes seems to conservative old me. But she learns quickly. You should hear her worry about the world political situation! The role of the anarchists in the revolution, marriage theory, dress, beards, sur-realism and a hundred things I never thought about before. But she is easily held down to earth by her 'bourgeois' interests. Charlie.

11. *Letter written by Lois to her family on 12 November 1936*

Since we first came here this town has become extremely bourgeois. All these women roaming around in the streets in their fur coats, and men in big expensive overcoats and shoes. Where, oh where are the overalls of yesterday? At last our money came, and I was all prepared to buy myself a lovely pair of overalls and a lumberjack, when I suddenly realized that no women were wearing them any more and, besides, that I have a job in the Generality, where people vie with each other in dressing more elaborately, especially the women. Breá made Mary quit wearing her overalls and trouser suits three weeks ago. Oh, gee, now I'm going to be suppressed. Because of course I'm not going to buy them now and look like the only proletarian in this whole dern town.

There are other signs that the city is going bourgeois on us. Of course the CNT has gone in with the Generality and the Madrid government in their policy of 'We are fighting to defend the bourgeois republic. Don't anybody mention the fact that there has been a social revolution, or our dear democratic friends, Great Britain and France, might stop being our dear friends....' or something dumb like that. Since the British are allowing Portugal to intervene actively against us, and since the French fascists are as busy supplying arms to Franco[48] as the Italian, German and English ones are. And, although I don't think the rank and file realized that they have been committed to a policy of suppressing the revolution, all revolutionary slogans of the CNT have been suppressed, and it looks pretty bad to me for the poor old revolution.

Of course, there is always one good thing about the Anarchists. Their long history of strikes and sabotage have been fought absolutely on individual initiative, or group initiative; they have no tradition of following their leaders, and whatever they are 'pledged' to, they go ahead as they always have and do what they think is right to defend the revolution. But a lot of them are getting good jobs now, and I don't know what about it.

Institutions that were taken over by the POUM and run for its members have been given back to their owners, cafés, etc. Not because we wanted to, but because we had to. The poor old revolution.

Of course, the military situation is so tense that really everything else fades into secondary importance, but if the bourgeois, who are never asleep, seize this moment of concentration on something else to take back control, that will be serious. However, the Generality, when it let the Anarchists in, didn't realize how they were going quietly and successfully to permeate every office and department with their men and take over control, at least so far as doing the jobs goes. And, after all, if you are the one who does the work, what difference does it make who gives the orders? Especially if you do the things you think ought to be done, and do them as you think they ought to be done. But, on the other hand, the Anarchists, since they have no definite philosophy of their own and are continually having to make new policies and new adaptations to the situations, are susceptible to the influence of anyone who has a strong determined policy: the PSUC in Catalonia, since the POUM is too small, and the Communist-Socialist coalition in Madrid. So the situation here is very unsettled. But all this is of no importance whatsoever if we don't win the war. And it doesn't look so hot. Today, the 12th, the Madrid militians are holding out ok. L.

12. *Letter written by Lois to her sister on 16 November 1936*

[...] I can sympathize and understand how you feel at the U. of L. I felt like a whole new world was being opened to me – tho to you, because your interests are different, probably it's just a broadening of the sources of information – things you were already interested in. And, of course, to any girl coming from Atherton,[49] and especially one brought up like you and I were, one of the most important new problems is men.

Of course, you may not face it consciously as that; I'm sure I never did. But you feel it: an increasing complexity in your relations – endless possibilities opening – with multitudes of combinations and all interesting and mildly exciting – giving life a pleasant kick that makes everything you do more fun. That, in a vague way, was how I first felt when I entered the U. of L. Back into the world of normalcy and men. Because, hell, men and sex and mild or extreme kicks are normal for women. [...]

Of course for men, all that is different. And any woman who wants a full, interesting life wants men and lots to do with them; and she wants – in spite of how modern, independent etc. she is – to understand them. Of course you must understand there are lots and lots of other things going into a life – and, hell, I know that as well as you; I'm not overemphasizing this men stuff – I'm just spending one whole letter on nothing else. Just as later on I might write you about nothing but the revolution.

Men are simple. Mom is right, tho I can never get her cynical – economic proposition of marriage – stuff. Her idea of romance etc etc is [illegible] disillusioned. Of course, tho, I've only been married 9 mos, so perhaps I shouldn't talk. Anyhow, she's right: men are simply biological, ideological [sic] creatures. Even the most intelligent, aesthetic one. Any man coming to a university, including a professor, notices women by their breasts, hips, thighs, etc. But he allows – if he is intelligent, a college prof, say – for this continual irritation of his sexual interest and doesn't pay any attention to it. He is first attracted to any girl by her vivacity and personality, maybe not first but fundamentally – C. was first attracted to me physically and then my personality had a leeway to express itself in (and receive some attention, I mean).

[...]

But with any college prof it's a question of interests. Where you begin to show intelligence and similar interests etc, you begin to stand out as an individual and not just another coed. Then you have a chance to get ahead (a) for marks (b) for anything else.

Another thing. While I'm unloading all this info – which you probably know already. I think unless I was absolutely serious, I'd not try to have an affair with anybody – college prof or no. There are a lot of reasons but mostly psychological (this one isn't of course). In the first place, to really perfect the sexual act and get the most out of it for both parties it takes 2 1/2 – 3 years. Going out for 2 months, or overnight stuff is usually not at all constructive – to make anything worthwhile out of the relationship, I mean, and just disillusions and discourages any young person. Besides, the factors (1) of security (economic), to provide for companionship (living in some apt. etc.); and (2) continued growth – individually and together, action and reaction; and (3) continued exploration and understanding of the other person's characters – all of these things are part, and a vital part, of any true marriage – and a fascinating part too. But it takes years and years. I just barely know C. yet, and he still presents infinite and varied and interesting possibilities to one. And what of this do you get from a drab or exciting 'affair' of several months – tho usually not that long – or a year?

Of course I don't see any reason why people should be legally tied together except in case of children. The thing that should keep them together would be continued love and interest in the other. If one fails to interest the other or if they find that they are really not well mated, then separate, otherwise be 'companions' – as they say in free revolutionary Spain, where nobody is tied to anybody. I think it's a lovely term – preferable to husband or wife. I didn't at first, but wife has so many north branch connotations for C. of duty, faithful, etc. I kind of caught his feeling.

I'm glad to talk to somebody about all this and hope you're interested; oh well, I know you are. I would be if it was you. I don't even think that companions need always be faithful to each other – men at least.[50] Of course, say what you will about double standards, there's a hell of a difference in men and women and I for one think they need and deserve double standards, otherwise whose standard will go – men's or women's? Up till now men's, of course. Mine'd be different.

Especially for men physical pressure gets pretty bad, although, of course, they can always stand it. But I wouldn't worry if C. wasn't faithful all his life to me. I certainly won't be all mine to him – in thought and deed. Of course, I can't tell if it would ruin anything else – just having intercourse; I'd have to see. It would be those other things that would matter.

Much, of course, depends on if you find somebody you like, feel affection towards and physically attracted to. And you ought to find such people – lots of times in your career. But as for me – I'd be careful just where I stopped. I would always stop. I wouldn't be promiscuous either, but if I liked somebody and wanted to pat him or pull his hair or kiss him, I would.

You didn't specifically ask for all this, I'm just telling you things I'd have liked to know when I went to the U. of L. Men like women to be vivacious and of course – somewhat in demand. Even the cream of the aesthetic crop find that it lends added enchantment to an 'intelligent' girl.

But men are really, besides being so biological, very idealistic and unrealistic. It's remarkable [...] how unspoiled and pure these cynical, educated lads all are. You won't understand what I mean until you meet them yourself. Especially among radicals, I s'pose, you would find these idealists. But among artists too perhaps. That's another reason why I like men. That is a quality rare indeed among materialistic women – nice, intelligent, radical women are still rare.

[...]

Well, C. is getting closer to a statistics job. Today he made great pals with a Russian who is organising an employment bureau for foreign technicians. No new news. We may stay here till next summer if he gets a good job & if I do too. [...]

13. *Letter written by Lois to Mary De Vries on 24 November 1936*

[...] Charlie's birthday was lots of fun.[51] For presents I gave him a pair of these Catalan slippers with rope soles and some elegant little cakes and candied oranges. But of course Charlie can't eat so much sweet stuff, so I had to help him. And that night Ted Fletcher, an English ILPer who is here organising an exhibition on the Spanish Revolution, came up and we had a party. That is we ate oranges and tomatoes and grapes and talked about Freud. Ted is a swell kid; he started to work at 16, after having to refuse a scholarship to school because of lack of money; he joined the ILP at 16. He has educated himself, as it were, read Freud, Pavlov, Adler and the other followers and dissenters of these movements; he knows his English literature, modern and past, to a T, and of course has practically memorized Marx, Engels, Lenin, etc. But in spite of all that, and oh yes, I forgot modern art and classical music, he's a quiet kid with a grand sense of humor and very proud of the fact that he's a worker and no intellectual. He's been arrested four or five times by the police for leading strikes, and has been labelled 'the most dangerous agitator in the Midlands'. Of which he is also very proud.

I don't know if I had this job in the Generality when I last wrote you, probably not. I work in the English Section of the Department of Propaganda of the Generality of Catalonia. This department was reorganized and members from all the parties put in, so I'm in for the POUM. I type stencils for the daily information bulletin put out in English, which is teaching me how to type, anyhow. I also act as a kind of control, along with Mary Breá, to see that our anarchist collaborator doesn't get by with any tricky stuff.

But you can't imagine the change between this place and the POUM. Here is a first rate bureaucracy, and very proper too. At the POUM, being as it was the revolution and we were all revolutionaries, we wore overalls, were improper in talking and not conventional in where we put our feet or how we sat or what we called people. Everybody was comrade; but, alas, them good old days is gone. Here I have been seriously advised not to wear my Catalan slippers, to try to look as nice as possible (which is difficult seeing how I have only my brown divided skirt and three blouses in various stages of disrepute), also we never say comrade, only *señor*, and besides this ain't a revolution anyhow, it's a civil war in defence of democracy. As the head of the Propaganda office said in an article which I translated for foreign propaganda, 'Barcelona has never been a town divided within itself. Between the suburbs of the rich, with their sumptuous and luxurious avenues and the decrepit homes of the lowly there has always existed a *comprehensive understanding*.' Underlining is mine. In another place, too, he was personifying Barcelona as a fine lady with a reserved sensitive spirit and no trace of *'plebeian vulgarity.'* Can you imagine a man saying anything like that in a revolution? It's fantastic. Plebeian vulgarity. I'm so simple that it really did shock me. I'd never understood how things had changed from the first exciting days until I ran into that. And did it make my blood boil to have to translate such junk for foreign consumption! But then I'm getting 12 pesetas a day for it, about $1.00, which is the first money I ever earned in my life, and which we can use very nicely for clothes, food, etc.

There was one other passage which was interesting. He was speaking about the street fighting on the 19th of July, 'behind it there seemed to be a flood of that light, so peculiar to Barcelona, and the *perfume of red carnations*.' That's how conscious he was of the revolution.

Of course, I like Barcelona too; it really is a wonderful city – so well-located with sea and mountains, and so big and clean. Except the part where we live, right in the center. There is a marked contrast to the rest of the city, as it is the very old part, and all within the old Roman wall. Most of the city is new, as it began to grow when it became an industrial city. But the main reason I like it is because it's a workers' city, not because of the 'luminous flood of light' or its reserved delicate soul. Hell, if it's got a soul, it's an anarchist one, a suspicious underdog one, dark and dangerous and ready to fight to the last drop of blood or the last stone for their first chance for any kind of a decent life. Not dainty and reserved and delicate, but strong and crude, and rough, just like any worker, and, in spite of the lovely stuff put out by the department of Propaganda, which, of all the dern places, is headed by Left Republicans, who use it to propagate their own ideas of capitalist democracy, when the showdown comes, it's the 'plebeian' people, with all their 'vulgarity,' who will take control and who will do all the fighting there is to be done. Just as they have in Madrid. There, the whole gov't was like the propaganda department here; but, when the fascists came, the workers went about putting up their barricades and tightening their belts in anticipation of no food, and keeping a sharp watch on these bourgeois with whom such a 'comprehensive understanding' had always existed, to be sure, so that they [the bourgeois] didn't betray them [the workers] to the fascists with whom they probably have an even more comprehensive understanding.

So you may gather from this tirade that I don't trust the bourgeois, and that every time I see an anarchist with a gun I feel good. Which is quite true. At first I wasn't used to so many guns, and I was a little uneasy around them, but now, when most of them seem to be at the front, I like to see them and wish there were more here.

Another of our friends here, a German refuge whom we call Willie, is in an awful mess. As are most of the 10.000 Germans wandering around Europe without passports or with ones just expiring. Willie is an artist; he is a theater director, and for such a sensitive soul has stood up very well to all the hard breaks he's had: working in a labor camp at the age of 14–15 during the war – one more year and he would have been at the front – ; losing all his money through the inflation after the war; finally, after working on the docks and as a violinist in a cafe, getting to

University and working in the theater and then loosing his job because he was a communist. He is a fine kid and can joke about it yet. He emigrated to Spain with his sister and her husband just after Hitler, four years ago. He found work off and on in the movies, but not much. Now, since his brother-in-law's brewery business here is going to collapse due to Germany's recognition of the Burgos Junta,[52] his sister and brother-in-law are moving to France, and he, with no job and no money, must go with them. It is breaking his heart because, as soon as the war is over, he has excellent prospects for starting a proletarian theater here. If he goes, he won't be able to come back, whichever side wins, because the fascists wouldn't let him and our side will ask, 'Why did you leave when things were bad?' He's so sensitive that he just can't go to the front, and the Red Cross is full. So we don't see how he can manage. He's been trying for months and months to get a job, and I doubt if he'll get one now in four days. Too bad.

14. *Letter written by Lois to her family, begun on 28 November and finished on 30 November 1936*

The weather here is quite peculiar. Instead of getting cold and snowing, as it does at home, it rains and rains and is chilly. The little raincoat that Dort and Fran gave me has come to pieces, and as soon as I can accumulate enough money, I am going to buy me a nice one. [...]
[...]
The food got so terrible in the free section at the Falcón that we had resolved to go out and eat, as soon as I got paid, but they opened there a sort of cooperative restaurant for POUM people where for 2 pesetas you could get a three course meal with wine and fruit. Very good food and very cheap. But they still keep the other place open and it is rank discrimination – bourgeois, I call it, to decide who can eat and who can't eat well by how much money he has. It sets up artificial barriers. But we eat one meal a day in there anyhow for the sake of our health. Charlie now gets a ticket for 14 meals in there a week and another for free meals. I get one for free meals too. So we alternate. In the good joint you get soup, a vegetable dish and a meat or fish platter with fruit or wine. In the other place, though, the average of the meal is not too bad. There you get one dish, wine, sometimes fruit and sometimes soup. We usually eat the classy meal at noon, because we need the energy to work with, I do anyhow, because I have to assemble bulletins for 1 and a half hours every evening. At night we eat extra fruit or whatever we have, and go to a cafe for *cafe con leche*, which is all *lait*, the way we take it. Ted, who

has to eat off his meals in the free one, goes with us for coffee, and then we have a party in our room, or at least a talk fest, and decide the fate of the world all over again. [...]

[...]

I've been talking about C's efforts to get a job.[53] But in Spain, everybody takes his time about everything. A POUM man in the Generality says they are looking for a statistician to work in international trade (the subject C. is taking his degree in) who must know German, French & English. C. can also read Italian and Spanish, so we are optimistic, but don't expect to hear anything anytime. If we do, we'll be pleasantly surprised, otherwise, we will forget it. The same guy also says POUM is going to start an Economic Planning dept. where they need C. So we may even stay here. We don't know, I may learn Spanish and go to the Univ, but our plans are as indefinite as a Spanish promise.

[...]

Lately, the milicians have developed a new costume here – round, high, Russian-looking hats of wool or furry stuff – (All militians – and Charlie – have beards here. You should see C's. It's wonderful – that he could grow one, that is. But the longer it gets, the more red and chestnut hairs it develops – it will probably end up by not being black at all. It makes him look dignified and, sometimes, Jewish.) The other outfit is a coat – cape – tent – pontoon bridge – blanket – parachute and what have you all rolled into one. They came at first only in khaki, but now blue, grey, brown-checked – one side rubber – endless combinations. They have hoods on the back, too. You get in thro a hole in the [illegible word]. [...]

[...]

Today is a lovely day – warm, sunny and not a cloud in the sky.[54] Every balcony on our horizon is fluttering with clothes – including our own – as it is the first nice day for a week.

Daddy, Charlie says to tell you not to stop writing us just because we have settled down. I already begin to miss your letters.

[...]

Last night – With John McGovern[55] & Ella Smith (distinguished middle aged lecturers) we went to a 'theater'.[56] Burlesque, I suppose. It was interesting – but only one good dancer – and the other women were built more or less like cows. The audience – men with sweethearts and wives – was fun – clapping time to the music, singing the songs – cat calls – yells etc.

The latest development here is that Friday (today is Monday) the Soviet Embassy sent a letter to all the newspapers requesting them to publish it.⁵⁷ It was a violent attack on the POUM, saying that we were agents of Hitler, paid to stop the revolution here, that we were counter-revolutionaries etc, signed by the Russian Ambassador. It was, of course, reprinted with great joy by all the Republican and PSUCist newspapers. In fact, every paper in town printed it Saturday, except the *Batalla* (POUM's paper) and the *Solidaridad Obrera* (the Anarchist paper). So we'll see. Probably, according to Mary, they are soon going to receive arms in large quantities and may even attempt force against us. That would be interesting. Of course, that's just a surmise. But if only the Anarchists would back us, we would be safe; but there are considerations and considerations in that. First is that our side needs guns and things to fight with, and if Russia says, 'Guns, no POUM; POUM, no guns,' then what? And, of course, Stalin, after the Moscow shootings, etc. etc., is more than capable of that. In spite of the CP's famous slogan, 'Workers of the world unite.'

McGovern, the Scotch MP, with Leon Green, the Anarchist guy who works with us on the bulletin, just got back from a trip to Valencia and Madrid. They saw lots of things, and McGovern, who is making, as I have probably told you, a study of the role the Catholic church is playing in this war – and has played in the history of Spain – in order to report the truth, whole truth and nothing but the truth to his Catholic constituency, has really learned the dope. Such as how the Church owned more than a third of the land in Spain and how they, in one or more definite cases, ran very questionable institutions for profit, burlesque music halls, and such. All of which was enlightening to McGovern, and will probably get some publicity in England when he gets back. We'll see.

I have been reading the papers, hunting up lies and dumb stories about the 'reds' that we can deny in our bulletin; it's one of our favorite indoor sports. But the military situation is getting more encouraging, and according to some inside dope which Leon, who is I suppose quite a big shot, brought back from Madrid, the whole scene has completely altered in the last two weeks. [...]

According to these men just back from Madrid, the morale there is wonderful. More guns, ammunition, etc. has put enthusiasm into the grim determination and tenacity of the militias there. It is a bad sign for poor old POUM though, that, in spite of how we are fighting, organizing relief and transportation there, the PSUCists have suppressed our paper,⁵⁸ and it ain't so hot. We were not allowed representation on the Madrid Defense Junta either, I think.⁵⁹ But it really makes me feel good to hear all those other things, and you can tell by the people here in

Barcelona that, if the city was bombed or blockaded, it would just arouse their revolutionary ardour even more. It's really wonderful; people like us, bourgeois people, just don't seem to have the guts and resentful bitter tenacity that these working people do to hold out for all they've got until the bitter end. [...]

[...]

I just came back from a meal – free – where we had real beef stew – tomatoes, onions, etc.[60] Boy, was it good!

I'm going to mail this now; just a few minutes ago a column of about 300 French volunteers marched down the Ramblas. Their band was playing the *Internationale* and was I glad to hear it!

Please write, and why don't you send me (a) pictures (b) a newspaper? Love to everybody. Lois.

15. *Letter written by Charles to Mary and Harry De Vries on 30 November 1936*

All is peaceful enough here, as yet. Everyone forgets there is a war, except for a slight shortage of food, slight as yet, but growing alarmingly these last few days.

[...]

We keep busy, but I dare say not nearly so much as you. It is just in comparison to Spanish slowness that we imagine we are tearing around. I have to work to 2 or 3 o'clock at night a couple of times a week, so I take that for an excuse to get up at 11 or 12 every morning. Lois has to get up at 9 tho & to work by 10. That is so early here!

I have not gotten any ec. or stat. job yet, but I have been appointed statistician for the new Economic and Technical section of the POUM, but with no time for or income from that.

[...]

Last night we took our old maid Canadian friend and John McGovern, the Scotch ILP member of Parliament, to the Burlesque! Last week we went to the bullfight, for the benefit of the anti-fascist militias!

I can't concentrate here or think about the revolution, except to say that it is in a state of suspension, going ahead in some economic lines – so slowly – and losing out in popular psychology.

[...]

I got sick twice this fall – usually light sore throat & bronchitis, but am eating better now & feel fairly good. [...]

16. *Letter written by Lois to her family on 1 December 1936*

I will send mama & Anne a couple of *Marie-Claires* after a while.[61] That is the new French women's weekly which is making history. Their styles are made by *Vogue*, incidentally. Expect them.
[...]

17. *Letter written by Charles to his aunt Mildred on 6 December 1936*

We did not write to you when we came to Spain partly because we were afraid you might unnecessarily worry about our safety, when there is no danger at all. And perhaps because we didn't know what you would think of this adventure. We do not have any guilty feeling about it, of course, because we know what and why we are doing, but it might not seem reasonable to you, I don't know.

To Mr. Culter, it seems quite foolish and unnecessary, whereas Mrs. Culter can understand our interest in humanity and all effect, political or religious or otherwise to better the lives of the people.

I feel sure you will fully understand our general attitude, but you may not understand the way we go at it. I wouldn't get so deep into political activity, of course, if I didn't have definite hopes of accomplishing some good.

We are working for the POUM, the Revolutionary Workers Party of Spain. It and the Anarchists are the only really revolutionary ones here, since the Communists and Socialists are both under the control of the Russian Stalinists and have become completely confused and reformist. Reformism may work in some Anglo-Saxon and Scandinavian countries, but anyone can see that in Spain today the only way to get a better society, more just, and on a more progressive economic footing, is to have a real change. The revolution is under way, so there is no question of fomenting one. It is only a question of correctly leading it, or else holding it back, as the Stalinists are trying to do – to avoid complications that might lead to a war between fascism and communism. [...]
[...]

18. *Unaddressed letter fragment written by Lois on 7 December*

I have been working at the Generality for a month and a half now, and it has reduced itself to a mere job, up every morning at nine o'clock, to work at ten, off at one thirty, back at three thirty, and work till seven or seven thirty.[62] Eat at nine, and then life begins again. The place continues to be flooded with interesting people, who all have lots to say, so we talk at the Hotel, we talk in the cafe, we talk on the Ramblas. Everybody has his own source of information and everybody has his own interpretation of what is happening. And, as the newspapers are unreliable, we, just like the Catalan peasants, learn what is going on by discussions. Moulin, the German journalist whom we met the first week we were here, through Erber, is back from Madrid, having been evacuated. He, you see, although he is a refugee, still has his German passport; and he was the only German working for the Madrid POUM – the only foreigner, I mean. The Communist-Socialist combine in Madrid is out to crush the POUM. The Stalinists in Catalonia are too. And if they had found that Trotskyist there with a German passport, there would have been no other interpretation given to it except that he was an agent of Hitler, as they have always claimed the POUM was anyhow. They are waging the most frightful campaign against us. Orders have come from Moscow, and I have this from a good Stalinist, to exterminate the POUM, and with violence if necessary. But the situation is very confused here – nobody is sure of his line or what he is going to do, except the Stalinists, and they are always dead sure, until they receive orders to do something else, and then they are dead sure of that. The anarchists especially have not decided what step to take. In their paper they write continual appeals to democracy, Britain, France, etc.; they declare the necessity for the united front, and then turn around and talk about the Iberian Proletarian Revolution, the inevitability of a world war against 'fascism' and the inevitable result from this war of the 'world revolution.'

[...]

19. *Letter written by Charles to his family on 8 December 1936*

Who said it doesn't get cold in Spain? It is a nice sunny clear cold, tho, & I suppose not so cold as it seems. But nothing is heated whatsoever. Your fingers get cold on this marble table cover. However we don't mind a few discomforts. We like it here and are building up lots of friends among the foreigners here. But our Spanish & Catalan don't progress.

[...]

[...] Does the daily Generality Bulletin get thru? That is the one Lois works on and we admit it is awfully dumb. I do our POUM one practically single-handed now, from translating & typing to proofreading & business. It keeps me busy.

[...]

I hope this comes in time to wish you all a merry Christmas! Eat an extra bite to supplement my beans or rice, as the case may be that day. We get oranges & dates to supplement. But sugar, milk & tobacco are no more. We get almond milk in coffee. We manage to eat well enough tho, with Lois being paid. [...]

I have no economic work yet, tho I am continually getting on new trails. They don't like foreigners here & refuse to try to learn anything. Too bad that Russia & Spain had to be the first countries for Socialist experimentation! But we are learning a good bit about organising a new society, if only by mistake.

Write once in a while. The longer you are away, the more you appreciate letters – the more you nostalgate all over them. *Salud*, love and merry Xmas. Charles.

20. *Letter written by Lois to her family on 12 December 1936*

The main thing which tempted me to answer immediately was Mother's crack that she was sorry I was a Trotskyist. Lady, I ain't no Trotskyist. You should read up on the position of the USA Socialist Party on war, etc., and you will find that it is exactly ye old leninist principle that the POUM stands for: Turn imperialist war into civil war. And don't think that just because it is the revolution here and we are thinking and acting and planning as if it were, that when we get back to America we won't be able to adapt our line to the situation there. I think we can. The best revolutionary is the realistic revolutionary, and anybody knows the revolution is years and years off in America – the land of the free and the home of the brave, or God's country, to you. And (I just feel it my wifely duty to take up for my husband) Charlie wasn't really so Europeanized that he was out of touch with the Socialist USA movement. He helped organize the socialist party in Michigan that, of all practical things, built up such a machine that it got 20% of the votes in Ann Arbor. He also did work with the Teachers' Union in Ann Arbor and all kinds of useful things, being a good revolutionary, and not an idle dreamer and griper like George Lighton. But *now* and *here* is the time to get our revolutionary theory down, though we may never need this experience in America. Probably we'll be just two more socialist school teachers and sociologists, and not the head of the state planning commission or the leader of the Socialist party.

I'm glad you like the posters, Ann. There are some even better ones now. My gosh, you all've got on good-looking clothes; me in my pants and new (!!!) blue pullover looks with awe and admiration at real civilized people. But no envy. Last night we went to a private 'spectacle' given by the CNT for Piscator, the German theater expert,[63] who has been in Russia directing some productions. Presence only by invitation. About 1.000 there and a strange combination of Anarchists and bourgeois. Saw typical Andalusian, Aragonese and Catalan dances, and it was swell. Tonight we are having a party at Willie's for Ted, and I must go now to get busy on the supper.

So long. I will write a real letter later. Incidentally, Merry Christmas, I'm considering presents, but we're awful broke. You'll hear more later. Lois.

21. *Letter written by Lois to Charles' family on 14 December 1936*

Yesterday was Sunday, the only day I don't have to work all day, and we spent the morning rereading our letters. We had just gotten one from you written the 2nd or 3rd of December, as well as two from Louisville. We took all those for the last two months and read them again. It was a cold rainy day; it always is here in Barcelona. Instead of snowing, it rains. And, of course, there is no heating, in houses or offices, so the only place where you can be really comfortable, all good revolutionaries agree, is in bed. On an especially cold day, everyone keeps to his own company, and not much interchange of ideas etc. goes on. This life in Hotel Falcón among the most intellectual of the intellectuals – each of whom belongs to some one or two-member fraction – who all have a particular line which they are trying to influence the POUM exec committee to adopt as the only way to save the revolution – life with about fifteen of these people has a lot in common with the life of the Catalan peasants. These Catalans, who can't read, learn everything from long discussions with their friends in the cafe or in the public square. Here in Barcelona there is one such square near our house, a very pretty one with a fountain, arched columns etc., where there are always three or four groups of fifty men or so discussing anarchism, fascism, marxism, etc. In our hotel, there is a general ignorance as to what is going on, most of the learned comrades can't read Spanish and have great difficulty keeping up on affairs. Each has, usually, one trusted source of information, his 'contact' in the POUM, Spanish contact. So we learn by long discussions when each expounds his line, his source of information, and what he has learned. Primitive. But effective.

The situation here is somewhat confusing now. The war drags on but the revolution doesn't make much progress. One or two of the obvious factors in the situation: attack of the Soviet Consul on the POUM; attempts of the PSUC (Stalinists) to put us out of the Generality of Catalonia, which have so far failed; much talk of attempts among the bourgeois parties to work for a separate armistice for Catalonia; POUM holds a big alarm meeting, where Nin once mentions 'Let's build soviets' and something very vague about leaving the government, and where Gorkin[64] explains reasons why we can't be put out (our strength in Lérida and Gerona[65]); thorough preparations of the city and population for bombardments – blue painted street lights, strips of paper on all shop windows, huge guns on the hills around the city, practice air-attack nights, much battleships in the harbor and much sailor boys swaggering around on the Ramblas; and continued appeals on the part of the bourgeois and PSUC press to the 'better nature' of Britain and France; continued denunciations of armistice from all quarters. But mostly we wait, and the routine things go on. Also unroutine things: the other night Charlie and I went with Willie, our German theatrical friend, who has finally managed to stay here through an unexpected gift of money from his pa, to a private 'spectacle' put on by the Union of Actors etc., in honor of Piscator, the German director who has been working in Russia but is expected to come here after he finishes some engagements in France. The 'spectacle' was to give him some idea of Spanish and Catalan culture. It consisted mostly of the dances of Aragon, of Andalusia, gypsy dances, songs of Andalusia and Catalan dances – the *sardaña*, which is really swell. There were some other junky things – selections from Catalan operas, recitations by local actors, etc., which were pretty terrible. The whole thing, as our friend Moulin says, could have been done just as well, probably better, before the revolution. Each actor saluted the audience, and at the end a men's choir sang the *Internationale*. The Russian consul, who was in the same box as Piscator, received a tremendous spontaneous ovation from the crowd, clenched fists, shouts, etc. He stood up and made a bow, much like the nobility at the opera. Piscator also, three or four acts later, was applauded and made a little speech – in German, which I could understand. Many of the audience were obviously bourgeois but the large majority were just ordinary people. With their children; Spanish people have a regrettable habit of bringing their children, no matter how young, to the theater and movies, to squall and squirm and make everybody else generally uncomfortable.

Yesterday Charlie went to a recital by Juli Pons, a noted pianist. He didn't enjoy it especially, but Ted did. A light program – Chopin, Schumann – and well attended. It really seems strange to me: real attempts are being made to raise the 'cultural' level of the people here, but you can't imagine what to. [...] At first, in the first great burst of enthusiasm, we were living in a workers' culture; it was the culture in which they had lived during the years of oppression. It was many movie magazines, much obscene propaganda against the church, free movies, everybody in overalls, streets full of such trinkets as caught their imagination – cigarette lighters, tom browns, mickey mouse, etc. – now, all this has receded somewhat. At least one is less and less conscious of it. Life on the surface looks much more like life in any bourgeois city. Culturally, Barcelona is still bourgeois, I think.

[...]

Food at the Falcón is improving. One of the front rooms, that used to be a reading room, is now filled with stacks of potatoes, loaves of bread – and delicious bread, crusty and substantial – cabbages and milk. For the militias and the refugees mostly, but, naturally, we come in on some of it. We've been having beef for meals!!! Ted, our English friend, is going back to Birmingham today or tomorrow, and he is looking forward especially to some real food – ham, eggs, Yorkshire pudding, etc. Incidentally, we've been having lots of eggs lately, especially (1) in omelettes with potatoes and served with green salad and (2) poached and served with a tomato and onion sauce, which you eat later with bread. There is, however, a shortage of cigarettes, but we don't smoke, so it really doesn't make any difference. I understand, though, that the militias at the front take it hard, and great efforts are being made to find some sort of supply. There is also a shortage of sugar, but you can get it with cafés, etc.

Saturday night we had a 'leaving party' for Ted at the apartment of Willie. Before Charlie, T., W., me, and an English girl had supper there. Willie only had three forks and four glasses, though, so we had to borrow some. Afterwards Moulin, our German Trotskyist friend, whom we met through Erber in September and who is just back from Madrid, and Bob, the Scotch lad, and Russell Blackwell, a swell American – NY radical and here as a gen'l information agent for his party,[66] all came. Willie, the good German, likes good wine and bought a huge bottle in a basket, which was purple and strong. Charlie had special lemons to make himself lemonade and nobody drank hardly any wine, but it was pretty to look at.

The other Sunday, when it was nice, we all went down for a walk along the sea. We came through a little shanty town where gypsies and very poor people lived. The houses were neat, homemade, with little courts or gardens. But so tiny, only one room half the size of your kitchen. There were very dirty gypsies there and their equally dirty children. Hundreds of children running around and playing in conditions of unimaginable filth. The little boys were gambling and the little girls playing with balls, each other or in the sand. There were quite a few of the children who were very blond and unquestionably German, probably with sailor fathers. The girls' hair looked, mostly, as though it had never been combed; all tangles and the most lusterless color. I could never have imagined such a place, and the thought of children growing up there is terrible.

My job has reduced itself mostly to a routine now: I get up at 9:00 o'clock while Charlie is still sleeping, get to work at ten – off at 1 o'clock – lunch at 2:00 – on again at 3:30 – work until 7:00. Eat at 8:30 or 9:00 and get to bed about 12. Life in Barcelona is normal until about 2:00 AM. Then the streets empty. Love to you all. Lois.

22. Letter written by Charles to his mother on 14 December 1936, in all probability an addition to the previous document written by Lois

We enjoyed the finely written letter of Dec. 2, as well as the one about two weeks before – where Fran stuck in a note about Dort being ill. We didn't enjoy that part though. I did not know she had to go to a sanatorium, and that got me quite anxious. I don't know what I can do about it, so I guess I should not worry any, except to eat more fruit and get plenty of sleep. But milk has been cut off now, diverted to refugee children & the front. So I get only fruit & bread for breakfast. I am eating lots of oranges and dates. Ask Dort what else I need. I take cod liver oil, but have forgotten whether it is calcium or phosphate which I should use to supplement it, calcium I believe. Calcium tablets come expensive here. Should I buy some anyway?

One thing, the sun shines brightly half of the days, and in the morning I go down and sit by the water, with my colored glass and the newspaper, and start my translating in the sun. That is the only time you are warm, except in bed, which we pack with newspapers & raincoats! My office is cold, but that of Lois not so bad. But they are moving to a bigger one, which body heat will not heat so quickly. It is hard to work effectively in the cold. But what can you do?

They have returned to an 8 page *La Batalla*, and are going to run my articles after all. I am writing some more of them.

John McNair[67] of the ILP and the London Bureau is here now and has his office next to mine. He is really our boss now. And I like him very well. We are changing the form of our paper, and it will come every 2 weeks.

[…][68]

Notes

1. This postcard was the very first sign of life sent back home by Lois and Charles after their arrival in Barcelona.
2. Ernest Erber was a key player within the youth politics of the American socialist movement during the 1930s. He had been elected National Chairman of the Young People's Socialist League (YPSL) in the summer of 1935, and by 1936 he had become a leading member of the Left wing of the American Socialist Party. Together with the majority of members of the YPSL, in January 1938 he split from the Socialist Party and joined the Trotskyist Socialist Workers Party (SWP).
3. The YPSL was the youth organisation of the American Socialist Party and a member of the social democratic Socialist Youth International (SYI). In the mid-to-late 1930s, the SYI radicalized in the direction of Left socialism and dissident communism, which, in the case of the YPSL, led in January 1938 to the organizational separation from the American Socialist Party. After separating from American social democracy, the YPSL became the official youth organization of the SWP.
4. This sentence of Charles' addendum to the postcard text refers to the print design of the card.
5. Emma Goldman, born in 1869 in the Tsarist Empire, pursued her lifelong devotion to the ideals of anarchism and anti-bourgeois feminism in a variety of national settings. Having made the United States her home early on in her career, she became one of the leading international spokespersons for the anarchist movement. Expelled to the Soviet Union from the United States during the Palmer Raids after the First World War, she returned to Western Europe in 1922. Her activity in defence of the Spanish Revolution was the last major campaign she led before her death in 1940. Her writings on Spain have been published as *Vision on Fire: Emma Goldman on the Spanish Revolution* (New Paltz, N.Y.: Commonground Press, 1983).
6. 15 September 1936.
7. The *Control Guerra* was in all likelihood one of the many committees or subcommittees that dotted the organizational landscape of Catalan towns in the summer and fall of 1936. From the context it is apparent that this committee had some sort of police function.
8. The World Youth Congress, meeting in Geneva, Switzerland, from 1–7 September 1936, was one of a series of international conferences in the late 1920s and 1930s, designed to be party-political neutral gatherings to promote peace and to combat militarism and fascism, but in reality dominated behind the scenes by the Stalinist organisers and their fellow-travellers.

9. Second part of letter, written the same day, 23 September 1936, 'later 7:30', the initial paragraph (not included here) begun by Lois and here continued by Charles.
10. Mary Low (1912–2007) was an Australian-born Surrealist writer who, together with her Cuban-born companion (and, after September 1937, husband), Juan Breá (1905–1941), a long-time activist in the Trotskyist and Surrealist movements, authored one of the most sensitive memoirs of the Catalan Revolution and the early months of the Spanish Civil War, *Red Spanish Notebook: The First Six Months of the Revolution and the Civil War* (London: Secker and Warburg, 1937). After her husband's death of natural causes a few months after their arrival in Mexico, Mary Low, after 1944, lived and worked together with the Cuban Trotskyist Armando Machado (1911–1982). In the wake of the successful Cuban Revolution in 1959, Mary Low, a talented linguist, obtained a professorship at the University of Havana. The creeping Stalinization of Cuban society, however, soon led to her growing estrangement from the Castro regime, and Mary Low was forced to leave Cuba in 1964, eventually settling down in Florida.
11. Second part of letter, written 'Tuesday morning, September 28', by Lois.
12. Third part of letter, written 'Wednesday, Sept. 30', by Lois.
13. A contemporaneously popular Soviet movie about the Russian Civil War.
14. Delirium tremens, a symptom of advanced alcoholism. The novel referred to in the letter is Émile Zola's *L'Assommoir*.
15. The stationery is imprinted with the name, address and telephone number of the *Fomento de la Vivienda Popular, S.A. Rambla de Estudios 10*.
16. The 24-year old Hans David Freund, known by the pseudonym 'Moulin', was one of the organizers of a Trotskyist grouping in Catalonia and Spain during the time that Lois and Charles Orr spent in Barcelona. He escaped the first wave of repression of dissident communists after the Barcelona May Days, but then vanished without leaving a trace after his arrest on 2 August 1937, in all likelihood perishing in one of the Stalinist secret jails.
17. The October 1934 revolt affected various portions of the Spanish state, though it was most widespread in the northern region of Asturias, where a coalition of Left-wing forces, led by social democracy but including most notably the Asturian federation of the CNT, staged an armed insurrection. This event, considered a last-ditch effort to stave off a dictatorship by the radical Right, became known as the Asturian Commune, and it ended in total defeat by the insurrectionary Left.
18. In Catalonia, the locally dominant CNT abstained from organizing protests in October 1934, and the Catalan contribution to the October revolt took on the overtones of a nationalist movement, though avoiding armed insurrection from the beginning.
19. The *Cardinal* was the student newspaper on the campus of the University of Louisville.
20. Addendum to letter of 7 October, with the handwritten notation '10:15 P.M.' at the head.
21. This was probably Hans Reiter, the head of the Josep Rovira Battalion, a subdivision of the POUM's Lenin Column.
22. The 'etc (!)' refers to rumours that the ship was loaded with military supplies for the Republican forces in the Spanish Civil War.

23. This 'Dutchman', later on in the text referred to by the name of 'Lou Litchfield', was Lou Lichtveld (1903–1996), who, under the pen-name Albert Helman, published many works of fiction. He lived in Spain from 1932 to 1938. In 1937, under his birth name, the Surinam-born intellectual of Native American descent, published his eyewitness account of his experience in Republican Spain, *De Sfinx van Spanje* (Rotterdam: Nijgh & Van Ditmar, 1937), devoid of any references to his activity for the POUM International Bureau. Subsequently an activist in the Dutch Second World War resistance movement, he later returned to Surinam, where he worked in a number of political positions between 1949 and 1961. Albert Helman then took up a teaching post at the University of Amsterdam. His home then remained in Amsterdam until his death.
24. Addendum, written on 'Thursday morning, October 15, 1936', by Lois.
25. This 'German Jewish friend', later on in this text frequently referred to by various misspelled versions of his name, was Willi Marckwald. Willi Marckwald survived the Spanish Civil War and later found refuge in Sweden.
26. This is the first partially typewritten letter in the collection kept in the Orr papers.
27. 'Socialism in one country' was a prominent slogan of the Stalin faction within the Soviet Communist Party during the 1920s, when Stalin was engaged in his power struggle against Bukharin, Trotsky and others.
28. This is the first sentence of the typewritten portion of this letter, introduced by the notation 'Later'.
29. Gertrude Stein (1874–1946) was an avant-garde American writer whose Paris home functioned as a salon for the leading artists and writers of the period between the First World War and the Second World War.
30. This is, in all likelihood, a reference to Juan Andrade (1898–1981). Andrade had been a member of the Spanish Communist Party in the early 1920s, then became a supporter of the Trotskyist Left Opposition, finally breaking with Trotskyism to become a founding member of the POUM.
31. Andreu Nin was a founding member of the Communist Red Trade Union International in 1921. He had come to Moscow as the head of the delegation representing the CNT. He became the Secretary of the Red Trade Union International and remained in Moscow, where he joined the emerging forces of the Trotskyist Left Opposition in 1923. Expelled from the Soviet Union in 1930, he returned to his native Spain, where he became the intellectual figurehead of the Spanish Left Opposition. Breaking with Trotsky in 1933, he eventually became a founding member of the POUM and Minister of Justice in the Catalan Generalitat from September to December 1936. He was captured in the wake of the Barcelona May Days by the Stalinist secret police, in whose hands he died.
32. A handwritten addition in the margins refers to this passage and indicates, 'latest claims are 200.000'.
33. This 'Scotch lad', Bob Smillie, was the nephew of Robert Smillie, the head of the Scottish Mineworkers Union from 1894 to 1918 and the head of the British National Union of Mineworkers from 1912 to 1921. Bob Smillie died under suspicious circumstances in the wake of the Barcelona May Days while in custody, probably from an ill-attended appendicitis.

34. This 'Belgian comrade' was Georges Kopp. Twice wounded on the Aragon front, he soon became a commanding officer in the POUM's Lenin Brigade, where he led the unit George Orwell fought in. Jailed by the Stalinist secret police, he spent many months in their custody in Spain before his release to a Belgian consular official in 1938. The most comprehensive biographical sketch of the colourful personality of Georges Kopp is now Bert Govaers, 'Comandante Georges Kopp (1902–1951). De Belgische vriend van George Orwell', *Brood & Rozen* 2007/2, pp. 5–21.
35. The British Independent Labour Party, founded in 1893, looked back upon a long tradition of socialist politics within or outside of the British Labour Party. In 1936/1937, it formed part of the same international association of Left socialist and dissident communist organizations as the POUM, that is the so-called London Bureau.
36. Jennie Lee (1904–1988) became the youngest member of the British Parliament when she won a by-election in February 1929 on the ticket of the Independent Labour Party. She was 24 years of age. In 1934 she married Aneurin Bevan, the Minister of Health and creator of the National Health Service in the Labour government formed after the 1945 election victory. In the same elections, Jennie Lee won the mining constituency of Cannock (now in the West Midlands) and returned to parliament. In the Labour government set up by Harold Wilson after the 1964 election victory, Jennie Lee held the post of Arts Minister, and she signed responsible for the creation of the Open University.
37. Edwin 'Ted' Fletcher (1906–1992) became a Labour Party activist after his return from Spain. In 1944 he was recruited into a team of young economists set up to develop plans for post-war economic reconstruction by the British Trades Union Congress (TUC). He soon became the head of the TUC's economic and research departments. He subsequently held further posts in several British and European economic research institutes.
38. Norman Thomas (1884–1968) was the undisputed leader of the American Socialist Party and stood as its presidential candidate in all US presidential elections between 1928 and 1948.
39. Most frequently employing the pseudonym B.J. Fields, the American Max Gould was active in Trotskyist circles throughout the 1930s. The Columbia University–educated intellectual founded the League for a Revolutionary Workers Party in the United States, a tiny splinter group from which he was eventually expelled, subsequently ceasing all political activities.
40. 'Kream' refers to William Krehm, who became a friend of the Orrs in subsequent months. The Canadian journalist 'Bill' Krehm led the Canadian branch of Max Gould's League for a Revolutionary Workers Party. Unlike its American counterpart, Krehm's organization for a while became more significant than the 'official' Trotskyist organization in Canada, although never gathering much more than a hundred members.
41. An international gathering organized by the London Bureau, the Left socialist and dissident communist organization then encompassing, amongst other groupings, the POUM and the ILP.
42. In fact, Francisco Franco's coup attempt on 17 July triggered a wave of bloody repression of real or purported supporters of Franco in many parts of Spain where the revolt was initially unsuccessful. Esenwein and Shubert

report, 'The principal targets were those who were directly involved in the rebellion itself as well as those who could be identified as "class enemies", namely the leading representatives of the Right. Literally thousands of people were summarily executed in the opening weeks of the conflict. Just how many were killed is difficult to say with any certainty, not least because many deaths were not faithfully recorded in the public registers'; see Esenwein and Shubert, *Spain at War*, p. 130.

43. Harold Laski (1893–1950) was a British political theorist and intellectual, a member of the British Labour Party and national chairperson of the Labour Party from July 1945 to June 1946.
44. Ramsay McDonald (1866–1937) was prime minister in the first and second British Labour goverments in 1924 and 1929–1931. He subsequently left the Labour Party to form a 'national unity' cabinet with Conservatives and Liberals in which he, once again, became prime minister (1931–1935).
45. This passage refers to the *Sagrada Familia*, designed, built but never completed by Antoni Gaudí i Cornet (1852–1926). See http://www.sagradafamilia.org/ for further information, including a virtual tour.
46. Third paragraph of a subsequent section of the letter begun on 9 November, headed 'Tuesday. 10th.'
47. Portion of an addendum written by Charles, addressed to 'Dear Culters'.
48. This is one of many unsubstantiated rumours which circulated in Republican Spain at that time, although individual cases of French citizens' support to Franco's forces undoubtedly existed in reality as well.
49. Atherton was a public girls' high school in Louisville, Kentucky, which both Lois and her sister Anne attended. In the 1930s, Lakeside, the part of Louisville Atherton High School was located in, was the equivalent of a suburb. Lois' comment should be read to indicate that anyone having attended Atherton had probably led a relatively sheltered life.
50. Starting with this sentence, this paragraph and the following one are crossed out by hand, and Lois has added the following sentences: 'Skip and come back if you wish. I cross all this out because I was just thinking aloud when I wrote it; I don't really know what I think on this subject.'
51. Mary was a sister of Charles Orr. She was married to Harry De Vries.
52. The city of Burgos in north-central Spain became the government seat of the Francoist forces after their military rebellion in July 1936 which triggered the outbreak of the Spanish Civil War.
53. First sentence of a subsequent section of the same letter, with the handwritten notation '[continued]' at the top.
54. Second paragraph of the section of the same letter, headed by the handwritten notation 'Sunday, November 29. 1936'.
55. John McGovern was a leading Scottish member of the British Independent Labour Party until his transfer to the Labour Party in November 1946. He served as MP for Glasgow Shettleston from 1930 to 1959. His memoirs are entitled *Neither Fear Nor Favour* (London: Blandford Press, 1960).
56. First sentence of a further handwritten section of the same letter, headed 'Monday'.
57. First sentence of yet another separate section of the same letter, started on 28 November 1936, a typewritten section headed 'November 30, Barcelona, Spain'.

58. On repressive moves by Republican forces in Madrid against the POUM as early as October 1936, see Reiner Tosstorff, *Die POUM im spanischen Bürgerkrieg* (Frankfurt: ISP, 1987), pp. 155–157.
59. On the exclusion of the POUM from the Madrid *junta de defensa*, see Burnett Bolloten, *The Spanish Civil War: Revolution and Counterrevolution* (Chapel Hill: University of North Carolina Press, 1991), p. 298.
60. First sentence of the final section of this letter, on p. 10, headed by the notation 'Later'.
61. First full paragraph on the fourth page of the handwritten letter to 'Dear family' written on 'Dec. 1. Wednesday' by Lois.
62. First line of an unaddressed, typewritten letter fragment, possibly an addendum to Charles' handwritten letter to his aunt, written by Lois, dated 'Dec. 7'.
63. Erwin Piscator (1893–1966) was a notable proponent of 'proletarian theatre' in the Berlin theatre scene during the Weimar Republic. He emigrated in 1934, first to Moscow, then to Paris, finally settling in the United States in 1938. He returned to Europe in 1951 and completed his career as a theatre director in West Berlin in the 1960s.
64. Julian Gorkin (1901–1986) entered political life as a journalist and member of the Spanish Communist Party. After briefly joining the Trotskyist opposition in Spain, he soon became a leading member of the Spanish section of the so-called International Right Opposition, Joaquín Maurín's Workers' and Peasants' Bloc, which merged in 1935 with Andreu Nin's Spanish Left Opposition to form the POUM. Gorkin became the POUM's International Secretary. Exiled to Mexico after the Spanish Civil War, he participated in the leadership of the exile organization of the POUM.
65. The railway town of Lérida took on a particularly prominent role after the outbreak of the civil war as a strategic centre for the provisioning of the Aragón Front. As the POUM was the dominant political force in Lérida, this elevated this provincial town to a position of particular salience in the context of rivalries amongst the Spanish Left. Another Catalan provincial centre, Gerona was likewise a stronghold of the POUM, though here the POUM was not in a position to dominate local politics. For a detailed social and political history of Lérida in the years of open civil war, see Joan Sagués San José, *Una ciutat en guerra: Lleida en la guerra civil espanyola (1936–1939)* (Barcelona: Publicacions de l'Abadia de Montserrat, 2003).
66. Russell Blackwell (1904–1969) started his political career as a member of the American Communist Party in the 1920s before moving to Mexico, where he soon joined the Trotskyist Left Opposition. Long before he arrived in Barcelona, he had already joined forces with Hugo Oehler's Trotskyist splinter group, the Revolutionary Workers League. In Barcelona, he also linked up with a dissident faction within the POUM under Josep Rebull. Blackwell subsequently became closely aligned with various anarchist groupings.
67. John McNair (1887–1968) was a leading member of the Independent Labour Party (ILP) from the 1920s onwards. From 1924 to July 1936 he lived

in France and was Acting International Secretary. For much of the 1940s and 1950s he held the post of General Secretary of the ILP.
68. The two letters penned on 14 December 1936, in all likelihood two parts of a jointly written letter, is the last extant (set of) document(s) in the Orr Collection for that calendar year.

5
Letters from Barcelona (Winter)

By the time of the first extant letter written after the Christmas and New Year period, penned on 4 January 1937, the POUM had been removed from the Catalan government coalition, reflecting the uncertain fate of revolutionary aspirations in the winter of 1936–1937. Lois' and Charles' involvement with POUM politics, however, deepened, with Charles taking over the English-language propaganda department of the POUM. In February 1937 Eileen O'Shaughnessy, George Orwell's wife, began to work as Charles' secretary, as her writer-husband fought at the front.

Lois now began to shed some of her uncritical naïveté regarding far-Left politics. In part no doubt because of the couple's close association with dissident thinkers operating in the colourful spectrum of activists with ties to dissident anarchist factions, non-conformist sympathizers of the POUM and an assortment of unorthodox Trotskyists, Lois developed a keen eye for faction fights within the powerful CNT and the far Left as a whole. A keen observer of detail, Lois confided that 'I get a feeling here that history concentrates on the little things.' Astutely aware of crucial ideological differences between the various factions on the Republican side, Lois soon concluded that 'it's all ordinary every day and seemingly petty things that might happen to anyone – this business of politics'. Still, Lois wrote in early February 1937, 'I am having a good time here and am satisfied – with living here, but am of course in a continual state of excitement and despair over the political and military situation.'

Yet her recognition that 'it's really the little points and shades of meaning that decide things' remained limited to the realm of politics as such. Though a curious observer of the world around her, Lois brushed off her mother's repeated exhortations to pay closer attention to 'local color', the culture and the habits of her Catalan hosts. Both Lois and Charles remained wholly uninterested in learning the local language, Catalan, and even their Spanish-language skills remained on a rather rudimentary level.

23. Letter written by Lois to her family on 4 January 1937

The weather is getting better and better here: warmer. The Ramblas are filling up again with stands selling tin-ware, Pop-Eye books, tom-browns, pornographic literature, pocket books, scarves, dolls, etc.

Last week was children's week, and everywhere were people carrying around toys, picture books (Mickey Mouse and Popeye the most popular; with also really good books for kids which had been put into cheap editions in the same format as Mickey and Shirley Temple), clothes, etc. The socialized stores featured giving presents with purchases of children's clothes, etc. This was organized especially for the refugees from Madrid, but I imagine that a lot of people who were afraid to give Xmas presents because Xmas was forbidden used this as an excuse for their own kids. The CNT and the UGT organised it. And all the little orphans were supplied with clothes, theater visits, etc. I saw a string of them walking along all in blue sailor suits and looking very chic.

I think I told you about a guy, Marzani,[1] who was the director of 'Winterset' on Broadway and several other things. He is at Oxford on a special scholarship and took advantage of the notorious freedom allowed students there to come to Spain two months ago. He has been out on the Aragon front with the *Columna Durruti*, in the sanitation and intelligence depts. He was sent around to see us by Willie, our German dramatist friend who works in the CNT German section. Those two got on fine together and planned out two movie scenarios in the course of one half-hour. Marzani, however, has gone back to England, so as not to lose his scholarship, as he thinks that nothing is going to come to a crisis here, probably, until the Spring anyhow. He had a lot of things interesting to tell; he is an Italian – left Rome ten years ago and has lived in the USA since, graduated Williams and of course speaks fluent Spanish. He says the soldiers at the front, at least in the Durruti column, are very disgusted with the way things are being run in Barcelona. They come back to the city on leave, remembering the exciting July days when they fought at the barricades and took over everything as their own, and find here, instead of any revolutionary spirit, a growing bureaucracy, the same graft as before, all Esquerra people in good jobs, everybody talking democracy and hushing revolution; the whole atmosphere disgusts them, and many go back to the front without finishing their leaves, all saying, 'just give us a quarter of our army here, and we'll go back and clean the place up'. But they don't know exactly what that means. Which Marzani found significant. We'd heard before that the soldiers were dissatisfied with things back here, and that the Catalan govt – the Esquerra and PSUC – were deliberately holding up operations on the Huesca front to keep the militia busy there.[2] How true that is I can't say. But the militia at the Huesca front are the real revolutionaries who captured Barcelona from the fascists, established the necessary committees, and then left for the 'front' in great groups of confiscated trucks and cars. A really wonderful spirit, you know. The people holding the jobs here – many of them – are not the militants of the parties that did the first important job. My own idea of why munition doesn't get to the Huesca front – and it is a generally recognized fact, even by the PSUC, that it doesn't – is that the central gov't, which has the money to buy the munitions, doesn't want them to fall into the hands of the anarchists. The central govt, dominated by the Stalinists, is already taking steps to institute another bureaucracy *à la Russe*: Valencia is jammed with Russian technicians – aeroplane experts, propaganda experts, economic experts, old CP stalwarts (Stalinists, of course), who are advising the gov't on every side. If it was just a question of proletarian solidarity, it would be swell, but they don't work with or for the proletariat, but the bourgeoisie.

It's interesting that, wherever there is an offensive to undertake – in Madrid, in Teruel, in Aragon, the 'International Brigade' or other trusted communist troops are shifted to the spot, supplied with the ammunition, and the attack begins. In Madrid, the anarchists were, according to bitter revolutionaries of the Durruti column, refused ammunition, weapons, even bread. By the central government. The Durruti column, which entered Madrid with such fanfare, had come trickling back one by one with always the same story – we can't fight, we can't eat. Durruti, too, the great anarchist leader and revolutionary, was shot; it is believed in all quarters because he was too dangerous.[3]

Mary Breá, as I may have told you, has gone with Breá to Paris, en route to Cuba, although probably they won't be able to enter Cuba. So Charlie is now the head of the English propaganda section of the POUM: he does the bulletins and the radio alone. Incidentally, they are making all the foreigners working in the propaganda department milicians so as to get them on the payroll. Charlie, but not me, because I, dern it all, work for the Generality and not the POUM. Of course, as always in Spain, this hasn't materialized yet, but, when it does, C. will be getting 10 pesatas a day and I twelve. Which is quite nice. Not that he doesn't deserve it, after working for the POUM three months for only that lousy food in the Falcón.

Oh, and talking about food. Willie took us out the other night to an old, old restaurant. It was a whole house of eating rooms, up to the fourth floor, with balconies inside and out. The kitchen is on the first floor and balconies look over it. The walls are a brown that only comes with centuries and were in some former time painted in bright colors with primitive pictures, which have been mostly toasted off. From the ceiling, which is three or four stories above the kitchen, hang huge bunches of dried and drying herbs. The staircases are very tiny and have a huge wooden snail on the post of the railing, worn smooth by so many hands touching him. We sat on a balcony where we could lean over and watch them cook – 65 people working in the whole house which has been collectivized. The cooks were all in huge white caps; and instead of making the food seem uninteresting, the smells and seeing things sizzle made you all the hungrier. There were two brothers who inherited the place. One of them was a sissy and ran away, and the other works as a cashier now. Before, all bourgeois came there; now the prices are down and workers come. And, last of all, the food: it was divine, of course. The best we've had in all Spain, Willie's cooking included. We had a salad of tomatoes, greens, onions, carrots, pickled cauliflower, ham, bloodwurst, another wurst, black big olives and little sharp ones, and was it good! We had also meat with tomatoes which was excellent. Willie had lobster with mayonnaise which was indescribable. We ran into Jenny Lee, McNair, and an American Anarchist, Frank, a swell fellow there. A very sweet purple wine, and strong, although we didn't realize it at first.

There is a fellow at the Falcón, an Albanian, who has chosen now – of all times – to go on a fast. It happens that he is a nature fad. He used to go every Sunday to the local nudist colony, where they put on plays and describe the present issue, not as socialism vs. fascism, or even as democracy vs. fascism, but as fascism vs. nudism. Therefore fascism must be destroyed, of course. He began to talk about eating only oranges to cure your eyes, etc., but of course nobody took him seriously. Then he decided to go on a fast and become strong. He hasn't eaten anything for 13 days today, refuses to see a doctor, stays in bed all day, and is becoming put out with all his friends for suggesting that he had better start to eat. He at first used to think about his wife, etc., but now he thinks only about his fast. After twenty days or so he believes that he will commence to become strong. We can't do anything with him, and all the revolutionaries are slightly disgusted: why did he pick *now* for this stunt? Of all inappropriate times, when there is other work for people to do than to try out his naturalism. I don't know what will happen to him.

I've been mostly working hard all the time, looking forward to Sundays when I can sleep all morning and try to diagnose the political situation. I got over the grippe in two days and now, after about a week, C.'s got it. He's in his second day now and is practically well. He eats hundreds of oranges and tangerines, and I even brought myself to peel three of them for him. I'm progressing, eh?

Ann, I stuck your all's pictures up on my mirror and am glad to record that I have had no less than three or four, or maybe even five, proposals for marriage for you. I guess I'll take back what I said about that not being a very efficacious picture. One was from Willie. Did I tell you what he did the other day? As he tells it. 'I went into the store to buy these oranges and there was a very pretty girl. She told how she liked my blond hair, so I said, come with me this night; and she said, only for marriage, and I said, we shall speak of that later; and she said, no, I will not.' – I wrote Xmas cards to my girl friends (I don't like that expression) and told (1) Va. D. (2) Weesie and (3) Starr that it was too bad that they weren't here instead of me as there were so many good looking and stray refugees, and also Englishmen here with no women. Wherever C. and I go, cafe, walks, movies, anywhere, there are always three or four men. We went to see 'Mutiny on the Bounty' the other night, but it was in Spanish and we couldn't understand a word. Which was infuriating, especially when we could see their lips moving in good, intelligible English sounds.

Charlie is doing a job for Andratta [= Juan Andrade], an Exec Comm of POUM member. He, And., is preparing a plan for the organisation of industry after socialism – for all Spain – and C. is to do the theoretical work, all the work, in fact. Very interesting.

I am beginning to pick up a little Spanish, but still very little. It's really awful to be here so long and not know any Spanish; I knew German enough to talk after two months, but here – no one speaks Spanish. Only Catalan.

I've had my hair cut very short: above my ears. It's very comfortable. All the Germans like it, and the French and Spanish don't. They like long curly locks.

[...]

Dear mom, I was just this evening in a bookshop that would turn your and Mrs. [illegible]'s hearts green with envy. It had a very very extensive English department with all the books by D.H. Lawrence, Joyce, Wilde, etc., that cannot be taken into America or England.[4] More D.H. Lawrence than I thought existed, and at ridiculous prices. 24 cents and 36 cents (for double sized). I plan to read as many of them as I can and as interest me – and then pass them on to somebody else – as it is practically impossible to smuggle them into the USA. Such a bourgeois library: *Fortune, Arts & Decorations* & the snitziest magazines including: *Sat Eve Post* up till August. Evidently prohibited since then as fascist. *Ladies Home Journals* current tho: probably considered innocuous.

NB do you all realize how much more you know and will know about the Spanish situation with me here? Though probably you don't really care so much – You'd like it here, mom, I'm sure.

24. Letter written by Lois to her sister Anne, begun on 6 January and finished on 22 January 1937

Between the time I wrote the 'Dear' and the 'Annie,' I was observing the new German Anarchist girl who has come to work in our office; why I know not. She has on a black skirt, a black sweater with just a little of baby pink in the front and the back, and huge round black beads over this. She has yellow hair and in some way makes me think of Paris, a room in the [Latin] Quarter, with primroses in the windows and smocks, etc. She & another industrious German are putting out a Norwegian or Swedish bulletin, I think.[5]

Life in this office is nothing phenomenal. There are more anarchists than any other one sect. There is one anarchist on each bulletin, with PSUC and POUM sharing the other posts. One PSUC boy is a Frenchman, or rather Italian brought up in France and unable to speak Italian, André, and a funny chap. When the other people in his department were working on a mimeograph machine with girls around and having some fun for a change, he comes up to me in the next room and says, 'You see, they are amusing themselves (in a most offended tone), but this can't keep up.' The other PSUCist is a German, Stacy, and also very nice. He says that, if this revolution comes to Stalinists vs. Anarchists, he is coming to America. He is another one who is always asking me about America. I told you how interested Muek was in America (Truper's wife). Evidently Stacy circulated in approximately the same culture in Berlin, where everybody among the moderns and radicals was interested in America. The main anarchist here – or at least the one who makes the most noise – is the one who works in the English department, Leon Green. He is a Russian who was a trade-union organizer in the Electrical Workers Union in the USA. I don't know how he had enough gumption to come over here, but he did and is one of these aggressive self-salesmen types who convinced some of the Spaniards of his great value. The only hitch about him working in this department is that he can't write English, as you may have noticed from the bulletins you've been getting lately. They're all full of Anarchist propaganda. But the English is atrocious, and Leon is so proud of himself and so touchy that he won't allow anyone to tell him anything. After Mary Breá left he was absolutely disgusted with the POUM because she was always correcting his English etc., so he took it on himself to get a PSUC person into her job, altho it is a POUM job.

For your information in all this politics, although POUM is out of the Generality, all POUM jobs, except those directly connected with the portfolios we lost, we have kept. Which I, although I am one of these people, can't exactly understand. It's a bureaucracy tho, and also a political machine which has to be fed.

As Leon had no authority to do this, people – there is a committee between POUM and the CNT for various things since POUM was kicked out of the Generality – are fixing it up, making PSUC unhappy. All terrific politicking, you see. Me, I'm just the secretary who does all the actual work to putting out this lousy bulletin. I don't take any responsibility for its contents, altho the boy whose place I took, did. It's too contrary to what I believe, and if I had to accept responsibility for the policy of the dern thing, I'd resign. Now, as just the typist, I have liberty to criticize and tell Leon what I think about it. Which I do, and because of which Leon doesn't like me and calls the POUM beggars, liars, thieves and other bad names – not to me tho. This in spite of the fact that the Anarchists are finding they have more in common with POUM than with PSUC and have issued several manifestoes against the PSUC and, in yesterday's number of our bulletin, Leon put in a long article about a meeting against the PSUC. He hates the POUM.

Last night I bought myself a new pair of shoes, Oxfords, with built-up wooden heels. About the equivalent of $4 shoes in America – for 20 pesatas – or $1. I don't know how long they'll last. We also bought Charlie a beret, with leather band and lined with silk. A little one; there are big ones here, they are the Basque. Basque in their own language is Euzkadi. But I don't like the big ones as much as the little French ones.

Charlie got paid for working in December for the POUM!!!! Not very much because Mary collected half before she left, but it's a good sign. Sets a good precedent.

Last night we went in to see the Albanian guy who is on a diet. He looks very emaciated but thinks perfectly, etc. Russell Blackwell, the American guy from the left wing fraction of the Workers' Party (the Trotskyists before they went into the SP – his fraction, about 150–60 people didn't go into the SP) went with us and worked his yo-yo all the time. He's a swell person. Super-super[6] intelligent, but given to bad puns. He always is at the bottom of anything and understands how all the wheels are going around, all the deepest of deep politics. But he's a very gentle person, talks softly, likes children and is extremely kind and never hurts anyone's feelings. If Bob,[7] the Scotch kid, makes a rough crack as he loves to do – Blackwell will always answer him back with another remark to repair the sore.

You know, it takes being in the POUM amid tens of tiny fractions to understand how wheels really work in a historic situation like this. Of course some people just know what they read in the papers, a very vague outline, others have an idea that the Communist party, the socialist party, the bourgeoisie are all working some way to make things happen. But when you are really in the know, it's the prejudices of the anarchist minister of justice or the personality of the fractions exerting their influence against two members of the execu. committee. It's the fact that Miravitlles[8] was kicked out of the POUM once – it's all ordinary everyday and seemingly petty things that might happen to anyone – this business of politics. I see after having written a paragraph that I can't explain what I mean; it's just a feeling of how unimpressive are the people who really make things happen, who really make history. And when you are close to all these things they look different.

It's really the tiny unimportant things, that most people brush aside when they say: 'These sectarian people, they can never take a broad view of things, a complete view.' But it's really the little points and shades of meaning that decide things; I get a feeling here that history concentrates on the little things. They're really the heart of political activities and the broad, generous, free-thinking people don't really understand. You can be vague and high-minded in America, but here you *must* understand and appreciate the tiny nuances, as well as having a broad oversight, or you are lost.

[...]

I started you a letter a week or so ago, but didn't have much to tell you, so didn't ever finish it.[9] Now I have a great desire to continue my progress, learning how to type without looking at the keys. All mistakes you note herein will be due to that.

I haven't had a letter from you all for over three weeks. Or from anybody. I think it's probably caught up in the Censor's office. I don't know why. It may be rank discrimination tho; don't know.

Life here continues much the same. The political situation is getting riper and riper. The French have just passed a bill prohibiting volunteers for Spain, which will undoubtedly be a blow to the prestige of those Pop front parties with the French workers. You there can't understand the feeling of the French workers. But they feel the way you read about in

Marxist books: when they occupy a factory, nobody talks about violating property rights, because the workers know dam' well, when they stick their red flags up in front of all the doors, that this is just practice for the time when they will take them over for good. They have a revolutionary spirit there that I never understood until I saw it. It's a feeling that an American can't very well understand. And they have a sure knowledge that their cause and that of the Spanish workers is the same. It's nothing they have to read in the books. They just know. And when the CP and SP prohibit them from flooding across the border as they have been doing, they will be very confused for some time, but I don't think the Blum government can stop them. I think that this is going to clear the minds of a lot of them. But we'll see.

And all these people that say, 'Oh, Blum knows better'; 'Stalin knows better', they're only being politic. I say a social democratic policy is the same no matter what color flags they carry in their demonstrations.

I'll get this letter finished one of these days.[10] Oh, I'll finish my polemic against popular front governments and their 'diplomatic maneuvers'. The French government *is* a bourgeois government and will continue to govern in favor of the bourgeoisie as long as the workers allow it to govern. Just because there are communists and socialists on it, this is no sign that it is a workers' government. It is dominated absolutely by the bourgeoisie. Oh, well.

This last Sunday I got a flood of letters. Evidently the censor has been sick or AWOL or something, because for three weeks nobody got letters.[11] And, oh daddy, the lovely bobby pins you sent me didn't get through. Evidently somebody picked them out and liked them too. [...]

[...]

I have been editing the English bulletin in the absence of Leon Green – the Anarchist.[12] Of course, legally, I am entitled to edit it regularly if I want to, but I don't. I don't want to take any responsibility for it because I disagree so heartily with every line it takes. The line of the Generality is frenziedly popular frontist. POUM wants us to hold our jobs here and strategically speaking it's an ok thing to do. So I stay. Glad to earn the money, of course, and also glad to have a job away from Charlie all day. And, of course, I learn a heck of a lot – facts about the situation here, political and economic stuff, and a lot more about how to get on with people, how a first class bureaucracy works, etc.

[...]

The weather is getting swell here again, warm and sunny all day. I have a new skirt, incidentally. There is a little Catalan girl who works here who went with me to a big market, under a tent like a circus, where they sell everything; material, stockings, dresses, underclothes, shoes, sweaters, tinware, furs, laces, everything you could think of. We bought there some blue woolen material, very lightweight. She measured me at the office with a string and three knots, and gave this all to a friend of hers, who gave it to her sister who cut and sewed the dress for me, for nothing. I wanted to do something for them, so they asked me to exchange English lessons with them, which I was very glad to do. 7 pesetas for the goods.[13]

Incidentally, there is an Austrian girl here now, who is head of an underground group.[14] She was working in the office – of the government department – which carried out the 'liquidation' of all the workers' organisations in Vienna, and she said it was wonderful how they didn't find a single typewriter in all the offices they inventoried. Disappeared. Vanished into the underground movement. She is a little short girl, with the broad face of a typical slavic-germanic type and very tiny. She has hands the size of a child's.

The girl I think I told you about in the first part of this letter is not a German at all but a real Swedish person. She is very sweet and Charlie and I have had her home to dinner with us twice. It was remarkable, the crowd of men who went with us that night for our usual *café con leche*: Tom, the Polish boy, the Swedish boy, the Greek, the one German, Fritz, Herbie, the very nice German YCLer who was in an insane asylum to escape from Germany after being put into a concentration camp, etc. And Bob, all of them came. She is a very flirtatious, capricious person, but, as she puts it, she never goes out with the same boy twice because she will only hold hands with them, nothing more.

Stacy, the nice German Stalinist who works here in this office, has been the whole morning and afternoon talking to a Dutch comrade who had just come here, orienting him to the situation. And, in spite of how the Stalinists' line is all and only for unity, peace within the working class forces, Stacy spent most of the morning telling him about the POUMists. All our crimes, etc. And, to listen to him, we and the anarchists must absolutely be done away with as counterrevolutionaries. *Then* we can have peace, cooperation, unity with the working class – between them and the bourgeois, he means. Just a little funny, tho, that these great advocates of peace and unity should spend the whole morning attacking another party in explaining the needs of the situation, etc.

I have some swell copies of *L'Il.lustració*, Xmas numbers, etc., which, after the library refused them on grounds that they already had them, we incautadoed from the home of one of the Nazi spies formerly here

(To *incautado* is to requisition or confiscate. All signs posted on buildings etc. say *Incautado por la Generalitat*, or POUM or CNT. Incidentally, if you saw this sign in good Catalan on a black wall, would you understand? *Recien pintado* or *Pintado de nuevo*. Or would you understand *Festa de fi de l'any* [= New Year's Festival] or *No hi ha pa* [= we have no bread] – that is the commonest);[15] from the same source I have also acquired 2 wonderful straw hats: big dippy ones, latest model from Paris, one black and one yellow, one pair white fine kid gloves – new – one pair brown suede – 1 marvelous belt with wooden buckle – brown – one black suede purse – also 2 vases for flowers & 2 ash trays & 2 plates – dishes for dates, etc.

The youth organizations of the CP and SP have fused and come out with this wonderful declaration: we are not Communists, Socialists, Marxists. We seek complete unity with the bourgeois youth. We think the Catholic youth are the key to the present situation. We are not deceiving you; this is not a strategy; we are sincere when we say that we have only one object: a parliamentarian democratic Spain, which will be respected in the concert of Nations. (Imperialist capitalist nations, please, are to recognize Spain as a fellow Nation!!!) As the Anarchists remarked in an editorial on the subject: If they aren't Communists, Marxists, socialists, or workers, what are they?

But the Stalinists continue gaining power here. There is a gasoline shortage, and restrictions are placed on the number of cars allowed to circulate. So the proportion of the Generality cars vs. CNT, political party cars has changed completely. Almost all the cars on the streets are Generality cars, very few POUM cars, and not half so many CNT cars as formerly. There has been a light shortage of bread here, due to the fact that when the Stalinists took charge of the supply dept of the Generality, they began to disband the local supply committees, which, created spontaneously by the workers after the July days, had been functioning ok. There was no organization to replace them. The PSUC is against the committees because they are too much like soviets, workers' control, etc. So the PSUC raised the slogan, 'Mes pa, minus comités', more bread, fewer committees. The Libertarian Youth, anarchist, began posting slogans against Comorera,[16] the PSUC minister, and the POUM did too: more bread, less reformism; Comorera must be replaced, as he is a reformist, and others to that effect. The Libertarian Youth were officially rebuked in the *Soli*[17] by the CNT. There is a split coming up in the CNT, I think, as there are elements there who are openly PSUCist, while there are others that are really revolutionary. The other day the *Soli* published an editorial showing the points where they disagreed with Marxism, and these were the characteristics of the PSUC – party dictatorship, etc. – not of the POUM. The POUM now comes out for a workers' democracy. I, personally, am not sure that that is really what they want. I am not sure that if they had the power they too would not set up a party dictatorship, perhaps with democracy within the party. I know there are some elements within the POUM who are working for a real workers' democracy, with different parties represented in a democratically elected governing body which would formulate policy and centralize authority highly in the administrative departments. The objections – one – to that is that, to have a really strong state, it is better to have one party and let the democracy lie within that party. But it is so easy to see the dangers in that system as exemplified to perfection in the party bureaucracy and dictatorship of this class over the rest of the workers.

[...]

It is so hard to realize, and it is a tragedy when you do realize it, that the revolutionary spirit and ideals of the workers are being slowly but surely stifled by this Popular Front talk, the necessity for putting the brake on collectivization, socialization, the necessity for compromise with the bourgeoisie. It is terrible to realize that the things that the workers took over for themselves, after years of oppression and misery, are slowly being given back to the bourgeoisie, and being given back to the power of the Generality, which is dominated by Esquerra and Stalinist politicians. It's stark tragedy; just as if, after five months of struggle, the Russians had turned things over to Kerensky, who would begin to work for 'social reform' by 'legislative means.' [...]

[...]

Charlie is making fun of me because I write so much about the Stalinists, but it's so terrible that I have to. What else should I write about? My happy marriage – C. and I are married almost a year – or what? Anyhow, I love you all very much and want to get a letter tomorrow. Love, Lois.

25. *Letter written by Charles to his family on 21 January 1937*

I have ten minutes to sit here before going on the air with my special Lenin's Anniversary broadcast tonight, so I will start a letter.

Yesterday, Bill Krehm, a Canadian Jewish fellow, head of the Canadian Rev. Workers' League at Toronto, arrived and has been engaged to help me, so I have a little more time to write. For the last month I have been too busy – ever since Mary Breá left me alone with the Radio & Bulletin. I was not too strong anyhow on account of the food – tho I was systematically supplementing it with oranges, tangerines, dates, milk and cod liver oil. I got weak in spite of this, and a week after that started to be serious, I had the grippe – not too bad a case. But I wouldn't throw it off quickly like Lois & have been dragging about for two or three weeks since. I worked too hard and finally had to quit. Then I went to the doctor, of the POUM, who sent me out to the Joaquín Maurín Sanatorium – swell houses and gardens taken from some 'fascist' – up on the side of Mount Tibidabo – they have given me a fluoroscope test, blood test, sputum test. The fluoroscope test & blood test were questionable. So I must go back in three weeks for a check. But the woman doctor, a German, thinks that the weakened condition is only a hang-on of the grippe. [...]

Lois is in a position of responsibility on the English bulletin of the Generality since Monday, Jan 18. Do you see any improvement in this week's? But next week she may only be typist again, if the Anarchist man returns. She doesn't want to be editor anyway, because they won't let her put anything revolutionary into it. The other editor is a PSUC (Stalinist) girl, & every argument between them is taken up to a board of an Anarchist & an Esquerra, who are People Front, democratic. So she can do little. She is quite a revolutionary – more so than I. And fairly keen thinker. Not quite broad enough or experienced enough to try to find the good on the other side tho.

She has a new skirt & me a new shirt. Since we came here 5 months ago I have had only one shirt – & no tie – so it was hard during wash days. And she wore her divided skirt right out. She had only a light dress besides. But dress is not important here! Now she has a whole slew of hats (which women don't wear here – but which will be good for India), vases, magazines, pictures, ring, finger nail implements and I don't know what all in her requisition from the [illegible passage] someone else would. I told her that it took a Bourgeois Vandal to really appreciate the loot. This Consul was found to have been the head of the Nazi spies here, and his PhD thesis now serves a useful purpose in the bathroom. The German refugees were given first pick of his home, which is now home for victims of fascism.

Tangerines are very cheap & I bring home about 2 dozen every day or so. And dates too.

More foreigners arrive at the Falcón to become revolutionary experts. An Austrian girl just from Vienna two weeks ago, a Pole, a Greek, an Albanian, a Dutch boy, a Swede, an Argentine Italian, etc.

Lois has a girlfriend who is a Swedish girl who works at the Generality Prop. Dept. Last night we went out to dinner again with our German theater friend, Willy Marqualt. So it goes, and Lois is perfecting her German faster than either of us our Spanish.

We have found a copy of the *Australian & New Zealand Travellers Gazette* for De. 1936 with an add of where to stay in Spain (each country). Under Spain is Barcel & under it is 'Hotel Falcón – Beautiful sunny situation – the Rambla – First Class Family Hotel – Every Improvement and Great Comfort – Very Reduced Terms – Principal Languages Spoken – Arrangements for Long Stays'

[...]

26. Postcard written by Charles to Lois' sister Anne on 30 January 1937

I don't know which we are more worried about – whether you ever got our book of impressions of the revolution which we sent. Or whether you all got washed out by the flood. If so, we invite you over here where it is safe and peaceful. Your big sister, however, has another worry – to hear from you and get an answer to the letter she once wrote you. Your letter must have been sent during Dec. – all mail for that period seems never to have come. But I want you to write to me instead, since I haven't had any mail since Nov. Lois has had 6 letters this month. [...]

27. Letter written by Lois to her family, begun on 4 February and finished on 12 February 1937

It just occurs to me that if I were a loyal Catalan, I would say Barcelona, Catalonia, and not Spain. However let it go. These people here are fiends on this subject of Catalanism. [...] But the interests of the Catalan worker are not at all different from those of the Spanish worker, the French worker, the English worker. This spirit of nationalism has no place in a worker's world, of course. [...] And so what does Thorez, Secretary of the CP-France, say in an address here in Barcelona? In a tirade against Franco's forces for calling themselves nationalists, he explains how the Spanish workers of the government's side are the true nationalists, achieved this that and the other *national* goals. Then he describes the great 'national' treasures of culture, etc., which the workers must and are defending. At first it was the culture and civilisation of the whole world that was being defended here, now it is only the culture and civilisation of Spain which is being defended from these fascist wolves. As if it were primarily a question of culture anyhow: primarily it is a question of economics, and not the defence of culture. What have these Spanish workers, who read only movie magazines, detective stories, pornographic literature, etc., ever known about this bourgeois culture which they are being urged now so heartily to defend? It's just another side track, another veil thrown over the real issues here.

Whew, what a paragraph! But here the revolutionary fervor, which Charlie and I could still feel slightly, when we came here in September and which was wonderful, has disappeared, of course, and now what goes on is political manipulations by the heads of the labor organisations, some of whom are labor bureaucrats, many of whom are Stalinists, and there are continual pacts and counterpacts and demonstrations and, in reality, much nullifying of what the workers did in July. I don't feel like I am doing anything constructive for the revolution working here in the propaganda office. Charlie is doing something interesting but, I suppose, if I weren't working here, we wouldn't be able to stay in Barcelona. What I really do here is observe and learn, theory and practice of revolutions. Charlie, who could be working constructively in industry, is absolutely unwanted.

We don't have meals at the Hotel Falcón any more because they are paying Charlie instead of giving him a meal ticket. We have been experimenting around at different restaurants, and for 3 pesetas can have a very nice meal: wine, salad, one vegetable, one meat or fish, bread and dessert (which here means oranges, apples, nuts, a paste of fruits, which is very good, or a little hard cake). For more, we can get correspondingly better meals. We ate at Carracoli's again the other night – We went with the Escuders,[18] who are Spanish Americans. She was born in America and went to college there; he was there ten years, doing advertising at a very good salary for 20th Century Fox. He is the editor of *La Batalla*, POUM's paper. They are very swell and interesting. Good friends of Anita Brenner[19] and other unaffiliated radicals in New York. They are not the fiends for the correct Marxist line that are the few other Americans here, but are realistic and very sympathetic. Most of the foreigners here come from little fraction groups that have the whole course of the revolution mapped out according to pp. 293, 277, 231, of CAPITAL, other pages of Engels and Lenin. But, as far as the peculiarities of this revolutionary situation are concerned, that is another question, which doesn't alter the prescribed line.

[...]

The weather is beginning to get a little nicer here already, although Mrs. Escuder assures us that there will be at least two more months of chilly weather.

I still don't understand German morals. One German woman, who works in our section, and was, to all appearances, deeply in love with her husband, who is at the front for long periods like three or two months, is now having an affair, before God and everybody, with a boy German, more than ten years younger than she. When we first came here to Barcelona I can remember her worrying and crying because she never heard from her husband who is an artist and a sensitive swell fellow. I think she's nuts. But she'll probably forget it all when her husband comes back. Such are Germans.

The campaign of the PSUC and the Communist International against the POUM is intensified. They use the Moscow trial as evidence that the POUM should be physically exterminated. They have claimed that more and more openly in their papers: that we should be liquidated as counterrevolutionaries and fascist agents. Can you imagine that? That the party with the history of the CP and the traditions of the CP could have come so far? They are unreasonable, absurd; they lie; they defame, and, what is worst of all, they are trying to strangle, when they attack us and the anarchists, whom they also accuse of being influenced by Trotskyist elements, the real revolutionary force in Spain. What do they want? It is evident that they do not want the social revolution. [...]

There is talk, and I can quite believe it, of a split looming in the CNT. There are elements there who have been completely carried away by the Stalinist line, which the anarchists, thank the lord, will not allow. We are hoping that, when this does materialize, the left elements will come into the POUM, or affiliate some way openly. But the Stalinists, of course, are hoping that they will be able to suppress them along with the POUM.

There is a scandal, of course, which has been going on these many months on the Aragon Front. This is the front where the fascists are weakest, as their materials and men are all concentrated at Madrid and Malaga, and only a skeleton force has been left to hold these positions. The soldiers on this front are mostly anarchists or POUM militias, not thoroughly under the control of the Stalinists at Madrid, whose organization maintains many of the original features of a workers' militia, and has not been thoroughly militarized. Altho the command has been centralized at Madrid. There has been absolutely no action on this front during all the long months since the beginning of the war. There has been no ammunition and no guns on this front because the Stalinists are afraid that, if they give them to the anarchists, they will return to Barcelona when they are through with the fascists and finish making the revolution, which must be avoided at any cost. One reason credits, supplies, etc., have been denied Catalonia is that they have not been able to comply with the terms of the Russian consul: stop collectivization immediately, eliminate the POUM. Then the CP has been attacking the workers' militias on the Aragon Front because they do not attack. Once or twice, with a few arms, obtained in spite of the Stalinists, the anarchists or POUM have attacked, or started manoeuvres, but in one case on the Barbastro front, where they were meeting with absolutely no resistance, they were stopped by their commanders. Can you believe all that? It's true, tho, really.[20]

And this, that I tell you next, is from reliable sources in the POUM and is absolutely true. One of the reasons for the bread shortage here, from which the PSUC made so much political capital, was that a shipment bought and paid for from Russia, was never delivered until months late. Russia, in spite of all the publicity she has been getting here and abroad as the proletarian brother of Spain, has only carried on the most business-like intercourse with Spain in distress. At first, true to the non-intervention pact, she refused to sell munitions, etc., to Spain, altho supplying machine gun parts, etc., oil, steel, to Italy to make 'toys for Franco'. Then, for gold, not for credits or for proletarian solidarity, but for cold cash, she sold guns and aeroplanes. She sold food, and now that we have a gasoline shortage, she says: 'For cash in advance, and if you come to Russia to get it, you can buy our gasoline.' And the Spanish workers here all are contributing to a fund for a new 'Komsomol' – Russian boat destroyed bringing *duly paid for goods* to Spain. Spanish pennies, which are few now, and had better be used for bread and milk. Oh, my, it's terrible, you know.

[...]

Lots of things are happening here.[21] But all political, and Charlie swears that he is going to start a campaign against me if I don't quit writing political stuff to you all. So what shall I do?

Now that Charlie and I are both getting paid, instead of getting meal tickets at the Falcón, we are trying all the restaurants in Barcelona, within a certain limit, to find good and cheap ones. Last night we went with a POUM student in the military school, a party militant, who fought in the streets and at the Huesca front, and was sent back to go to military school because he was pretty able. He is a nice kid, twenty-three, I think, and very ambitious. He knows French already and is learning English from me. He has already studied a lot but has never spoken.

We ate with him and two friends last night in a typical Catalan restaurant. It was quite large, a bar at the front and a big room at the back with tables with wooden tops. There was a sign up, *sols 5 de pa*, which meant 5 grams of bread, or no, it must have meant ounces because all the bread is rationed here. A meal usually consists of *ensalada*, which is not counted as a 'plate', a soup or plate of potatoes, cauliflower, cole, rice (Valencian), chick peas (which are very good, but a Mexican dish, I don't think you ever had any; they are yellow and fat, shaped like a round nut with a very distinctive flavor), mixed peas and beans (but never the kind of peas we have in America – these are used only in the swell places to decorate with; they are a luxury) – but never more than two or three of these dishes are available at any one place to choose from. After that comes a meat, fish or egg dish. You are only supposed to have two plates in a restaurant, but if you have a pull you can get more. For meat there are small beef steaks done in tomato sauce, veal with peas or sauce, stew with potatoes and turnips, big fish with their tails in their mouths, ten or twelve little fish, or pieces of sole or cod fish – the last two are sent as relief products from the northern countries. One of these, or eggs cooked over a spicy tomato sauce which is delicious, or tortillas – omelettes – or hard boiled eggs with a sauce and peas over them.

But only two dishes, with salad and not much bread, and with a pasta – dessert afterwards – doesn't really fill you up, I've found. However. There are apples, oranges, dates, figs, raisins, nuts, and *membrillo* – a conserve of fruits which is sliced and very good – or cheese. There is another wonderful thing here, which Blackwell assures me they have in Mexico too, called *turrón*. It is a candy of almonds and honey and is made in different combinations, and with other nuts or fruits in it, and is really wonderful. But expensive now. Lino, the military student, says that, before, it was very cheap, but evidently some source of supply has been cut off by the war. [...][22]

I am reading, did I tell you, the *Plumed Serpent* of D.H. Lawrence, and I must say it is not so good as *Sons and Lovers*. It is too much on the same theme – Mexico, dark, love, manhood, womanhood, how to love your man, in the same marvelously described Mexican landscape, but there is not enough action in the book, and about the fifth ecstasy he goes into over the perfect mating of a man and a woman, you begin to wonder, well, what's going to happen next, having lost interest in what's happening now. And, me being a socialist, his mystic answer to the problems of misery and injustice doesn't quite satisfy me. After all, he advises all races to go back to the gods for their own race: Mexicans to

Quetzalcoatl, Germans to Thor, etc. Well, Hitler has gone back to Thor, and carried this idea of race along the same direction as Lawrence. [...]

But I thoroughly enjoyed the book, as he is a master and writes with a style that is perfect, and his descriptions are fascinating.

[...]

There is another big fight here, too; and that is about the workers' police. Of course, who has the police power and the guns controls the state. So the first thing after the revolution, the workers organized what they call the 'Patrols of Control', which are composed of militants of all the workers' parties: POUM, CNT, UGT, PSUC. They kept order here, had a political police service to safeguard the revolution, which kept a careful control over all activity in Catalonia, made all the citizens have passes to travel, set up this censorship to discover fascists, etc. And, altho it wasn't talked about much, it was continuously discovering fascist plots, etc. And was also discovering plots against the POUM on the part of the PSUC and a big plot, originated by the Estat Català, a bourgeois party, against the anarchists and the POUM, to kill all the leaders. A real workers' police and, in any showdown, these patrols would hold the city and the province for the revolution. There were more anarchists of course than any one party. Now the cry has been raised to give the police control to the Generalitat, to abolish the patrols of control. The PSUC and the UGT have withdrawn all their men from the patrols, much to the disgust and confusion of the men, more than 300 of whom have come over to the anarchists alone, and many of whom have come over to the POUM. So now the patrols are practically in the control of the POUM and the Anarchists. And they got very disgusted about all this posting of slanderous stickers, etc., and one night some POUM and anarchist policemen caught a bunch of stalinists at it and beat them up fearfully.[23]

[...]

But, to continue my little non-political discussion, there is another factor which may weigh largely in the business: the fall of Malaga and the advance of the fascists. This, naturally, tends to stop the factional struggle here. But if things go bad, it will come to this: every party here will attack the other, blaming him for the disaster, those who are hindering the formation of a 'popular army'. (This business of a popular army is this: an army without a class character, commanded autocratically by professional soldiers in Madrid, those who *happened* not to be in on Franco's schemes.)

And, gee whiz, nobody can see better than me and us the real need for unity. It's fatal to be all cutting each other's throats while the fascists come closer and closer. But when the Stalinists use this need for unity to strangle the revolution, when they never loose sight for one minute of the fact that they must use all means to exterminate the POUM and the anarchists, what else can we do, as revolutionaries, but fight for the revolution? Fighting, at the same time, of course, as well as they will let us, against the fascists at the front. But the fact, which even my stalinist girlfriend says is incredible, that in such times of crisis the stalinists who control the Madrid government and the USSR that controls them, would deny arms to their revolutionary worker opponents, is monstrous. And tells much.

But, really, I'll lay off politics. I'm going over to the POUM library, which is just across the street from where I work, and get myself another book to read. It is run by a German, Konig,[24] and is in a swell old house. Everytime the POUM caught some fascists who had a library, the books were brought to this library, and there is a very good collection of French, English, German and Spanish books. Much Lawrence, Buck, Anderson, Sandburg, Dos Passos, Sinclair Lewis, etc. etc. Dickens, Thackeray, Gibbons' *Decline and Fall*, much detective stories, and romance junk.

I am writing this at Charlie's office now and there is a very bad typewriter ribbon. I just got a new one for my machine at the Generality and gave the old one, which was not very much used, to Blackwell; I should have kept it and given it to C.'s typewriter instead. However.

There is a very nice little restaurant where we eat often with Willie, who is working very hard for the anarchists, but is also unhappy because he can't make a theater. It is near the University Place and, as usual, is in the back of a cafe. It is very clean, a low ceilinged room, with white table cloths and clean glasses. It is not collectivized, because it is part of a chain of cafes and restaurants here owned by *Cafés Brazil*, which, as foreign capital, is very scrupulously respected by this bourgeois Generality. It is nice, but not so terribly Catalan. They serve their wine in bottles, not in the little Catalan holders, and the service, etc., is slightly European. Not too much so, and every night at about 10, 10:30, when we are finishing our meal, the whole family who cook, wait tables, with a small child of 3 or 4, and a grandmother with an old shawl, all sit down and eat their dinner. Which is fun. Willie can make a noise like a cat and nobody can tell where it is coming from; he amuses the child for hours with this, and there is a big fat Catalan individualist who eats there who can make a noise like a cock, although he is not so good as Willie. So it's great fun. The little Swedish girl we like eats there too. She is uninformed politically and says, 'I am the friend of the PSUC *and* the POUM; I have many friends in both.' So Krehm, from Canada, who has been working here with C. in a superior fashion, says, 'and when your friends of the PSUC start shooting your friends of the POUM, what will you do then?' and the girl said, 'be sorry'.

I am having a good time here and am satisfied – with living here, but am of course in a continual state of excitement and despair over the political and military situation.

The other latest thing is that C. had an interview with Santillán,[25] the Anarchist Minister of Economy for Catalonia.[26] He is a young chap and, C. says, somewhat gawky. Santillán suggested that he give C. a job either in the department of foreign commerce or in the planning bureau which they are trying to establish. He talked to him and found out just what he could do and then said that, since nothing was well enough organized yet, there wasn't a place for him at this minute, but that they could use him. And he took his name and address, etc. So that may mean something, and maybe not. He told him that there hasn't been a revolution yet. Which is by and large true.

We got a copy of *Time* from an English guy here in the Generality, Donald Darling, and am I happy!

Green's wife has come to Barcelona, and is she a pill! Incidentally, you can continue to observe Green's spelling around our bulletin, lousy as ever. She had some lovely bracelets and rings with big green heads and silver Indian things, which she said were 'the rage around the Village and the lower end of the city, especially among the radicals. You know New York, of course?'

Charlie's beard is flourishing and he really looks very dignified. Of course he occasionally loses a morsel of food in it, for me to pick out. It has a funny smell, too, although he washes it quite often with soap. I don't know why beards would smell any different than heads, but this one does. It is dark brown, the body of it, but the hairs around the top are a reddish gold color, which looks a little funny. He is very proud of it tho, and I am afraid will not want ever to cut it.

[…]

28. *Letter written by Charles to Lois' family on 11 February 1937*

We are still anxious about our people and friends in Louisville, having heard nothing since the flood.

We are getting on well enough and feel better than we did just after the grippe. The sun is getting warmer and the air is clearer already. We have our windows open all day and don't bother about top coats. It will be really nice in another two weeks I think.

Lois is finding herself socially, at last. She is very attractive and likeable when she gets going, but was a little reticent ever since she left home, until recently. About half the men want to take English lessons from her or something. She has become accustomed to working regularly and no longer complains about it being tiresome etc. Of course the working conditions here are ideal – so she should not mind it – except one or two of the people she has to work with. But you always are having to work with people that just don't suit – at least most people are – tho I have had good luck almost always – congenial people to work with.

Lois is showing the *Time* magazine to a German boy, and he is calling her a 'flapper-girl' – which she is denying – and trying to explain the difference between flipper & flapper & flip & flap! Soon we go over to eat in our new boarding house (pension) where we are making a try. I finish broadcasting at 8:15 but we can't eat until 8:45! It is cheaper and better & more (which is important here) than the restaurants or the Falcón. They pay me in money now, so we can eat anywhere.

[…]

The loud speaker is roaring out in front on the Ramblas – to the crowd which always gathers. I have been stuck into a new office – a corner of one, but it has the advantage of being in front on the sunny, but noisy side.

[…]

29. *Postcard written by Charles to his sister Dorothy on 18 February 1937*

The day before yesterday, I got 27 letters – the first I had received in 3 months! It seems that the new managers of our Hotel Falcón didn't know they had a box at the P.O. – since they often delivered letters anyway – only not to me.

I was glad to know that you weren't dying or something. I am busy. Krehm, my helper from Toronto for a month, has left. Just as I was being swamped again, 2 So. Africans and a British boy just turned up & I have put them all to work, sharpening pencils and typing, but Lois came in and got them talking about splinter politics. […]

30. *Letter written by Lois to her family on 18 February 1937*

I sent you all a post card today, but I will follow it with this letter. This one is for the family ensemble but, poor daddy, it just has to have some politics in it, because that's the most important thing here now.

Except, of course, that Charlie and I were married a year yesterday. I remembered it the first thing early in the morning when I woke up (9 o'clock) but as Charlie was still half asleep when I left home, I didn't wake him up by talking to him. Then I forgot all about it. But Charlie gave me a big bunch of red carnations to remember and I put them in one of the vases we got from the German Consul's home, and they look lovely. We still love each other very much and, after due consideration, are glad that we are here together instead of scattered over the American continent apart. I had a Spanish lesson yesterday with a very nice Spanish boy, who can't stand Spanish women, but likes foreign women; and we ended this memorable day at 12:30 coming out of a POUM party meeting, where Andrade spoke and the members discussed the policies of the POUM.

We are eating in a pension now, where we get more than enough to eat but all the people are either fascists or monarchists. Middle class people and do they hate the revolution!!!!! They say, to prove they are not fascists, that they agree with the PSUC in this and in that – in every reactionary step the PSUC has taken. Moulin, the German Trotskyist, whom we met when we were first here, eats there too and is very nice. He is against everything, tho, and works with a few other 'bolshevik leninist' comrades to reform the POUM. They are not members of the POUM, most of them, but are working up an organisation against it. You know, of course, that the official Trotskyists are bitter against the POUM. The official line of the party – of the old man[27] – is that there is no revolutionary party in Spain and that all support must be for the Bolshevik Leninist fraction here. Which is stupid, as there is no more time to build another revolutionary party here – we must work thro the POUM. In it, not against it, as they do.[28]

[...]

Since the fall of Malaga, the revolutionary spirit of the workers has risen, and they are demanding compulsory mobilization and arms. Also, they are demanding that the bourgeois behind the lines be mobilized for fortifications, trenches, etc., building and digging. The CNT and POUM youth organizations, along with several stooge bourgeois groups have formed a 'revolutionary workers' youth front' which is demanding arms for the Aragon front, mobilization, a unified command under revolutionary workers' control. This is significant. The PSUC refused to attend the great demonstration held in the Plaza Cataluña (12,000–15,000 people) because the POUM youth was also invited to attend. It's about 8:15 and the POUM Juventud Comunista Column just marched down the Ramblas with POUM banners and the band playing 'Internationale' and 'Vanguardia'. It's stirring, you know. They're going to the front. Aragon or Malaga, I don't know. But, with the defeats of the last week facing them, the workers show again their grim determination and courage to win this war and make the revolution.The atmosphere here in Barcelona is changing; the Patrols of Control (workers' police) are coming into the foreground. It's really wonderful, you know, the spirit of these workers. The cards are stacked terribly against them – British, French, German, Italian imperialism – but they are just going to fight for what they know and want, until they die. It's simple, dogged and, well, wonderful.

[…]

31. *Letter written by Lois to her sister Anne, begun on 24 February and finished on 2 March 1937*

I just got your typewritten letter on the subject of the Trotskyists. I showed it to Moulin, our 'official' Trotskyist friend, with whom we happened to be eating, and he laughed and laughed. Thinking you a very clever girl. He is 25 – younger than Charlie; but oh, such cynicism, political, I mean, personally he's very nice, and clever – not too sophisticated.

There is a very nice girl here, whom I like. I think I may have told you about her vaguely. Angela Guest – PSUCist who worked before me at this job in the Generalidad, but left for the front. Wears overalls and a Durruti-cap and has short muddy-colored straight hair. She is very simple and direct, and does – within vague restrictions – whatever she feels like. We get along swell. There's a Polish journalist here – Honig – good-looking chap, but such cheek! Mon. nite he makes a date with Angela for 6:30 & Tues. with me at 6:30. Angela had an instinct – that he wasn't all above board etc. Me, I hadn't given it such consideration, being married etc. I wanted to learn about Russia from him – what was really happening in there. So A. was 1 hr. late and brought four or five friends there with [illegible] she said 'You know, I find that kind of thing awfully boring, don't you? Especially with an old man.' So, not knowing that I was wiser by this, I came 1/2 hour late to my appointment and he insisted that we walk thro the Barrio Chino – or red light district of Barcelona – which is picturesque, with funny old cafes, stores, children, dark winding streets, etc. So after a while – when he tried the same stuff on me, I said, when he asked when to see me again, 'If you can give me interesting political information, I'm interested, otherwise absolutely not.' So – twice in 24 hrs – he was thoroughly squelched. But a brilliant well-informed chap. Such tripy stuff.

Lino, a very handsome Catalan lad, is much in love with Angela. So, when he is inarticulate with emotion, she introduces him to a PSUC boyfriend who starts to argue politics – Poor Lino utterly incapable of answering back – Then she assures me that he's convinced of the merits of the popular front and [illegible] on his back. She tickles me.

The PSUC drills men, with much music, up and down the Ramblas every night – 7–8:30 – for a publicity stunt, great excitement, congestion of traffic, a few very daring girls drill, great masses of spectators, much shouting for the bourgeois slogans; *viva* the republic, popular army, etc, *visca* is Catalan for *viva*.

Mrs. Eric Blair (Eileen O'Shaughnessy[29] before marrying), whose writer husband is at the front with POUM, is working in C.'s office now just to be in Barcelona. There is another Irishman here – French – tall good looking [illegible] chap – young & a Marxist Grouper (variation on the strict Trotskyist theme to you unenlightened) speaks slowly as if he were thinking over each word, and seems a bit hesitant about saying it – a charming, childish way of speaking.

We are organising – Escuders, Blackwell, C., Oehler[30] (an American with the worst middle western accent I ever heard who is here with Blackwell) and me – a campaign between us & the Anarchists for aid to the POUM – if you are contacted, do your darndest for the old revolution –

[...]

You know, I don't spend all my time on politics – not by a long shot; but, somehow, when I write home, I want to write about the most *important* thing, so I always come to what is the center of life here: revolution. A letter like today's, I keep on feeling, oh well, I'll tear it up: it doesn't say anything. Incidentally, try to save the stuff – as well as letters – we send you, because our copies of back numbers of Bulletins, etc., are running low.

Mother says: I hope your experiences now don't form you too much. I don't; and, of course, they are bound to form me. I shall probably [illegible] the labor movement all my life; it's the most interesting, exciting thing that I can imagine doing – but we are a long time from America yet. I'll see – Also, mom, it's not me who makes cracks about sentimental bourgeois mothers; – that's Ann. I'm quite sentimental myself – like pa more than Ann. Sweet child [illegible] she is.

[...]

I would like to see you and have a long talk – wouldn't you?[31] About more things and in more detail than you can put in letters – I wrote a very good letter to [illegible] the other day about love and life – but don't mention it to anybody, especially her. Love. Lois.

32. Postcard written by Charles to his mother on 2 March 1937

[...] We are moving from the Hotel to that apt. of the Consul – with ten huge rooms, hot water and all for us 2 alone, tho at any time we are subject to receive a batch of refugees, if more should have to come.

I am very busy again – all the work alone again, except an Englishwoman as stenog. but she can't translate. It is now like April here, but windy. Am feeling fairly well.

33. Letter written by Lois to her family, begun on 4 March and finished on 7 March 1937

So life goes on, of course; the international situation and the internal situation get graver and graver every day, Charlie and I moved the other day, we eat at a pension now, I never have any work to do at the Generality, I just go there and sit all day doing POUM propaganda, I read *Winesburg, Ohio* by Sherwood Anderson. What else? There have been some nice people around here – English, I mean. I haven't been paid yet for February.

We moved to the house our pal Blackwell lives in, that of the German Consul. 10 rooms. We have a very nice room, hot water, etc. We are eating at a little pension with Moulin for five pesetas a day, and we are getting so much to eat that we have both started to take on weight again. The food is swell. Simple, and piles of it, plenty of vegetables and green stuff too. And I even eat an orange every day – two of them. [...]
[...]
Yesterday one of the South Africans came back from the Aragon front, where he had gone taking pictures, and, among other things, he brought back a huge loaf of bread with him. Did we enjoy that! It was better even than cakes or cookies. He is Jewish, Sapperstein is his name, and he always wears spotless blue shirts open at the neck under a fine leather jacket. The other English people is a girl named Eileen Blair who is nice but very vaguish when she talks and is eternally smoking cigarettes. I was never so glad I didn't smoke as now. There is a shortage, and all the people we know spend their time (1) worrying about where, how to buy

cigarettes (2) searching the streets for cigarettes (3) discussing how terrible it is and what they did, would have, etc., done in London (4) hunting for matches – there are none and everybody used tiny fireworks made for children on little sticks and then they ran out, and now they use a cigarette lighter, made of a cord and two stones that spark, which never work – (5) sparking their cigarette lighters (6) sparking other people's, trying to make them go – all the men especially love this as it makes them feel like mechanics, etc. etc. But I don't even worry.

Another thing that everybody does all of the time – everybody in Barcelona, I mean. That is drink – vermouths, absynths, beers, Malaga wine, cocktails, etc. etc. C. and me favor coffee with milk, all milk, only a little flavor of coffee, and *nata*, which is a delicious white substance that you eat with a spoon made from whipped cream, egg whites and sugar. But it has a fresh good taste, partly because it is made from goat's milk, I suppose.

Besides eat, you see, and talk about the revolution, we only write and sleep. The revolution is practically life here, and when I talk about anything else, I am automatically limited to describing living conditions.

Blackwell, our American friend, is still here, although he is trying to get to Paris. He is a nice guy. Another member of his party in America, a bird named Oehler, came here too, but has already left for Paris.[32] It was he who found the formula for a revolution (deduced from the realities of the Spanish situation, of course): buy a thousand rubber stamps and hire a thousand guys to work 'em up and down and the revolution's made.

Mom, you're always worrying about the local color here, etc.[33] The great Catalan national customs, etc. I notice things about them and funny differences between America and here, but, after all – this isn't a tourist cruise and the most important thing about the Catalan workers at this particular moment is not that they wear red hats or drink wine from such funny bottles, but the fact that they are the vanguard of the world working class: Emphasis on the things they have in common with workers all over the world.

I'm not unnoticing and theoretical, of course, but this great local color and Catalan culture was supplied by the idle bourgeoisie and is now manufactured by the Commissariat of Propaganda of the Catalan Generality. Really, Catalan workers and peasants are much the same as workers everywhere: blue denim, dirty, uneducated, uncultured etc. etc. – tons of kids, black fingernails, but with a vision – a touch of it – that American workers don't have. But not wonderfully brilliant, duped by their leaders to reformism. On the whole, your local color really consists of difference of architecture, of food, speech, etc. All important to people who had time to cultivate them – but not to workers who had to work all the time, and now these bourgeois are not much in evidence and their 'culture' for the time has taken a back seat. It's unobtrusive and unimportant.

I may wonder when I read my letters over again, what about the local color, meaning bourgeois culture, but I don't do it. It is too superficial & far from the heart of the situation here. (Anyhow Catalan culture is only Spanish culture under a different flag because these people are so nationalistically nuts.)

34. *Letter written by Lois and Charles to Charles' sister Dorothy on 5 March 1937*

You should see our 10 room magnificent appt.![34] Up on the hill, with a view of the sea from our dining room balcony! It was a bit too good for 2 people, so we have arranged with this Austrian woman and her two kids to come out and take over 5 or 6 rooms and keep the place clean. We have hot water, electricity & all. No one collects! I don't know how long it can last, but don't think the revolution doesn't pay some people some of the time. We are working hard tho, and don't feel that we are abusing our opportunity very much.

[…]

35. *Postcard written by Charles to his mother on 10 March 1937*

I have just gotten permission and a ride up to the front for about 4 days – to visit the English boys and to take some pictures. This will be very interesting, inasmuch as I have not even been out of the city more than 4 miles in the 6 months since we came. I want to see the villages and the political situation among the peasants – whether I can see the front or not. The sector of the Huesca front where we are going has not been active for 5 months – so don't worry.

I am getting to talk a little Spanish now – but it is mixed so with Catalan that it makes a funny mélange. Lois will take my radio for this time & an English girl is coming to stay in the apartment with her. Since cleaning Sunday morning, it is quite an attractive home – richest I ever had.

36. Letter written by Charles to Lois' sister Anne on 10 March 1937

While I am here sitting, waiting for this Irish friend, so he can come home with me, I might as well answer your sweet, saucy letters, so I can rate another of them. I just got back from the front last night after a four day trip, full of excitement and interesting information, especially political, but some military too. If I ever get to be a General or something, it may come in handy. A Belgian friend of ours, whom we all thought was funny and supercilious when he first landed here last October or November, has got be a Major or something already! He was in charge of the ILP boys and that whole sector around Huesca – and it was nice for us – got us free transport and all. I got it fixed so Lois can visit the front, if we decide it is wise. She is just dying to go. I felt mean going and leaving her behind, but it couldn't be helped. I suppose her parents will think this foolhardy – but there is no danger much. No activity at all on this front.

Yesterday I got up at 3:50 am, spent most of the day in Red Lérida – a POUM city. It was great! They have their POUM headquarters in the Casino which is really a luxurious, tastefully arranged club. Their barracks is the former monastery – which has place for 5.000 men, but is mostly used for a cooperative garage, woodwork shops, sewing, etc. They have a swell cheap restaurant (the POUM has) and free medical service for everybody. That is the way to run a town. Everybody who isn't POUM there is Anarchist, but I think the POUM controls the Anarchists there anyway. A city of about 30,000. They can get 25.000 peasants out to a POUM peasant meeting.

With you asking me about your love affairs reminds me of Angela – our English girl friend, who is having quite a time and also asked me for advice today. But how can I give girls advice & tell them anything. It's hard enough to know for yourself, let alone all the nice gals. But Lois thinks I ought to be able to tell you if you are in love – or else it proves I never was, or something! Yes, Lois has quite a time with poor un-passionate me for her husband! She still likes me in spite of my being no good. What makes it interesting; [illegible] the other men like Lois too! For which I can't blame them. So you see I aid your love life by turning to my own problems. A lot of good that is. I guess I am trying to write as disjointed a letter as yours, but it is easier after so carefully mulling over articles all day.

[…]

37. *Letter written by Lois to her brother Billy on 13 March 1937*

So, after I was away from home about a year, you finally got around to writing me. I won't wait so long to write you, though.

It is Saturday afternoon and I don't have much to do. I am at the English office of the POUM, which is on the fourth floor of this building on the main street. It is a very nice day, and as usual there are huge crowds of people walking up and down the Ramblas, doing nothing. Just below our office, which, like all offices and rooms in Spain, has a balcony, there is a man yelling, singing rather, with a huge crowd of people around him. [...]

As I started to tell you, Charlie has gone to the Huesca front for a week, what to do, I don't exactly know. There was a column of the POUM – sixty or so men – going up to join a division, and so C., John McNair, a man who works here in the Eng. dept., and an English woman who was working here whose husband is at that front, have all gone up there. I could not go because of – sex discrimination, I call it. *They* said they didn't have facilities for women, so, if I had been a man, I could have gone. That's outright discrimination, I think, especially since the other woman went. And, being a believer in equal rights, etc., it makes me somewhat indignant, but not too much. All the men around here are very nice to me and look after me, taking me to the movies and such useless things, so I don't get lonesome. Also, I've been doing Charlie's radio for him and looking after the English office which, in addition to holding my own job down, keeps me pretty busy.[35]

I suppose all the political stuff I write in my letters bores you stiff. I wouldn't be surprised, anyway, if it did. But there are plenty of things going on around here that you would be interested in, military training: learning to handle guns, Mausers, pistols, machine guns, submachine guns, anti-aircraft guns, and a hundred in-between varieties of firearms. There are rather big looking pistols that have a wooden handle that pulls out and makes a rifle out of them, there are repeating rifles, and automatics, and old fashioned pistols, and the big kind of guns cowboys have. There was a Cuban here who had a tremendously long pistol; it seems that all men in Cuba carry them.

Every worker that has a gun is very proud of it, and they keep them polished and cleaned to the n-th degree. There is a great sale of little oil cans and things on the Ramblas to keep guns clean, and all the milicians spent their time arguing about the relative merits of their own particular brand of gun. The reason they are all so different is that they came from a hundred different sources: some from the arsenals in the churches

(believe it or not!!!!), some from the old anti-strike police, some from the soldiers and the barracks, some from the stores, etc., many from the homes of private capitalists. [...]
[...]
I am interested, my lad, to hear about your girlfriends and your heart-throbs. That is a very important part of your life, and, honest, I think it must be rather difficult in the artificial bourgeois circles you move in. I mean, most people aren't honest with their daughters and sons, and that makes it harder for you, whose parents were (I think, at least they were with me) honest with you. By bourgeois, I mean with such affected ideas of *what's right* and *what's wrong* and *what you do and what you don't do*. Such unbiological ideas, etc.

While Charlie is gone, I am wearing his regulation POUM shirt, which is very nice. Dark blue, with straps at the shoulder for a Sam Brown, and a zipper and stitched in white. I am going to join the Feminine Secretariat of the POUM and have one of the women's uniforms. I'm glad those dern Generality bulletins are of use to somebody. I told you about the mad anarchist who worked on it. He's gone now and just me and the PSUC gal work there. They have a wonderful new machine to make the things with, you'll get a copy of one of them eventually: it photographs a typewritten page and prints the sheets from that. Everybody in the office was so excited about it: it took them over a week to get it operating, but during all that time nobody even considered making bulletins on the old machine – oh no. It just sat there useless, and we just sat in our offices doing nothing until the new machine was ready. So I did lots of POUM propaganda, stuff for the radio. It was lucky for me, because otherwise I might have had a little difficulty holding down two jobs at once.

Another very interesting thing around here is *La Batalla*, the POUM paper. They have a fairly large printing shop and offices which, before the revolution, belonged to a reactionary Catholic newspaper. In fact, in the old picture files of this Catholic paper, in the *La Batalla* office, were some very revealing things showing the close connection between the Catholic Church and the fascist rising. Such as mass being held with armed members of the fascist organizations as choir boys, and guns with some holy symbol on their barrels, bullet cases embroidered with sacred designs, etc.

The Huesca front, the closest front from Barcelona, is about twelve hours ride on the train. There hasn't been any action there as the fascists don't have any equipment. All the men do is sit around and play cards all day. Because, as you probably know, if you've read any of my letters, the capitalists' agents, who run the Catalan government, don't want any action on this front. The front runs through one tiny village after another and is mostly in the country, which makes it even less exciting. There hasn't been any offensive on this front yet, in spite of all the wonderful things Franco has told the foreign press. Right now there is an offensive on the Guadalajara front north of Madrid, and everybody here is sending reinforcements, etc., altho they won't use help from the POUM or the anarchists. Isn't that crazy? Here we are ready and eager to help, and it is the *workers'* government that won't let us. God, it makes me sick.

[…]

At our new house we have a hot bath, and all our friends have been coming there to use it; it makes me feel like a public benefactor.

I will enclose the receipt I got for the letters, and you can exercise your Spanish on it. There is a parade outside now, at least a band and a few men collecting money for the refugees, probably. There is a new magazine just put out by the Generality for the women, full of movie stuff and sob stuff. Why don't they ever treat women like intelligent equals, instead of dumb little things who have to be amused with movies, etc? The main reason being that that is what all women *are* here, but you don't cure them by never talking anything else to them.

Notes

1. Carl Marzani (1912–1994), born in Italy, came to the United States in 1924. In the Second World War, he worked for the United States' Office of Strategic Services. Suffering the consequences of McCarthyism, he went on to a career as a writer, publisher and polemicist.
2. This is another one of the many unsubstantiated rumours that made the rounds of Barcelona and other Spanish cities in the course of the Spanish Civil War.
3. On the circumstances and activities of the Durruti Column, see the monumental biography of the Spanish Anarchist leader by Abel Paz, *Durruti en la revolución española* (Madrid: Anselmo Lorenzo, 1996). Buenaventura Durruti (1896–1936) was in all likelihood killed in an accident.
4. Strict enforcement of obscenity laws kept many literary works off American and English bookshelves until the relaxation of such censorship laws in the late 1950s.
5. This last sentence, added in handwriting to the typewritten text, has been crossed out.
6. A handwritten marginalia explains, 'C. says just one super [illegible]. I think he's jealous. L.'
7. A handwritten addition explains, 'Bob, bored with life here, has gone to the front with the ILP column. Jan. 20.'

8. Jaume Miravitlles had been a leading member of the BOC when he joined the *Esquerra* in 1934. He was the *Esquerra*'s representative in the central committee of the anti-fascist militias at the beginning of the civil war and then the head of the Propaganda Department of the Generalitat.
9. Typewritten letter fragment by Lois to 'Dear Annie', 'January 16, 1937 Barcelona, Spain', which continued the letter begun on 6 January 1937.
10. This is page four of the letter started on 6 January, this third instalment dated 'January 20, 1937'.
11. A handwritten note on the back of page four adds, 'night. 22. we were just talking to Willie – we had supper with him; he used to work in the censor's office, and he said they aren't over the Xmas rush yet. Being Spaniards they wouldn't be.'
12. Thus begins the second paragraph of the section of the same letter after the subheading 'January 21'.
13. Here, for the first time, Lois spells 'pesetas' correctly, after having continuously misspelled the Spanish currency as 'pesatas' in all previous letters.
14. This is the second paragraph of the fourth section of the same letter by Lois to Ann, this installment entitled 'the next day', that is 22 January 1937.
15. Lois' and Charles' difficulties with the Spanish and Catalan languages show even in this excerpt. The original text by Lois renders the Spanish or Catalan words with many mistakes. I decided to include what appears to be the closest equivalent in orthographically correct Spanish or Catalan, so that what Lois refers to as Catalan writing on the wall in actual fact sometimes appears to have been Castilian Spanish.
16. Joan Comorera (1895–1960), the general secretary of the Unió Socialista de Catalunya (USC), participated in the Catalan revolt of 6 October 1934. Jailed in the wake of this unsuccessful rising, he was liberated in the wake of the electoral victory of the Popular Front in early 1936. He led the USC into the newly created PSUC, and he became the PSUC's first general secretary. Forced to leave Spain towards the end of the civil war, he returned for clandestine work in 1950. Jailed in 1954, he remained incarcerated until his death.
17. Founded in 1907, *Solidaridad Obrera* has remained until the present day the principal newspaper of the anarchist CNT.
18. The Catalan Josep Escuder emigrated to the United States in the 1920s, working in New York as a journalist. Returning to Barcelona, from 1934 to 1936, he worked for a newspaper of the *Esquerra*. After briefly returning to the United States, he returned in the autumn of 1936 to work on the POUM daily newspaper, *La Batalla*. Jailed by the Republican government in July 1937, along with other members of the POUM leadership, he was eventually released.
19. Anita Brenner (1905–1974) was best known for her publications on the Mexican Revolution and Mexican culture. During the Spanish Civil War she worked as journalist in Spain for *The New York Times*.
20. The issue of Soviet aid to Republican Spain remains a bone of contention until today. For a recent discussion of the role of the Soviet Union, see Gerald Howson, *Arms for Spain: The Untold Story of the Spanish Civil War* (New York: St. Martin's Press, 1999).
21. First sentence of a new section of the letter started on 4 February, written on 'February 9, 1937' by Lois.

22. A handwritten marginal comment in Lois' handwriting alongside this paragraph reads: 'I seem to be repeating myself. You can see what is important in my life outside of politics.'
23. The *patrullas de control* were dissolved on 4 June 1937 by an executive order in accordance with the legislation approved in March 1937 providing for the dissolution of the patrols and the Assault and National Republican guards, dominated by moderate forces within the Republican camp, and mandating their incorporation into a single internal security force; on this, see Bolloten, *Spanish Civil War*, p. 492.
24. Ewald König (1894–1945), a member of the German section of the so-called Right Opposition (within the Communist International), worked as a bookseller in Germany during the 1920s. He came to Barcelona in 1934, where he operated a combined bookshop, lending library and newspaper kiosk on the central Plaça Catalunya. Jailed by the Republican side in 1937, he was expelled to France after several months of incarceration.
25. Born in León, Sinesio García Hernández (1897–1983) emigrated at an early age to Argentina, eventually returned to Spain, and under the pseudonym Diego Abad de Santillán became known as an anarchist journalist. In early 1937 he held the post of Minister of the Economy in the Generalitat.
26. This is the first sentence of the third paragraph of the third section of the letter started on 4 February, written on 'February 12, 1937' by Lois.
27. The 'old man' refers to Leon Trotsky, who was sometimes referred to in this manner by his sympathizers.
28. On the Spanish Trotskyist movement, see the extensive documentation by Agustín Guillamón (ed.), *Documentación histórica del trotsquismo español (1936–1948): De la Guerra Civil a la ruptura con la IV Internacional* (Madrid: De la Torre, 1996).
29. Eileen Maud O'Shaughnessy (1905–1945) had met George Orwell in 1935 and married him the following year. She died while undergoing routine surgery in Newcastle upon Tyne.
30. Hugo Oehler was a one-time American Communist Party organizer, who was then a leading representative of the Revolutionary Workers League, one of several competing Trotskyist groups, an organization to which Russell Blackwell belonged as well.
31. Third paragraph of the second section of Lois' letter to her sister begun on 24 February, completed on 'March 2, 1937'.
32. From 6 to 7 March 1937, a conference of various anti-Stalinist splinter groups unaffiliated to the Fourth International took place in Paris.
33. First sentence of a new, handwritten section of the same letter by Lois, dated 'March 7, 1937'.
34. Beginning of the second paragraph of Charles' handwritten portion of a letter written by Lois and Charles to 'Dear Dort' on 'March 5, 1937, Barcelona, Spain'.
35. The present tense employed by Lois in her description of Charles' visit to the front in this letter casts doubts over the accuracy of the dates heading this letter and/or the preceding letter by Charles, supposedly written on 10 March, in which he refers to the visit as a past event. I have retained the original datelining employed by the letter writers in the original versions of their respective letters.

6
Letters from Barcelona (Spring)

Sometime in the late winter or early spring of 1937 Lois vacated her paid employment at the Catalan regional government propaganda department, where she had worked for half a year on the Generalitat's English-language bulletin. Having filled 'downtime' at the Generality with secretarial tasks for the POUM, she now devoted most of her time to this voluntary labour. In April 1937 Charles became a member of the POUM, with Lois remaining a critical observer on the POUM's periphery. She now identified rather closely with efforts to fashion a new revolutionary party out of dissident factions within the POUM and radical circles within the CNT, crystallized around the Amigos de Durruti.

It was in the spring of 1937 when Lois – after a Sunday spent hiking in the Catalan countryside in the company of Charles, Eileen O'Shaughnessy, who had become a close personal friend of the American couple, and George Tioli (on the latter, see Chapter 7) – suddenly informed her mother that 'you are right about getting to know the Catalan people. I don't really know them or understand them'. Yet with the political situation further deteriorating in Lois' eyes, she was never able to really begin familiarizing herself with the peculiarities of Catalonia. The twists and turns of Spanish politics soon took their toll. 'You can judge the pace of the revolution by the fact that the gov't was able to prevent any May Day celebrations' on the International Day of Labor, Lois observed. 'I am restless to leave Spain as I feel the revolution is going so bad, and I am no help.'

Yet the political drama of Catalonia and Spain cut short – but eventually accelerated! – this plan to leave Spain. In early May fighting erupted in Barcelona between Republican government forces and grass-roots activists in the ranks of the CNT and POUM. The Barcelona May Days, made famous in George Orwell's autobiographic account of these events which he witnessed while on leave from the Aragon front, saw Charles and Lois Orr helping to construct barricades. Lois had been ill in bed for two weeks when news broke of the fighting. Charles reports, 'Ten minutes after she heard about it, she was out with me helping build barricades. I am an expert now, worked on five or six wounded and one killed in my principal station. My neck was grazed.'

38. Letter written by Lois (and Charles) to her father on 23 March 1937

There are some funny people here – the wife of the *Manchester Guardian* correspondent for example.[1] We went out to have a milk coffee one afternoon, the first I'd met her, and she immediately told me 'aren't the men in Barcelona dull? I haven't even found one to tempt me to be unfaithful to my husband.' Too bad. And if you saw her husband once you might understand; even so, she needn't go around telling strangers about it. So, naturally, I started to go over all the men I know – in my mind – and see which ones I could propose. But such a nut. Then she started to tell me about women – how, if they were put into an institution at the age of, say, seventeen, they could be trained to be reasoning intelligent beings. I suggested faintly that maybe it would be a little hard to do that because of women's psychological make-up but she poo-pooed that.

I am very unhappy today, and I was yesterday too, because I am cutting two teeth very violently, and my whole mouth is very sore. I can't chew anything hard or even firm, and it makes me feel tired and weak for some reason. But, still, I suppose everybody goes thro this – at least everybody that sees me (my cheeks are very swollen) tells me terrible tales, varying from constant misery for six months, to monthly misery for two years. And everybody, when I explain my grievance (because, not being a baby and able to bawl, I have to relieve myself by telling somebody about this every half hour or so), tells me that in *his* language they are called wisdom teeth – Albanian, Spanish, Catalan, German, French, etc. [...]

The cigarette shortage let up for a while, but now it is getting bad again, and everybody, even the nice dainty little English girl who works in Charlie's office, is smoking the most horrible big cigars, which smell simply terrible. There is a German in this office now smoking one and that made me think of it.

You asked me about Charlie and me. We get along swell. I think he's a fine person, and we never fight about anything. For a while, after we were first married, I found it was kind of hard to think for myself, etc. I mean, my personality was a little unhinged. Now, not at all. We work in different offices and have acquaintances apart and do things apart, which is good, and still enjoy each other's company immensely. We have both learned a lot since we came here – I probably more than Charlie. There are some things, of course, that we aren't quite settled on, but not any one thing which might some day become important. He is more careful about everything than I am, more methodical about cleaning up after himself and picking his clothes up, etc. He doesn't like to go into cafes and sit; I do. He likes to take long walks and look at everything around him, I don't. Etc., but none of these things are really important. One day I give in, the next day he does. I try to be more careful, he tries not to always tell me about it, etc. I am earning more money than he is, and I have my own money, which is a good thing, because he would always be suggesting things – he is really very good about money, we haven't had a tenth of the trouble that everybody anticipated.

He has a good mind and can think straighter than I can as yet, but I am catching up with him. I think I probably have a good mind too, when I can get it trained. He is a very honorable, upright person. I think that my sense of justice and right, altho reasonably ok, is not so good as his. But I think that men are naturally that way more than women – I'm not sure.

[...]

[...] She is getting to be a good typist, isn't she?[2] She has held down that job for almost five months, and she is getting bored with it, which is quite understandable, and she is looking about for another. At first I used to discourage her from changing because I thought it would do her good to know that she could live down a routine job for a long period (she does not agree on my puritanical theory about learning to work at disagreeable work – thinks that one should always find interesting work), but now I think she has shown herself what she can do and I am trying to help her get a change. She has her eyes on 2 or 3 other jobs, but –

[...]

39. *Letter written by Lois to her family on 4 April 1937*

Here I am using this French typewriter again, and I refuse to be responsible for the finished product. I don't work at the Generality any more. There came a new bunch of Stalinists who objected strenuously to my making POUM propaganda there, and as I absolutely refused to spend the whole day sitting around doing nothing, I quit the job.

Now it seems like it was a smart thing to do, because for two weeks there has been a crisis in the Generality, which means that Catalonia has been legally without any government. And the thing of it is that nobody knows how the business is going to be *resuelto*. It started over this business of the patrols of control, which were to be dissolved into the old bourgeois police. The bill was passed nicely, signed by the Anarchist ministers and everything was lovely. There was another bill too, mobilizing men to fight in the 'popular army,' and another one demanding that all guns in private hands be turned over to the Generality to be sent to the front. There were also bills implementing the dissolution of the workers' police, the patrols of control, saying that all guns should be turned over to the Generality 'to be redistributed,' ha, ha. Well, you see, in essence these decrees were aimed at disarming the workers, at a time when there was a bourgeois government in power, when the revolution was only half – a quarter – made, and when the counter-revolution was advancing openly, when the Valencia and Catalan governments[3] were both trying their derndest to sell themselves out to British and French Imperialism, which isn't quite ready to take them on yet. So the idea was that the workers should give up their arms to the 'authorities' and then find themselves powerless to stop the hastened rhythm of counter-revolution. Well, in spite of the fact that their ministers signed these decrees, the anarchist workers refused to give up their guns, and very sensibly.

So the bourgeois raised the old cry of 'give us a government that can govern,' also the Stalinists shouted this. But the hard truth is that it is impossible to govern in Catalonia without the anarchists. So, finally, the anarchist ministers presented a list of demands to the government, which in effect would stop these disarming and bourgeois army measures. So the government had a crisis because they weren't prepared to stop. Stalinists (both CP and SP people) raising as much hell as they could, demanding a 'strong government,' a 'popular army,' dissolution of the patrols of control, etc. Damn their hides. If there has ever been a worse betrayal of the revolution and of the interests of the working class than this one perpetrated by the Comintern, well, there couldn't be. They are trying their very hardest to sell out the Spanish workers to British and French Imperialism – to the 'great sister democracies of Spain,' which have set out from the first to let the Spanish working class exhaust itself against the forces of Hitler and Mussolini.

[...]

It's just before dinner on Sunday, you see, and hence I can be so violent. I'll lay off politics, which is the most important thing going on just now and tell you about our joint cases of trench mouth. Charlie picked it up first and has had a worse case than I. I was being treated by a dentist at the same time for my teeth, and he just put on some blue stuff that cleared mine up in two days. C. had a bad fever and had to stay in bed almost a week; the doctor gave him some iodine stuff and his are almost cleared up. He is rather weak tho, as he hasn't been able to eat anything. He's around now, and I feed him two or three extra times a day – milk stuff, etc., which I of course must eat too, to keep him company. So I am even more scrupulous about feeding him.

Our English and American friends – somehow I am getting so I always say English, without thinking, for anybody who speaks that language – have all come back to Spain, they were smuggled over the border by professional smugglers. Russell Blackwell, Bill Krehm and Oehler. The middle one is staying at our house now, the others in a pension and all work there. They had gone to Paris for a conference.

While they were gone, I had some meals with the bourgeoisie, and good ones too. There was a journalist here from the *Daily Express*, which is a reactionary sensational paper in England. It has come out for the government in this war, but mostly because Beaverbrook, the owner, realized that public opinion was against Rothermere, who, his traditional enemy, was of course for the fascists. Both are black reactionaries.[4] Anyhow, this man was always trying to pump us for information, so Eileen and I, as John McNair was at the front and Charlie was in bed, amused ourselves by eating swell dinners in all the fine places at his expense, without divulging information of course. Really, tho, it is disgusting the number of people that go to those snitzy bourgeois places and pay 30 pesetas or more for a meal – when ordinary people pay from 3 to 5. They tell me that in the first days of the revolution that type of good restaurant was always empty. Naturally. Of course, the price of the peseta on the foreign market is going up because it looks like France and Britain are going to come to the 'support' of the Valencia gov't.

There is some excitement within the POUM these days, as people are investigating the 'Trotskyists.' The POUM, you see, has many faults, one of which is that they are afraid of being called Trotskyists. They really aren't of course; probably they would be better revolutionaries if they were. But that is a debatable question, and I'm not convinced. [...]

So I always get back to the same thing. Of course, when I am just living, I don't spend all my time thinking about such things, but when I start to write a letter this is just naturally what I write about, other things really aren't important.

[...]

40. Letter written by Lois to her parents, started on 11 April and finished on 12 April 1937

Honest to goodness, your letters about leaving Spain have of course all come through ok, and I want so bad to make you understand what it is like here, how peaceful, etc.

I am so honestly sorry that you are always in a stew about me, because you certainly wouldn't be if you would be reasonable about it. I don't mean any kind of reproach in that because I know that people can only be calm and reasonable on the basis of solid and believed information; and, unfortunately, it takes my letters three weeks to get there, but all the other stuff you read makes you unwilling to think that I know what is going on around me. And, of course, you don't trust my judgment at all, having got worked up into a kind of a state. I can understand it, honest, and I am so very very *sorry* that you feel so bad. But all I can do is tell you the truth about what is going on here, and if you will feel like people in the Middle Ages when people left for long unknown trips, gosh, I wish you could take it calmly like Charlie's family. This is just another town like Jeffersonville, or New York, full of quite ordinary people, the overwhelming majority of whom just get up in the sunshine every morning, go out to buy their cabbages or oranges, or to their woodwork shops or factory jobs, now collectivized, who play with their kids, go to interminable movies, etc. etc., just like a Spanish family in New York.

I mean, life is so calm and ordinary here, that my main problem now is to find something to do to keep from getting bored or fighting with Charlie (the latter is just theoretical as yet). This Sunday, for example, we went for an all day excursion into the country, and it was simply wonderful. Everything is growing, growing, the grapevines are starting, there are potatoes, many many small truck garden patches, and the country is so mountainous and beautiful. We went with Eileen, the English girl, and George, the Italian boy I told you about in connection with Angela Guest (who, incidentally, has gone to Albacete, the headquarters of the International Brigades – George is quite a civilized and interesting person now that she is gone).[5] We climbed part way up a hill and lay in the grass for a couple of hours in the sun eating candy and talking. The view was too magnificent to describe. We talked about all joining the FRIENDS OF MEXICO, because, George being a member and a Friend of Mexico, we just thought that we'd like to be friends of Mexico too. Charlie especially since he has been there. We decided that he would have to address the association on Mexico, its climate and geography. Then Eileen said that if a world war came we could all go there, but George thought that Iceland was better. Anyhow, we could all forget politics in Mexico, but then Charlie said we couldn't, because Mexico was very political, but we could go into the mountains and live with the uncivilised Indian tribes, which would have the advantages that they didn't speak any language but Indian and that we would be within a couple of hours ride of Mexico City, the most modern city in all Mexico. But George said that this just went to prove that Americans were all Indians, and he is absolutely determined never to come to America, and particularly the United States (he might go to Mexico, as, after all, he is a friend of theirs).

Then, at about one o'clock, we started to walk to a little town that we could see across the fields. We came to two men who were cooking their meal by the side of the road, in a terracotta flat dish. It looked very good, and they were in a nice grassy place, full of very small pretty daisies. Rabbit, *havas* – big green beans – snails, greens, onions and things, all done in oil. We watched them for a while as we were very hungry and then went on. The wagon trail into the town was shaded with plane trees – very much like sycamores, but with all the branches cut every year to make firewood – they were all carefully tended fields, with different flowers growing along the side of the road, and always hills and trees of all colors of green in the background. We got to the village and found a place, with white table cloths, napkins, etc., and had our dinner.

We had – and here, daddy, we go into another description of food – first vermouth and pickled artichokes that you eat with a toothpick, then I had chicken and a meat and vegetable salad, bread – not rationed for once – and wine. Afterwards more bread and Dutch cheese (with the red outside, pineapple shaped, only we just had a slice, of course), oranges, raisins and coffee. I write about food because people think and talk about food here. People are conniseurs [sic], I'm sure that's spelled wrong. Altho I don't know what a *crèpe suzette* is as yet.

Afterwards we walked around this little town, and outside it. We crossed vine fields and meadows and came to a pine forest which was on a hill that looked for miles and miles over the country. So on a path going out of it, we found some soft green grass and sat down again. We talked about tea, and George decided to start YE OLD TEA SHOPPEE on the edge of this forest in deepest Catalonia. Then we talked about founding: ELS AMICS DE CATALUNYA, oh, no, ELS AMICS ESTRANGERS DE CATALUNYA, since George and Eileen hate Catalan so (after a lively and prolonged argument, because I disagreed in principle). We decided to get a rubber stamp, two flats, three cars, a bath, an office, three typewriters, etc., for this organisation, ELS AMICS ESTRANGERS DE CATALUNYA. Nothing on earth of course could give you an idea of what that sounds like in Catalan.

So then we started back to the railroad station, at half past five, and after about an hour or so, got there and went to a little place to wait a half hour for the train. We sang, had more bread and cheese, and grenadine, which was very bad, like rotten cherry pop.

Then, having an hour and a half before dinner, I decided to write you this letter because it's so bad for you to feel unhappy about me. I have been wearing Charlie's blue overalls around as they have shrunk to be much too little for him.

You know, mother, you are right about getting to know the Catalan people. I don't really know them or understand them. Of course, it isn't as if I had been spending my time here in a vacuum, because I have learned a tremendous lot about the hearts and lives of the foreigners who travel around – refugees, journalists, these sophisticated people of the Parisian culture, and lots of things. We are thinking, tho, of me going perhaps to spend a week or more in some village around here to learn Catalan, and get to know a little more about the people.

Since I left the Generality, I haven't found a job as yet, altho there is some political work I can do which won't pay. If I can get a job that pays, I would start to do some of this work, but jobs are scarce now.

The other day George and I went out to Sabadell, where for ten years an Argentinian has been running a 'modern' school – in the most primitive and simple of conditions. The children discuss among themselves their problems, make their own discipline, and aren't taught normal handbook mathematics, geography, etc. He uses Van Loon's *History of the World* to teach them history, and also thinks his geography very good. Ferrer's (I think it is spelled like that) system of teaching history.[6] He has very interesting stories to tell about the things that happened to him under the dictatorship, when he wasn't giving religious instruction or inculcating the monarchistic ideas. He calls his school 'rationalistic;' and he is now one of the 'men of the FAI' (which means a lot in any Catalan town), and his school is under their auspices. The FAI is a wonderful organisation. These anarchists are men well worthy of their salt. They are radicals who are always willing to experiment and learn, and their idea of direct action is magnificent. In intellectual fields, artistic, economic and political. They are absolutely determined to have democracy here. Boy, and in everything, for the kids going to school, and everybody else, whether they want it or not.

Charlie is hungry and wants to eat, so I will close this for the time being. Life is so normal and ordinary and interesting here, and so undangerous. [...] Incidentally, Emma B. would like the anarchists and the men of the FAI. They're a fine lot.

It is a rainy day.[7] I got up at 12 o'clock, and at one arrived at Plaza Catalonia where I had my hair cut. As usual, they cut it too short, and it looks like hell. I had it done in a men's place where it would not be shampooed etc., to the great astonishment of the natives who expected me to walk about ten blocks in the rain to get it done.

This afternoon, if it ever stops raining, I will wash my hair and go over to the CNT-FAI house for a new bunch of posters to send to you all. And, incidentally, if you get a couple of rolled up packages of Spanish handbills, magazines, etc., they are to be put away and kept carefully – after Bill has tried his Spanish on them, of course.

I am writing to the address that you gave us in Albacete for the papers, etc., of this boy from Louisville. I will have them sent to you, and you can turn them over to his mother. But I imagine that she will get them through the proper sources in time. And, tho it won't do any good to tell her this, there have been five or six cases of English boys reported dead when they really weren't, with eulogies etc. in all the British liberal press for them. And another thing about the international brigade, but you needn't tell this to his ma either, because of course it doesn't prove anything, is that many men desert from it and join the anarchist and POUM columns, and have to be registered as dead or they will be shot under monarchist military code – or at least not allowed to fight in Spain any more.[8] Because there are a lot of things screwy, not what they should be, in that Stalinist-controlled brigade. I was very sorry to hear about the death of this comrade, and I wish you would tell his mother for me that he died fighting for something worthwhile. I'll do all I can to get anything he has left to her.

Charlie and I are both feeling well, and the spring is a very nice time in Barcelona. Much love to you all. Lois.

41. *Letter written by Lois to her family, begun on 26 April and finished on 29 April 1937*

I am writing this in bed – which I should not be doing, of course – as I have the flu again. I have been in bed since Sunday a week ago – feeling ok but running quite a temp, 101–3 usually, now it's much lower and is just one degree above normal in the morning – about 99 – all thermometers here are in centigrade. So I have to be just approximate. I didn't get a thermometer until Wed. and my lightest was 39.5. 36 is normal and 39.5 is about 103–4.

Everybody has insisted on coming to see me, altho the risk of flu was something. George brought me some lovely orange and yellow roses, and on my birthday (whose main excitement was that I took a laxative which didn't work) the German doctor brought me a huge bouquet of roses gathered at the Maurín Sanatorium. C. gave me some chocolate candy for a present, expecting me not to eat it. I did eat too much, of course, and felt a little sick afterwards.

George bought a big bottle of a very expensive sweet liquor and left it up here to cure me. *Crème de cacao.* It's delicious and we use the fancy little glasses of the German consul to drink it with.

Bill Krehm, the Canadian boy who lives in the house with us has also been very nice to me. He is waiting for money from his organisation to go back to America; he has been in Europe and Spain since October, attending the Brussels Congress, etc. Now he is very bored and disgusted and wants to go home to do some real work – He reads me the news – or tells it to me; he also reads me a French novel we have here – [...]

[...]

Charlie has joined the POUM, is a member of a cell, has a little red book, etc. Me no. I think the *partit – el nostre partit* – as the Catalans say – is pretty bureaucrat-ridden and varies so far from bolshevistic Marxism – and the leaders are dirty cowards – politically, not personally. However, a split at the party congress next month might have important results for the revolution.[9] These roses by my bed smell so very very sweet. I am getting tired of not having any clothes to wear.

This morning I took a hot bath which I needed and enjoyed, but which also tired me out.[10]

Yesterday I got mother's letter of April 7 with *Cardinal* enclosed. Yesterday, the 'English boys' (as John McNair, who babies them mentally, morally, spiritually, etc., calls the ILP men who are fighting on the Aragon front) came to Barcelona on leave. All just paid, of course. And it was yesterday, naturally, that all the chocolate, cigarettes, etc. that the ILP sent got here. They suffer for it at the front, but now they give it away. I have 2 huge 1 lb bars of the best English chocolate, with raisins and almonds in it.

[...]

Bill Krehm was just talking yesterday to a man from the International Brigade. An Italian or a Pole, I forget. But he was a left oppositionist.

So he was sent forward to an advanced position under enemy fire one day. Then the C.P. Brigades at his back opened fire on him too. There was a German machine gunner in the trench with him who, when he realized what was happening, shouted a warning to those behind and turned his machine gun on them. The adventures of this Hungarian (or whatever he was) would fill a book. He was thrown in jail, escaped, captured, escaped. And finally got to Barcelona, where he sat in a cafe & told Krehm all this. There are lots of deserters from the Intern. Brig. in POUM and Anarchist columns. Many are listed as dead, as one German I was talking to – *getoted* [sic]. There is also the case of a crack Italian aviator who was with the Brigades, and suspected of being left oppositionist. [...] He was sent up when the sky was full of fascist planes on an impossible attack.... Anyhow, he flew away –

Did I ever tell you about the nice German aviator?[11] Young, about 23 and professional flyer – couple or three hundred hours – doing underground work in Germany, Marxist classes for workers, etc., CP member. The CP, you know, following their general line of colossal blunders and sacrifices of the working class, having lost hundreds of their best militants in the 1st year of Hitler through open pamphlet distributions, meetings, etc., has now organized a popular front in underground Germany – a united front of workers, bourgeois, liberals, Reichswehr officers invited, 'sincere' Nazis invited!!! This kid had to leave Germany last June because 2 Social Democrats who knew him were caught, and it was that he was incriminated in their confessions. Later, it was learned that they died without confessing, so last December he returned to Germany, having been instructed about the new popular front line. He goes back to his classes to teach, this class collaboration stuff, to the bitter, discouraged and frightfully punished German workers, as the way they would be saved. But they just laughed at him and said, you'll sell out to the bourgeoisie; you've betrayed us too; we don't trust you any more. So he couldn't work. He gave his addresses to the Left Communist Opposition – the SAP[12] and came to Spain to fight. A tall, handsome, nervous, sensitive lad. We had supper with him one night before he went to the front. Now I hear that he's been killed.

There is going to be a POUM party congress in a couple of weeks. It is very important, as on its outcome depends the rapidity or slowness of the development of the real Bolshevik Marxist party that is the only hope of carrying the revolution through at this late stage.

[...]

Here there is friction coming into the open between the Stalinists and Socialists.[13] Isn't it incredible that Stalin's obedient fools of the III

International would become even too rightwing for the *social democrats*!! What this will lead to is not clear. Probably if an open split comes, many people will reevaluate the SP and believe that now, being rid of the Stalinists, the social democrats will make the revolution. Which of course is absurd.[14]

I just thought, poor Billy, if he wades through this letter. All the Trotskyist theories, etc. There is one of the defense planes flying low. It's a gorgeous warm, sunny morning. The days are wonderful now.

We would like to stay here until the beginning of September, but unless I get a job – or cash – my Xmas check – it might be a little difficult.
[...]

Yesterday I had a lot of company.[15] George Kopp, a Belgian who is a very important commander on the Huesca front – lieutenant colonel, and whom we knew before he even went to the front, came here in the afternoon with a huge box of chocolates. (...) Bob Smillie, the Scotch boy, is also back from the front and he came about 7 pm and visited me until 11. He brought me a supper of eggs, bread, strawberries with cognac over them. Charlie was busy last night introducing John Dos Passos[16] to Nin & Andrade – and also attending a cell meeting – which didn't take place.

I have a chance of getting a job in Valencia next month, that is – at the beginning of June. I don't know if I want to or not – working for an American newspaperman.

They are still trying to disarm the workers' police here, but haven't as yet succeeded. Last night the gov't had evidently made some kind of decree or ultimatum, as the Patrol Guards were everywhere on the streets in groups of 6 or 7 armed – the streets were full of them – and there were a lot of Civil Guards – gov't police – around too, but no trouble as far as I have heard: and no workers disarmed either.

There is trouble in some of the border towns too (Puigcerdà) where the Generality has sent the old customs officials (*carboneri* or some name like that) to take over control of the frontier from the Anarchists. Last night a POUM controlled town near Puigcerdà was telephoning repeatedly for men to be sent there – not to play games of course, but men with guns.[17]

All these signs mean that the revolution is still alive, and *that* means that there is still a chance of the workers winning the war.

I think I'd better finish this long letter, and let Charlie mail it. I wish your mail got thro more regularly, but I usually get it eventually. Much love to you all, Mother, Daddy, Annie and Billy. Lois.

42. Postcard written by Charles (and Lois) to his mother on 1–2 May 1937

Dear Mother. It must have been three weeks almost since I have written you, and the same since I got a letter from you. You see, I have been busy taking care of Lois who has had the grippe or something which has left her in bed with a considerable fever for 15 days. It is lower today.

It is still staying quite low, so we took her out to a restaurant for Sunday dinner.[18] We are on our way home now and are sitting in a little three-cornered park under palm trees. But it is not warm – just about like May 15 at home. You see, we are north of you all.

You can judge the pace of the revolution by the fact that the gov't was able to prevent any May Day celebration – i.e. parade, on the pretext of working for the war. But the Anarchists are raging mad for having given up their principles just to go up a blind alley of reformism. They are stirring and may someday act.

I'm OK & greatly object to having my health subject of international discussions. Gosh.[19] Charlie just had his beard trimmed & looks like Lenin – honest, he does. So many people gave me chocolate while I was sick – it made me worse. Plenty of bread too when the English column came back from the front. I am restless to leave Spain as I feel the revolution is going so bad, & I am no help. Lois.

43. Undated letter fragment written by Lois in the first half of May 1937

May Day passed without any demonstration: the Generality forbade demonstrations, and no one challenged their authority.[20]

[…]

I can't think of much excitement to tell you. The ILP English column is going to break up. A lot of the men aren't even revolutionaries and don't stand up to inaction – or action. Some want to go to Madrid or Bilbao. Eric Blair, not of the ILP – whose wife, Eileen, has been working in C's office – is off to join the International Brigade. Eileen is going to Valencia to get a job to be nearer Eric.[21]

John McNair is going to Paris for two weeks to attend to his business. The German doctor who has been taking care of me is going to Barbastro. Charlie is itching to go to Valencia or Madrid and see more of Spain. I want to go to India.

[…]

Pat French has gone to England but couldn't tell me goodbye because he has TB & would catch the flu from me.

John Sapperstein & Sappire, the two South Africans, are back here from Paris and England. Sitting around the Cafe Ramblas etc. Sappire working for the BLers.

[...]

I just got back to bed again – it is afternoon late – 6:30 – so I will write you some more.[22]

I just got a 3 page typewritten letter of daddy's. You can tell Teresa from me that I miss her good cooking over here – but it's hard to cook when you have to queue up at 6 am for milk – or bread – or meat – or sugar – or potatoes – and send your family to line up for the other ones as you can only stand in 1 queue at a time. She could learn a lot of new ways to cook things here – all smothered in olive oil – à la descriptions. Yesterday, a man had an omelette for dessert with some kind of sherry or cognac burning all over the dish – it must give it a funny flavor. But mostly – and at the front especially – people just eat beans – garbanzos – & artichokes.

I can always write about food.

You remember Willie, our German stage manager-director friend? At last, after doing political work for the Anarchists, he has a commission to 'make a theater,' and he is so radiantly happy. He wanders around with 10 or 9 volumes of plays, in German and Spanish, in a satchel under his arms.

He came to see me this afternoon. He is such a simple direct friendly likeable person. I am sure I would fall in love with him if I weren't married, and could speak more German.

I got up again for lunch – altho C. makes me stay in bed all afternoon. George Tioli, the Italian child psychologist (who, like most psychologists, has such an individualistic outlook on life, and who finds it almost – no, completely – impossible to see events from a social point of view; he doesn't want to) had dinner with us at our little restaurant here. Good dinner. Afterwards we had cherries which are cheap and fine.

It is a cloudy dark day, with black clouds. The hills out our windows look green and bright and fragile against the sky. There are a lot of black birds wheeling and crying, darker than the clouds. From our windows here we see four or five of the hills that dominate Barcelona – all unsettled and green.

I bought some lovely rose perfume for 12 pesetas – a day's wages but only 50c American money.[23]

I'm sorry this is so delayed.[24] I've sent you another in the meantime. I got a letter from daddy with a letter and poem from Ann enclosed.

Love, Lois[25]

44. Postcard written by Charles to his mother on 8 May 1937

Dear Mother.[26]

This is to tell you that we are all right. The workers were wonderful + after a series of counter-revolutionary provocations, they went out into the streets en masse – made a general strike, threw up barricades, disarmed police and almost took the power to make the revolution – all quite spontaneously, not only without any leadership, but actually against their leaders, and against all newspapers. They were double crossed and betrayed by their reformist leaders – or they would have won easily – with the least organisation. L. had been in bed 2 weeks with a strange fever after the grippe. 10 minutes after she heard about it, she was out with me helping build barricades. I am an expert now – worked on 5 or 6 wounded and 1 killed in my principle station. My neck was grazed. But it would be worth dying for, if it went thru. We are quite o.k. – a little hungry – Bill.

The fighting is evidently finished – but no one has won.[27]

45. Letter written by Lois to her family on 11–12 May 1937

Well, the excitement and the shouting dies, etc., so I will write you a letter to send with the others I have been keeping because the mails aren't functioning – weren't rather. Now the Valencia government has stepped in and taken control, restored order, etc. Eight thousand Guards with Russian rifles have come from Valencia and are patrolling the streets in groups of eights and tens.

The POUM English Column was back on leave during the excitement and stood guard around the POUM buildings, but weren't allowed to fire, altho there was fighting in the Plaza Catalunya which their position dominated. Some of the boys, thanks to the ILP's clear revolutionary policy, are Stalinists, and others are not even revolutionaries, and these elements are quitting and going back to England. They had finished getting their stamps from the Catalan Generality and now they have to start all over again getting them from the Valencian government which has taken over public order and controls coming and going in Catalonia, as well as censorship, etc.

[…]

There is another Englishman who has just come through, hiked over the border, and, after some difficulty due to the fact that he came through with some comrades of the PSUC and they were passing through Anarchist territory, arrived in Barcelona yesterday.[28] An ILP man – a politico, not a militian.

Since the Government has taken over the town, the food situation has improved, bread is more plentiful and other commodities too. This makes good propaganda for the government and against the anarchists.

Charlie and I are scheming how to buy some new clothes as he needs a new suit and I need some slips etc. He also needs shoes. As I have no job now, and he earns just enough to cover the food, we will probably have to change some of our foreign money. Of course, since the events of last week, the peseta has fallen still lower on the foreign exchange – Weisbord, an American who also landed in town in the middle of the fighting, got 37 to a dollar.[29]

The market is full of cherries and strawberries. The cherries are very big and black and cost only 70 centimes (at 37 for a dollar a peseta is worth about 3 cents) a pound. They fix the strawberries here by putting sugar on them and then pouring wine or cognac over them. I would much prefer them with cream, or in a real honest to god shortcake.

I am working around the POUM office, typing etc. Things are very disorganised up here, because there is a great campaign against the POUM as the provocateurs who started this uprising. It's hot air, of course, but there is a real danger that the POUM will be suppressed.

[…]

46. *Letter written by Charles to his mother on 15 May 1937*

Your last letter, written April 12, says that I was at the front the last you heard from me. Well, the front came to me instead of me going back there. We have seen and learned a lot during the last few days, and expect to be driven underground at any time now. We are breathing free for a few days, however. Most of our comrades taken prisoner have been released, but the streets are patrolled by 8.000 guards brought in from Valencia & Madrid.

The lines here, between the revolutionary workers and the middle class reformists who want to halt the revolution and play ball with

Russia, France and England, are now clearly drawn. But the counter-revo. is on top. I am not so sure that it will remain peaceful, however. We hear that some 'undesirable' foreigners are being deported, so we may continue our trip earlier than we expected.

Our faith in the sound instincts of the working class – as opposed to its leaders – has gone up tremendously. It was a great experience to live even 4 days under workers' power.

47. Letter written by Lois to Charles' family on 18 May 1937

We have been living a very tranquil existence here the last weeks. The POUM people have gone into their holes waiting to see what will happen.

Sunday was the first bullfight of the season, but neither one of us went. I finished D.H. Lawrence's *White Peacock* and Charlie went exploring the old fairgrounds, a huge park full of buildings etc. left from an exhibition here in 1928.

Yesterday we had dinner in a very expensive restaurant with a Belgian POUM army officer and the English girl who works in C.'s office. A marvellously prepared and exquisitely served meal. Kopp, being a gourmet, talked about food the whole meal. Eileen too. We thought it was interesting, but to spend all our meals on such endless discussions, exchanges of recipes etc., would bore me. Funny people, don't want to talk politics in the middle of the world's most exciting and interesting situation. We are enjoying ourselves thoroughly here – altho reaction is advancing rapidly. It's like being in the nerve center of the world's imperialist struggle.

I haven't got a job now and have decided to start a bit of heavy reading, so as to occupy my time profitably.

As Barcelona is in the midst of a truck gardening center the market is flooded with spring vegetables and cherries, strawberries, little pink peaches, etc. The food situation is easing up. Bread is easier to get – partly because the Valencian gov't, which had sabotaged the Catalan economy before, has now taken charge here and is seeing to it that we get convinced that their rule is preferable to Catalan autonomy.

[…]

I am working on a project to take care of refugee children – a *Comité Femenina pro Infancia Proletaria*. It is not affiliated with the POUM – *nor* the Stalinist-controlled North American Committee for the Defence of Spanish Democracy. It has equipped a home for children and is doing good work. […]

I have just acquired a fine blue-green heavy English-tailored shirt which is alleviating the clothing problem somewhat – not much. All our clothes are still in Marseilles. I am living with 1 blue [illegible] shirt – 2 cotton shirts, this new one, and 1 red cotton blouse. Also Charlie's cover-alls, which I borrow when my shirts are at the laundry.

It's a lot of fun tho. The weather here is getting nice.

48. *Letter written by Charles (and Lois) to his sister Dorothy on 24 May 1937*

Here we are still safe & sound, and still on a continuous wave of excitement and learning a-plenty – all different ways not to make the revolution. It came pretty near being made the other day – in spite of the betrayal and dumbness, respectively of the Stalinists and Anarchist leaders. The workers are fighters and could handle the military side of it if they had a little leadership. But the leaders have all gone bourgeois, and the Anarchist organisation is demoralised and splitting.

The weather has been wonderful for a week now and is supposed to stay so from now on. We will stay here likely till August, on account of it – not on account of the revolution, which is evidently lost for the time being – tho there still is a general 'revolutionary situation' from which anything can develop.

We have known several MDs here. There are lots of funny ones, as well as good ones, who come here to help, and they all have trouble being assimilated. Many wander around – get the run-around – until discouraged and then go away. One was the [illegible] sister of the President of the Univ. of West Virginia. I don't know where she is now. We know a nice German woman, Dr. Carlotta, with red hair. She was at the front and then for a long time at the Maurín Sanatorium of our party. They made it hard for her tho, wouldn't let her discipline the patients etc. I don't know why tho – I guess the patients, being often influential party members, had more pull with the Red Aid than she. Now they have fired her – I don't know why, because she seems to be a very able Dr., better than the average here. When we brought pressure to get her put back, they said she took opium, which she proved she did not, by giving up her supplies. Now they say she drinks. I am trying to find out why they don't want her.

We are having a party next Sat. evening in our spacious apartment – we have invited her because she knows English & you always lack women at anything in this country.

[…]

I am taking exercises every morning to keep limber.[30] I would record here that, during the first four exciting days of the week of May 3rd, Charlie, who had been complaining vaguely of bronchitis, tired, etc., became extremely healthy, never tired, was on the go – walking, running up steps – all day, helped build barricades and only got very slightly stiff – always stayed up 3 hours later than I and got up earlier. Claimed to not be the least tired, feel bad, or even weak from not getting anything to eat. His one and only concern, the sweet soul, was to make the revolution: the cure for his various maladies, I deduce, is to make the revolution in America to make him and everybody else well and happy.

49. *Letter written by Lois to her family on 25 May 1937*

It is about nine o'clock and I have just been typing some political documents so I will relax my mind and dash off a letter to you all.

The weather is getting very hot here, but I enjoy it, and it seems to make Charlie feel healthy, which is a good thing. If I don't talk about the political situation, which is all-absorbing, I mean very interesting and tight, I would tell you that Sunday we made another excursion into the mountains, got lost, wandered around in a thickish wood and finally stumbled into an old tavern on a hill just as the moon and first stars were getting bright. It was lots of fun – we were with a Dutch lad, Dereck, and a Scotch girl. My German is better now that it was in Germany, that is I know lots of complicated verb forms that I didn't know before. I am always hearing people talk German, and I absorb some of it. Of course, I think that, considering the number of words, I know rather less, altho I have learned new ones here about fighting, guns, etc. We are planning to go to the beach to do some swimming next Sunday if possible. There is a swell in the number of English people here – altho Bob Smillie is still in jail in Valencia. He will be out soon, we hear, is fed well and is quite happy.

I am so glad that you all were more sensible and intelligent than C.'s brother-in-law – his first, Mary's husband. That dumb bunny sent a letter to the American consul asking him to find out if we were sick, wounded, etc. And, to our great surprise, we learn that they didn't have any idea, at the headquarters of Am. Imperialism in Spain, that we were here. They inquired at all the recruiting agencies if we were at the front, rather if C. was at the front, and finally found us at the POUM. C. mistrusted the man at first and wouldn't tell him anything. Then he saw the letterhead from Buena Vista, Iowa, and thought it was somebody that Harry had sent to him. Now the fact that C. is working for the POUM goes into the file behind his name at the State – or is it Justice – department. Heck. When we get to India, no matter what sort of a typhoon or earthquake or famine or whatever they have there, you won't do that, will you? Those two kids in Iowa, who think Roosevelt is a radical, just didn't understand that revolutionaries are trailed, letters opened, names, profiles, etc., recorded and that the more revolutionaries are away from the state department the better.

[...]

Well, these are exciting days. I wish you could be here in the heat of everything. I know you'd learn a hell of a lot and – well, you wouldn't like it of course. However, lots of love, and I haven't had a letter for three weeks.

I just read three C.-J.s (which are coming quite regularly, thanks) about how the Trotskyist POUM's paper was taken, etc., etc.[31] Also saw an article on how streets were running with blood. I suppose that you all took that with a grain of salt. Of course neither report is true and both inspired by the Stalinists. C. and I were the first to go to *La Batalla* – it was surrounded by police barricades but there weren't any shots fired around there, nor was there any fighting there. Thursday this week there was a truce, and we went there and found 30 marooned people, including the Escuders, so we told them they could leave and we all left. *La Batalla* is still coming out, giving their screwy line.

Incidentally, if you get a *Spanish Revolution* telling about the events, don't believe it. That is, believe it instead of the bourgeois press, but even that's not the way things happened.

The Generality council has begun a discussion of 'isn't the collectivization decree of Oct. illegal?' The majority say yes. And so soon, probably, will come either nationalization and institution of state capitalism or even more obvious forms of private ownership. Ho hum. I guess the anarchists will learn that when they have the factories – but they haven't got credit, or raw materials, or a workers' government – they ain't got nothing. Long live the revolution; the revolution is dead.

C. and I are having a party Sat. nite. It'll be great fun. L.

50. *Letter written by Lois to 'Dear Genie' on 28 May 1937*

Charlie and I escaped quite unscathed through the fighting here. We helped with the barricades, etc. What really happened, as you may have gotten rumours of by this time, is that the government decided to take the initiative against the small remnants of workers' power left (control of the telephone building, certain revolutionary workers' police bodies – out of place remnants of the July days of revolutionary law and order in the bourgeois 'popular' front regime of today – and now against the factories which are socialized or collectivized). It attacked the telephone building, a provocation par excellence, and the workers throughout the city responded immediately by throwing up barricades all over the city. In all the little towns throughout the country they prepared for an attack by preventive measures: taking over the headquarters of the reactionary Catalan nationalist and Stalinist (SP-CP) parties, and the trade unions controlled by them.

As Companys himself said, everyone was against the 'legal' government: it had not men enough to support itself. With one important exception: the leaders of the Anarchists and the POUM. They called their people off the streets, pleading with them not to smash the bourgeois state that was crumbling in anticipation of their coming. The workers, confused, were paralyzed; they couldn't leave the barricades, many of which were under fire from small isolated groups of government police, and they had no leadership to guide them in the attack

The result of course was a complete defeat. [...] The offensive against the POUM is a direct result of this defeat (the present one I mean): today *La Batalla* was suspended indefinitely, soon, the POUM will go underground.

[...]

And so what are the revolutionaries doing, you ask, and what are they aiming at in the immediate future? The revolutionaries (except a lot of fair-weather foreigners who are all leaving the country) are working frantically to build an organisation that can give the necessary slogans and lead the masses to victory – a revolutionary marxist party that understands and doesn't fail at the moment of action, as the POUM always does. [...]

[...]

So we revolutionaries are preparing for the POUM congress, which is due June 15. If the POUM goes underground, I don't know if they will have it or not. There, a growing left opposition will state its position and try to win the support of the majority of the party. If not, we will see what. There is also a left wing which has developed in the CNT-FAI with which a reformed POUM could work.

I still don't have any job, so I am devoting my time to educating myself. I am reading a very good biography of Stalin and a history of bolshevism by Souvarine, in French.[32] Also some other things. Next I'll start

on Engels, or Marx. I am also giving a party Friday in our requisitioned apartment, which I should be home scrubbing now. It's pretty clean tho.
[...]

51. Letter written by Lois to her mother, begun on 2 June and finished on 6 June 1937

I just mailed a letter to Ann yesterday, but I will start another as the typewriter is free, and I can't do anything. The reason for that is that my upper left wisdom tooth has started to come in and is very painful. I went through a siege the last month with the other three, and that front has been quiet for about seven or eight weeks, but now this one has started coming and I have terrific pains, neuralgic, I suppose, all on the left side of my face. I can't concentrate on anything. I have an important piece of work to finish, but it is utterly impossible; there is also a copy of Joyce's *Ulysses* lying around here of which I have read thirty pages, but I can't even enjoy that. [...]
[...]
It just occurred to me, in the letter to Ann I forgot to say that we weren't hit during the last aerial bombardment. Our house, up in the snitzy residential district in the hills, has a tremendous set of French windows overlooking the city. We saw the bombardment from there – saw our guns answering with little red lighted bullets, saw their planes fly away, etc. It was just coming light, and the evening star was still bright, but it was very hard to see small black spots in the changing light.

As I think the POUM is opening and stopping my mail, I changed my address at the post office, but you can keep on addressing yours here, as this other address, at our apartment, is not permanent. We may move if it is too uncomfortable living there without electricity (we aren't going to pay our electric bill as the collectivity of inhabitants can't afford it.)

Bob Smillie is still in jail. John McNair is in Paris. [...] There is a scotch girl, Ethyl MacDonald, here who is very nice. She has a pale complexion and sandy hair and should wear very bright clothes and much lipstick, but wears black and dark blue and no lipstick. I am almost tempted to give her the Coty's I bought before I was married. It is hardly used at all, and I never touch it. She helped me clean our apartment for my party last Saturday, which was a very nice party. Everybody had just enough wine to feel bright and happy, and we played games that were a lot of fun. [...]

I have been working this morning and have now decided to have a rest.³³ There is not much excitement here. Many foreigners are leaving Spain, as they think the excitement is over and the revolution is dead. There is some sporadic fighting throughout Catalonia in [the process of] the collection of rifles, etc., from the workers. Other foreigners are being put into jail, etc.; Albert Weisbord, a phoney revolutionary, who in America is so intransigent that he never has more than eight or nine in his organisation, 'The Communist League of Struggle', was asked to write an article on the American strike movement for the POUM international paper. He did so, expounding his own ideas that [the] Lewis movement³⁴ should have absolutely no support, that Roosevelt is a fascist and his regime the first step towards fascism, etc. Landau,³⁵ the editor, said he would have to put an editorial comment in, demarking his and POUM's position from that of the article. Weisbord said: 'Oh no, oh no, you tell me the POUM line, and I'll change the article.' (!!!!!) Landau was shocked, of course, and I don't know what ever happened to the article.³⁶ Weisbord has left here thro the American consul on a French ship. If he ever shows up around where you are, he's a phoney. [...]

Norman Thomas has been here and gone on to Valencia. He got here just after the May events. He's a credulous person. C. wrote him a note telling him that he would be glad to be of service to him if he wanted to make contact with the POUM, etc. Thomas wrote back that he was having a 'delightful personally conducted visit' to Montserrat (an old historic and beautiful monastery and mountain 50 miles from Barcelona). Miravitlles, head of the propaganda department, led this tour himself. They also showed Thomas, according to the Generality English Bulletin, the '14th century courtyard of the Municipal Building in the moonlight' – gee! – and he drank a toast to 'Catalunya and the other democratic nations.' Then he passed on to Valencia. That in the midst of a revolution from a supposedly serious leader of an American political party. They took him 50 miles from Barcelona so he wouldn't see the barricades in the city streets, and the hundreds of armed guards patrolling the workers' sections. He probably got lots of 'local color' from his Catalan guides, but as for serious political investigation, well, he will be in Barcelona on his way back, but I don't expect that he will meet the POUM leaders – altho he assured C. that he wanted to have his point of view. [...]

It is after lunch now. You would absolutely go nuts in Barcelona this week. It is the festival-of-books week, and all over the city there are hundreds of book stands set up. The main streets in Barcelona are very wide with broad promenades in each side shaded with plane trees. Every party, the trade unions, all the bookstores, every little or big society, all the departments of the Generality, etc. etc., have got stands and are selling their literature. The POUM has very conspicuous and well-gotten up stands. The *Editorial Marxista* stand is very modern and is in the form of a big book. They have published many many pamphlets and books, several of which are sold in other stands than the POUM's (Bebel's *The Woman* in a red binding with big scrawling white letters is one that is on every stand). The purpose is to buy books to send to the front, or to your kids, or for any purpose, but just buy them. There are some lovely editions of Zweig's,[37] biographies of hundreds of different people, many books of Ludwig that I hadn't seen before, and lots of big colored history of Catalonia books, many interesting technical books – one set of Freud, Adler, Jung, extremely cheap. And, of course, the hundreds of books by Spaniards on the October rebellion, on Russia, on Marx, Lenin, etc. There were, especially in the Stalinist stalls, many books about Russia, about Lenin and Marx, but few by them. It is very colorful as every stand is gaily decorated, and there are so many colored varieties of editions, etc. We just walked down to the second hand stalls which are very interesting. There are many old German books, lovely editions, taken from fascists' houses. We found some old 1600s manuscripts on parchment, evidently taken from an abbey or nunnery. There was a huge stand full of them and they were undergoing some very rough treatment there. There were lots of fine leatherbound collections on every subject under the sun taken from confiscated houses – in red, brown, blue, and that sort of tannish color.

If we were going straight home, had the money, and knew Spanish, it would have been a regular paradise. It was the intellectuals that the revolution has brought to the front. Instead we saw a very small little artificial rooster made of real feathers by a Catalan, who had 40 or so to sell at 50 centimes a piece. We bought one in memory of our many adventures with Catalan roosters. They are like no other roosters, incidentally, in that they crow all night long. Every Catalan family has three or four that live in cages on their back balconies – in a city of one and a half million, mind you. That is part of the great campaign that the Catalan government has on – *la lluita de l'ou* – or the battle of the egg, which has for its end the noble aim of making Catalonia self-sustaining in eggs by the end of four years. They have compiled hundreds of statistics on the subject, and so the roosters crow all night. It is a standing grievance of all foreigners. Ordinary roosters only crow at about five or six, don't they?

Tomorrow the [POUM's] Feminine Section and the Communist Youth together are sponsoring a picnic – all day picnic to the sea. It leaves from the Plaça Catalunya at six o'clock in the morning. We are going. It will require manipulation to get the food together, as it is impossible to buy bread for sandwiches, and you can't buy food at the seaside. However, as this is Saturday afternoon and I want to go, I'll have to get busy about the food.

Boy, am I sunburned![38] We got to the beach yesterday morning at 8, and it was really swell. A place where the barbed defence wires broke through. It was a fine white sand and very clean; there were no people anywhere around, and it was a natural beach. It was the first time I had ever been in salt water or in the ocean. I had great fun riding the waves when they got bigger, in the afternoon.

Late in the afternoon we exchanged songs with the Spaniards – boys and girls of the Young Communist group. They did much better than we English, C., David Crooks, Bill K., and Stafford, *el piquena Inglesa* [sic]. There was one girl especially, who had a lovely high clear voice. She sang a 'flaminka' (flamingo) [sic] – that kind of Spanish song that is very high with many many trills, the longer they trill the better it is, and at the end of a particularly good one everybody interrupts the song to clap. There were some Polish and French Jews there too who sang some lovely Hebraic and Russian songs. I am going to study Jewish music some day, as I like it very very much.

[...]

52. *Postcard written by Charles to Harry De Vries on 7 June 1937*

[...] Elsa is not working now, but I am, and as long as my job lasts, we will stay.[39] It may end at any time, however. [...] We have been mountain climbing every Sunday, until yesterday when we went to the beach with about 50 Catalans – a swell beach they have. It was the first time Elsa swam in salt water. My boss is away, so I have several small things to do – but the main work is halted by abnormal political conditions. Sincerely, Albert.

53. *Postcard written by Charles to his mother on 11 June 1937*

[...] I am writing you by candle light, because the Electric Co. tried to make us pay for the German Consul's bill.[40] We offered to pay our part since Feb. 15 even, but they wouldn't bargain. So – no more hot baths – a luxury here. [...] We are nearly broke, but just bought 2 bathing suits today anyhow. Cheap – 5 pesetas for mine (37 to a dollar). I am not very busy now – so am reading James' *World Revolution* and Souvarine's *Staline*. [...] Wrote today for ship booking for late August. Your cards came, but no letters for a month. Sunburned – Paul.

Notes

1. A handwritten notation in the margins identifies the woman as 'Mrs. Jellinek'. Frank Jellinek, the correspondent for the *Manchester Guardian*, published in 1938 his reminiscences of his time in Spain, *The Civil War in Spain*.
2. Handwritten addition by Charles to 'Dear Mr. Culter', written on the back of Lois' typewritten letter.
3. In early November 1936, with Francoist forces on the outskirts of Madrid, the Republican government of Spain decided to move the seat of the central government to Valencia. Later military setbacks resulted in a further move of the seat of government from Valencia to Barcelona in November 1937. Madrid itself held out until 27 March 1939, literally five days before the end of the Spanish Civil War on 1 April 1939.
4. Lord Beaverbrook, born William Maxwell Aitken, first made a fortune in the cement business in his native Canada. One year after moving to Great Britain, he became a Conservative Member of Parliament, and quickly managed to obtain a controlling interest in the *Daily Express*. In 1918 he was appointed Minister of Information in David Lloyd George's wartime cabinet. In the interwar period the *Daily Express* became the most widely read newspaper in the British world. Lord Beaverbrook was rewarded with several ministerial posts in Winston Churchill's wartime government. Lord Rothermere, born Harold Harmsworth in 1868, was the key personality behind the successes of three mass circulation dailies in Great Britain, the *Evening News*, the *Daily Mail* and the *Daily Mirror*. In the 1930s, Lord Rothermere repeatedly and publicly expressed his admiration for Oswald Mosley and his National Union of Fascists.
5. For more on George Tioli, see Charles Orr's observations included in Chapter 7.
6. Francisco Ferrer, born near Barcelona in 1859, early on became an anarchist and a Freemason. He devoted much of his time to a series of wide-ranging and radical school reforms, and he opened up his first Modern School in Barcelona in 1901. Within a few years more than 50 schools, modelling themselves on Ferrer's Barcelona *Escuela Moderna*, sprang up throughout the Spanish state. Always most popular in the Catalan region, Ferrer's principles of liberated schooling were widely applied in anarchist-dominated areas of Republican Spain at the time of the Catalan Revolution.
7. First sentence of a new section of the letter, headed by the comment 'Monday, April 12'.

8. Lois refers to an unsubstantiated rumour, which is not borne out by the relevant literature.
9. In the spring of 1937, some political reconfigurations occurred within certain milieus in Spanish anarchism, exemplified by the formation of the *Amigos de Durruti*, a dissident grouping which criticized the CNT's continued willingness to cooperate with moderate political parties and which called, instead, for a return to what they regarded as a revolutionary strategy for the forces on the radical Left. The *Amigos de Durruti* were influenced in this thinking by ideas emanating from the POUM, but they likewise had connections to the forces associated with orthodox Trotskyism, amongst them the close friend of Lois and Charles Orr, the German activist, Hans Freund, known as 'Moulin'. Such new departures from within Spanish anarchism also led to a reinforcement of Left-wing critiques within the POUM itself. Here, a tendency around Josep Rebull, aided by another friend of Lois and Charles Orr, Russell Blackwell, called for a more radical course on the part of the POUM. It is most likely this emerging division within the POUM's rank which is alluded to in this passage by Lois.
10. First sentence of a new section of the letter, written by Lois on 'Tuesday', 27 April 1937.
11. First sentence of a new section of the letter, begun on 26 April, written by Lois on 27 April, '11:40 PM'.
12. The German Socialist Workers Party (SAP) emerged out of a leftwing split-off from the German Social Democratic Party (SPD) in the second half of 1931. It remained a marginal force in German politics, despite attracting locally important SPD dissident forces to its ranks. The young Willy Brandt, many decades later the Chancellor of West Germany, was a young activist of the SAP. Although spending much of his exile in Norway, Willy Brandt played a certain role in German emigré circles in Barcelona at the time of the Spanish Civil War. Brandt operated from Barcelona for much of the time when the Orrs lived in the Catalan capital city.
13. Second paragraph of another new section of the same letter, this one headed 'Wednesday', 28 April 1937.
14. In the spring of 1937, at a time of growing dissensions within the Spanish and Catalan Far Left, Spanish social democracy also underwent a considerable evolution. As the counter-revolutionary nature of Soviet-controlled Spanish communism – increasingly allied to the moderate factions within the PSOE around Indalecio Prieto and Juan Negrín – became ever more pronounced, the important Left-wing faction within the PSOE, headed by Largo Caballero and closely linked to the leadership of the UGT, went increasingly on the offensive. Unwilling to join forces with the radicals in the POUM and CNT, Caballero and his co-thinkers were nonetheless equally disinclined to countenance or even tolerate the openly regressive policies supported by Negrín, Prieto and the PCE team. It is this emerging division between the PSOE-Left, on the one hand, and the PCE and PSOE-Right, on the other, which Lois is referring to in this passage.
15. Letter portion written by Lois on 'Thursday, April 29'.
16. John Dos Passos was already then one of the most well known American novelist, who at that time was influenced by Left socialist and Trotskyist ideology.

17. The town of Puigcerdà and the surrounding Catalan areas of the Cerdanya were solidly in the hands of the Left-wing factions on the Republican side. The head of the local paramilitary border control troops, known as El 'Cojo de Málaga', became the bête noir of the conservative forces in the Spanish government. A first high point of conflict between the local anarchists in Puigcerdà and the counter-revolutionary forces aiming to enforce the centralizing and simultaneously moderating impulse emanating from the central state occurred precisely at the time when Lois wrote this letter. On radical politics in the Cerdanya, see Joan Pous i Porta and Josep M. Solé i Sabaté, *Anarquia i república a la Cerdanya* (Barcelona: Publicacions de l'Abadia de Montserrat, 1991).
18. The remaining paragraphs on the card were written on Sunday, 'May 2'.
19. These and the remaining lines on the card were added by Lois.
20. This letter fragment was most likely started on 2 May, but with the last hurried lines written on 14 May 1937, that is after the intervening 'Barcelona May Days'.
21. George Orwell had indeed been planning to leave the POUM militia and to join the International Brigades. He had been planning to use his leave from the Aragon front to effect this change. At the time Lois wrote these lines, however, he had not yet left Barcelona. Caught up in the whirlwind of the 'May events' (see Chapter 1), where Orwell participated in the armed defence of the conquests of the Catalan Revolution within the ranks of the POUM, Orwell switched his mind and decided to continue fighting within the ranks of the POUM. A recent biographer put it like this: 'His attitude towards the Communists had altered and hardened', and the result of having joined the POUM's forces in armed combat on Barcelona rooftops and the city's streets 'had been to strengthen his ties with the POUM. He was afraid that by joining the Communists he could be used against the working class'; see Gordon Bowker, *George Orwell* (London: Abacus, 2003), p. 218.
22. First paragraph of the subsequent portion of Lois' letter, written on 'Monday', 3 May, addressed to 'Dear Mother'.
23. This is the end of the portion of the letter written on Monday, 3 May 1937, when the small-scale civil war, usually referred to as the Barcelona May Days, erupted in downtown Barcelona.
24. These lines were added in hurried handwriting by Lois on 'May 14, 1937'.
25. Lois then added another line: 'you'd better address – no'. All words of this last line were crossed out by Lois.
26. This is the first card where Charles signs off using a different name, here 'Bill', and fabricates a fictitious name for his mother, in this case 'Mrs. Emma Orhlinge', in order to lead astray any potential censors in the aftermath of the May Events. The card was addressed to 'Mrs. Emma Orhlinge, 1513 So. University Ave. Ann Arbor, Michigan EE.UU' (her correct mailing address).
27. The postscript was added on the margins of the postcard.
28. First sentence of a new portion of the letter started on 11 May 1937, headed 'May 12, 1937'.
29. Albert Weisbord, born in 1900 in New York City, was a leading activist within the US Socialist Party in the first half of the 1920s. An organizer within the Communist Party in the second half of that decade, he briefly joined the

Trotskyist Left Opposition before setting up a rival organization, the League of Communist Struggle, which existed from 1931 to 1937.
30. Addendum by Lois to 'Dear Dort'.
31. First sentence of the second portion of the letter started on 25 May 1937, headed 'May 26, 1937'. The mention of 'C.-J.s' is a reference to *The Courier-Journal*, the local paper in Louisville, Kentucky, Lois' hometown.
32. Boris Souvarine's 1935 biography of Stalin (*Staline: aperçu historique du bolchévisme*) was one of the first serious and substantive critical appraisals of the Soviet leader. Boris Souvarine had been a leading member of the French Communist Party and the Comintern in the early 1920s. In the second half of the 1920s he sympathized with the general position of the Trotskyist Left Opposition before evolving slowly towards more moderate positions.
33. First sentence of a second portion of the letter begun on 2 June 1937, headed 'June 5, 1937'.
34. John L. Lewis, born in 1880 in a small town in Iowa, was perhaps the most influential American labour leader to help found the Committee for Industrial Organisations (CIO) in 1935. The CIO, initially operating within the traditional US labour federation, the American Federation of Labor (AFL), set itself the goal to represent the unorganized industrial workers, who had traditionally been disregarded by the craft-oriented AFL. Though a staunch anti-communist, in 1938 John L. Lewis and the CIO were expelled from the conservative AFL, and the CIO changed its name to the Congress of Industrial Organisation.
35. Kurt Landau was the editor of the Austrian Communist Party's daily in the mid-1920s, when he began to move close to the position of the emerging Trotskyist Left Opposition, resulting in his expulsion from the Communist Party. Continuing his engagement in the milieu of dissident communist organizations in Germany and France, he took a position of responsibility in the POUM's International Secretariat in Barcelona. Initially avoiding the Stalinist secret police after the May Days, he suffered arrest on 23 September 1937 and perished in the secret jails of the Stalinist apparatus.
36. The article was published, entitled 'Le mouvement ouvrier des Etats-Unis', in *Juillet* (the French-language international publication of the POUM) 1 (June 1937), 33–36.
37. Stefan Zweig, born in Vienna in 1881, was a poet, dramatist and pacifist. After the First World War, he began to concentrate on short stories, a genre of writing which made him world famous. Forced to leave his native Austria after the crushing of democracy in 1934, the Jewish pacifist writer spent the subsequent years of exile in a number of countries. He committed suicide in February 1942 in Brazil.
38. First sentence of the third section of the same letter started on 2 June, headed 'Monday, 6th June'.
39. With the rapid increase in punitive measures meted out to the POUM, Charles once again had recourse to pseudonyms. 'Albert' is, of course, Charles, and 'Elsa' refers to Lois. The card was addressed to 'Prof. Harry De Vries, Buena Vista College, Storm Lake, Iowa', his brother-in-law's correct name and address.
40. Again employing precautionary pseudonyms, the card was written by 'Paul' [= Charles] to 'Dear Mrs. Palmer' [Charles' mother].

7
Reminiscences by Charles Orr

Charles Orr, more than ten years older than Lois, had already led a somewhat itinerant life by the time the newly-wed couple settled in Barcelona for ten months. After obtaining a degree in economics, in the late 1920s Charles for a while worked for the International Labour Organisation in Geneva. A cultured and articulate man, by the mid-1930s Charles became a leading activist in the Ann Arbor, Michigan, branch of the Young People's Socialist League, the radicalizing youth branch of American social democracy. He was thus well poised to take advantage of the unusual confluence of independent spirits concentrating in Barcelona, which provides the backdrop to the countless letters by Lois and himself.

Amongst the outstanding experiences in the Catalan port city must count the chance encounter with George Orwell within one hour of the latter's arrival in Barcelona. Still largely unknown, but having just secured the Left Book Club's contract for The Road to Wigan Pier, which provided the final take-off for Orwell's stellar writing career, Orwell arrived in the Hotel Falcón to speak to his designated contact, John McNair of the British Independent Labour Party. Charles Orr's astute psychological portrait of Eric Blair will be of interest for anyone wishing to understand the personality of one of Great Britain's most famous and most controversial writers. This intimate portrait was facilitated by Charles Orr's close association with Eileen O'Shaughnessy, George Orwell's newly-wed wife, who became Charles' secretary in the offices of the POUM for four months in early 1937. For Eileen had become one of the young couple's closest personal friends in those months.

This chapter closes with Charles' suggestive observations on one of the very many Stalinist spies employed by Moscow to help turn the tide against the Catalan Revolution. George Tioli, however, was unusual in that, in Charles Orr's view, he, like others in succeeding years, developed second thoughts about his political and personal role. Whether for political reasons, out of personal loyalty or because of a combination of these two factors, George Tioli, a close friend of the Orrs, repeatedly behaved in a rather enigmatic manner. His contradictory behaviour in the spring and early summer of 1937 helps provide authenticity to the life-and-death issues which then came to the fore.

54. *Homage to Orwell – As I knew him in Catalonia*

Orwell wrote *Homage to Catalonia* a few months after the events.[1] His plunge into the Spanish Revolution was still sharp in memory. I am writing my recollections of Orwell and of the Revolution almost half a century later. But such events, accompanied by strong emotion, one never forgets.

What Orwell describes so vividly in *Homage to Catalonia* I can only confirm. He shows the war and the revolution, and he reveals himself – fully and honestly. Here I recall certain incidents and personal relationships which may reveal Orwell's character more fully still.

First day in Spain

Early one morning – that is about 10 AM Spanish office time – in December 1936, I was working at my office in the administrative building of the POUM on the Barcelona Ramblas. A little militiaman, in his blue coveralls and red scarf, trudged up the stairs to my office on the fourth floor. The lifts, as usual, bore the familiar sign NO FUNCIONA. This militiaman was one of the guard-receptionists whose duty it was to block and check any stranger coming to the main door.

There was an Englishman, he reported to me, who spoke neither Catalan nor Spanish. He wanted to see my boss, John McNair. Inasmuch as McNair was away that morning, I went down to see who this Englishman was and what his business might be.

There I met him – Eric Blair – tall, lanky and tired, having just that hour arrived from London. He had come to volunteer for the anti-fascist war. I invited him in and we climbed those long stairways, back up to the fourth floor.

Exhausted, but excited, after a day and a night on the train, he had come to fight fascism, but did not know which militia he should join. However, an acquaintance in England had advised him, before enlisting, to contact John McNair in Barcelona. McNair was the representative of the ILP, the British Independent Labour Party, in Spain. At first, I did not take this English volunteer very seriously. Just one more foreigner come to help, but not a party man, apparently a political innocent, blundering into a milieu which placed a premium on political acumen and partisan pedigree. Lucky, I thought, that we could lay hold on him before he fell into communist hands.

Yet I liked him: frank and refreshingly enthusiastic. I too had been naïve in the view of professional Marxist-Leninists when I had first arrived. Another point in common: we both knew French. I asked him how he had learned the language and he told me about his adventures in Paris where he had managed to live by working as a kitchen help. I too had been down and out in Paris and elsewhere and I knew that an intellectual needs a good quantum of self-assurance to undergo such an ordeal. For that, at least, I had to respect this gawky, stammering adventurer. There might be more to this man, I felt, than meets the eye. He told me he was a writer. Later, I learned that he wrote under the pen name 'George Orwell'.

Two important events within the past few days were to change the life of Eric Blair. First, he had made it to Spain to risk his life in the anti-fascist cause. Then, as he proudly told me, his manuscript for a book called *The Road to Wigan Pier* had just been accepted for publication by the Left Book Club. It would be published in an edition of several hundred thousand copies, and this hitherto obscure, aspiring writer would now become well known. He had learned this good news just as he was leaving London. Thus Eric Blair arrived in Spain already a different man.

I spent an hour or two with him, awaiting the return of John McNair. Under the emotion of having arrived in Spain, he opened up – the one and only time that I was with him alone and that I found him in a mood to talk. I remember that we talked about his life as a tramp in Paris. This seems to confirm what literary critics have deduced from his writings: this experience had a profound and enduring effect upon Orwell.

McNair returned to the office in the afternoon and soon persuaded Eric to join the International Militia of the POUM. Just by accident, so it seems, Eric Blair ended up in the ILP-POUM contingent on the Aragon Front, rather than in the communist-controlled International Brigade in Madrid. He went to the POUM's Lenin Barracks in Barcelona, and a few days later left for the front. That might have been the end of my contact with Eric Blair but for the fact that, before leaving for the front, he arranged for his wife, Eileen, to join us in Barcelona as our secretary.

Eileen

Orwell was his pen name. To us he was just Eric. More formally, he was Comrade Eric Blair, militiaman in the ILP-POUM Brigade, one of a small band of foreigners, mostly British, fighting on the Aragon Front. We knew, of course, that he was a writer who had already published a couple of books (of which we had never heard before). That in itself caught our attention and set him apart. That, and the fact that he was tall and lanky and that he had a beautiful wife, Eileen. She came to work with us in Barcelona, as a secretary to John McNair and myself. As editor of the fortnightly review, *Spanish Revolution*, and as a reader of the daily news broadcast, I needed the services of an English-language secretary.

In *Homage to Catalonia* Orwell scarcely mentions his wife. I cannot avoid mentioning her, because it was only through Eileen that I came to know Eric in a personal sense. I had met him and had that one long conversation with him on his first day in Spain. Our contacts, thereafter, developed through Eileen, with whom I worked closely for four months, while Eric was at the front.

Orwell had married Eileen O'Shaughnessy in the Spring of 1936, half a year before they decided to go to Spain. Eileen was a round-faced Irish girl, prim and pretty, with black hair and big dark eyes. Eric was tall, lean and gangling, to the point of being awkward. In stature and physical appearance, they were opposites – and in other ways too. He was tongue-tied, stammered and seemed to be afraid of people. Eileen was friendly, gregarious and unpretentious.

Eileen was an excellent secretary. In addition to being attractive, I found her to be intelligent and self-confident. Everyone liked her, women as well as men. The reader may think that I over-idealize her, but working in the same office every day one comes to know the character of a fellow-worker. When I compare her with the refugees, reformers and revolutionaries who made up our office staff, and others in our political milieu, Eileen stands out as a superior person.

Eileen had studied at Oxford and was a trained psychologist, who was not too proud to accept a job as secretary-typist. Her sister, back in Britain, was a medical doctor. The two were in constant correspondence and her sister sent us some pharmaceutical products which were not available in Barcelona.

Eileen's hero

By 1984 Orwell had become a popular hero. For example, in 1982 the dissident youth of Lausanne, Switzerland, named their youth center *Café Orwell*. The police soon raided the premises, gratuitously smashing the furniture, as if to fulfill Orwell's own vision of a heartless police state.[2] But already in 1937, Orwell, a struggling young writer, unknown to the general public, was a hero in the eyes of at least one person – his wife Eileen.

Eric was up at the front, his life in danger, without a break for 115 days. For all that period and for at least a month before, Eric and Eileen saw each other only once.[3] At the office, Eileen just could not resist talking about Eric – her hero husband, whom she obviously loved and admired. It was my privilege to hear about him day after day. Not that I paid much attention. He was still just an unknown would-be writer who, like others, had come to Spain to fight against fascism. But I learned to respect him as a solid character.

One might respect a man who risks his life for a cause. One might also respect a writer whose book has just been accepted for wide circulation – who is about to 'arrive'. As I came to know Eric better – through Eileen – my respect grew. First, because of Eileen herself. A man who could win a woman of such quality must have some value. The man she revealed to me was a good man, a profound man, not just some blundering adventurer.

Apart from her natural beauty, why was Orwell (who married late) attracted to this outgoing gregarious Irish girl? He needed, no doubt, a socially extrovert wife as a window to the world. Eileen helped this inarticulate man to communicate with others. Though married for less than a year, she had already become his spokesman. This relationship – Eric's outreach to the world via Eileen – is illustrated by an incident which occurred during a visit to Barcelona by the famed American writer, John Dos Passos.

I had been asked by the POUM to arrange Dos Passos' tour, to find him a hotel room, to make his appointments and to accompany him about. I recall taking him to the headquarters of the CNT-FAI to meet Emma Goldman, the notorious American anarchist. I also arranged for him to meet Andreu Nin, the Secretary of the POUM. Eileen, as my secretary, helped to make these arrangements.

At the time Eric was, at last, on leave in Barcelona. The aspiring young writer wanted to meet the great Dos Passos. He could have asked me directly – he dropped by our office every day. But, no, Eileen brought me his request. Could I find some excuse or some way for Eric to meet John Dos Passos? So I arranged that he should meet Dos Passos in the hallway in front of Nin's office, where they chatted for a few minutes. I wanted to invite him to accompany us in. But who was I, to drag this husband of my secretary, this militiaman – in his baggy, tan coverall uniform – into a private interview? So we just left Orwell standing in the hallway. I regretted it at the time, and I have regretted it ever since. Orwell waited half an hour, sitting on a bench, until we reappeared, and he was able to speak with Dos Passos for a minute or two again.

A few days later, Eileen brought me a message: 'Eric wants me to thank you from the bottom of his heart. He asked me to thank you for him, because he knows he can't talk.'

55. *The repentant spy*

The most intriguing of the communist agents was George Tioli, a refugee from fascist Italy.[4] I will relate his story in some detail, because it shows that some of the people caught up in the Stalinist apparatus were indeed human and could not accept the brutality required of them. I met George in November or December 1936. He pretended to be a journalist. He was friendly and helped us in many ways....

He had an extraordinary facility for getting our post into and out of Spain, at times when nothing else seemed to work, supposedly through his 'connections at the Turkish mission' – or so he claimed. A year later, when I was in Paris and Tioli was still in Spain, we were able to communicate through a mysterious Parisian lady who lived in a large villa. In short, George had unusual connections and facilities. [...]

Towards the end of *Homage to Catalonia* Orwell describes a police search of his wife's hotel room but he omits the part played by George Tioli. Orwell does mention George elsewhere in the book, accepting his claim to be a journalist. Orwell speculates as to why his wife, Eileen, was not arrested along with the rest of us, but he does not question why George Tioli was not arrested. I believe that by June 1937 Tioli had been assigned either to survey Orwell and Eileen or, more likely, just to gather information from the talkative, but non-political, Eileen.

In June 1937 following my release after ten days in a communist prison, I met Eileen, together with George Tioli, in the streets of Barcelona. They told me this strange story: In the hotel the two of them happened to live in adjacent rooms. Eileen had permitted George to store a roll of supposedly incriminating maps on her balcony. When George noticed that the police were searching Eileen's room, he reached across from his balcony and took the maps. When the police left her room on their way to search his, he handed the maps back to Eileen's balcony. Were these maps intended to incriminate Eileen and the POUM? Did George, then, try to protect Eileen? Or was this just another play – an episode contrived to cover George's role as an inter-party spy?

But George was different from the other communist agents. At times he gave me enigmatic tips which – if I had understood them – would have saved me and others much trouble. Later, when I was in Paris, he tried to denounce to me the lady whom we later discovered was the topmost agent planted in the POUM's military committee. Was George planning to escape from his own position as a communist agent and trying to protect me on his way out?

Another incident which points to George's ambiguous role: one afternoon in June 1937, Andreu Nin, the secretary of the POUM, was arrested in Barcelona by the then communist-directed police. On the way home that evening, I went out of my way to observe the central police station where Nin had been taken. There I saw Mrs. Nin, who had come to inquire about her husband's whereabouts. (She never saw him again. A few days later his body was found in the street, outside a prison in Madrid.) Among the crowd which had gathered in front of the police station, I met also George Tioli. He promised me – at first I thought it was a joke – to bring me blankets when I, too, would be in prison. On the way home, I decided that in the morning I would look for a place to hide. Little did I know that by early morning I would be arrested in my flat and locked up, at first in the basement of that same police station. And George, true to his word, did send me blankets, badly needed in our cell.

As far as I have been able to ascertain, Tioli disappeared in Spain. If indeed he was killed by his communist masters, it would not have been the only time they suppressed their own agents in order to forestall their defectors or to cover their trail.

Notes

1. The following pages reproduce the first half of a 1984 unpublished document written by Charles.
2. When writing this reminiscence, Charles Orr lived near Geneva, which explains his example drawn from neighbouring Lausanne.
3. Note by Charles Orr: 'That was in mid-March [1937] when Eileen, John McNair and I made a brief visit to the front. Except for that one day, Eric and Eileen were 250 kilometers apart. (It so happened that Jenny Lee – later to become Mrs Nye Bevin – was up there to visit the front and to encourage the ILP boys on the very same day.)'
4. This excerpt is taken from a January 1992 manuscript by Charles Orr, entitled 'Some Reminiscences of the Hotel Falcón during the Spanish Revolution', which he wrote at this editor's suggestion.

8
In Stalin's Secret Barcelona Jail

On 17 June 1937, Lois and Charles Orr were rounded up and arrested along with many other Catalan, Spanish and foreign revolutionaries residing in Spain. It was part of a crackdown operation nominally undertaken by Republican authorities, but instigated, inspired and supervised by Stalinist operatives then congregating in Spain. As the hot spot of revolutionary activity anywhere in Europe at the time, Barcelona had become the temporary home of anti-Stalinist revolutionary Marxists from around the world. The Soviet leadership, then engaged in a series of show trials in the USSR, designed to snuff out any potential for the revival of a revolutionary anti-authoritarian tradition at home, intended to extend their field of operation to other parts of the world, in order to crush opposition currents which operated to the left of the Comintern.

Helped along by the conniving neutrality of the moderate wing of Spanish social democracy, headed by Juan Negrín, the Soviet operatives, having recourse to Republican counter-espionage organizations and the regular law enforcement agencies, thus brought to bear the full brunt of their repressive moves against, above all, the dissident communist POUM. Andreu Nin, the undisputed head of the POUM and a former high official of the Communist International, was only one amongst many victims of this vicious calculated act. But, as the two accounts reproduced in this section make clear, the range of targets far exceeded the numerically limited forces of the POUM. The entire range of revolutionary forces, whether Marxist or anarchist, experienced the repercussions, though within anarchist circles the strength of Spanish and Catalan anarchism, coupled with its leadership's increasing moderation, ensured that repression against anarchists mostly focused on the frequently homeless and stateless foreign anarchists on Spanish soil.

Charles and Lois Orr's accounts may well provide some of the most detailed extant reports on the Stalinist prison complex in underground Republican Spain. The facsimile reproduction of the list of foreign revolutionaries *imprisoned together with the young American couple may well cast some new light on certain individuals' fate. The final document, a letter by Lois written in 1938 from Paris, establishes that the two protagonists of this volume had taken up temporary residence in France, carrying out solidarity work with their Spanish and Catalan former hosts. Politically, the Orrs had moved ever closer to the beleaguered forces of international Trotskyism, fighting, along with some others, a rearguard battle to salvage the revolutionary heritage, which had first come to world attention with the success of the Bolshevik Revolution in Russia, but which was nearly totally defeated by Stalinism 20 years later on the battlegrounds of Republican Spain.*

56. Some facts on the persecution of foreign revolutionaries in 'Republican' Spain (by Charles A. Orr)

Our apartment was thoroughly searched for two hours – to the bottom of the garbage can.[1] They found things that we had lost and could not find ourselves. Inasmuch as this apartment had formerly belonged to the German Vice Consul, they were able to collect such things as Nazi song books and thousands of German government tax stamps. They also took with great care the Monarchist colors with which we had decorated our bathroom door. They evidently were instructed to take all possible evidence for a frame-up trial. With all our papers and letters, Nazi song books and colors, we were packed into cars with the armed guards and taken to the Chief of Police. No warrants nor charges were ever produced. Against our vigorous protests, we were searched and thrown into the general pen, where we found about eighty other prisoners, the majority politicals too.

While being taken into the building, we happened to see two young ladies, Scottish and American, who were there to visit a Dutch Anarchist chap who had been held there several weeks without charges. When the authorities saw that they knew us, they arrested the two ladies as well. Being Anarchists they were released that night. The police were not ready to start on the foreign Anarchists at that point, but the Scottish girl has been taken again since then.

We learned that dozens of Spanish comrades, taken in the raid on the Hotel Falcón, had already been released, but all foreigners were being held. Spanish comrades of known importance in the POUM were held as well as the men and even young boys who worked for *La Batalla*. Every few minutes another foreign comrade would be brought in. Some were taken for walking past a POUM building and looking in to see if it were safe to come in. Thus several foreigners not connected with the POUM or any party were taken and are still being held.

Hugo Oehler was brought in soon after us. He had been taken two days earlier, however, at Puigcerdà, a border town. He had not attempted to cross the border illegally nor had he committed any illegal or irregular offense, he assured us. He had approached the police authorities (who were conducting a veritable reign of terror against the Anarchists who had until recently held this town and the customs there) and had asked them if he could proceed to leave the country without the proper permit stamp of the Valencia Government or whether it was necessary to await the stamp. They told him that they would gladly help him out. In the meantime, however, they telephoned Barcelona to see if he were especially 'wanted'. It seems that the police list of foreign revolutionaries was already prepared at that time, with Oehler's name upon it, and he was sent back to Barcelona to prison, arriving soon after us. He was searched and a political thesis in manuscript form was taken from him. He also carried a French grammar, with words underlined in red; the examining officer thought he had found here a spy code! Scarcely had Oehler time to tell me this when the police must have discovered that he was an important revolutionary figure, for he was taken out of the pen and put in strict isolation from all prisoners. This isolation was not very perfect the first day, however, for the police station was so full of prisoners that they had no place for him and made him sit in a stairway all day. To get to the men's room we had to pass him.

This trip downstairs also led us past the women prisoners and members of the POUM Executive Committee, held in smelly damp cells in the basement. Walking down the row, one saluted first Gorkín,[2] Lewin – the Secretary of the lively German Anarchist Section[3] – and another Anarchist; next were eight women (six of whom were political) all crowded in one small cell; then came Arquer; then David Rey, Bonet, young Maurín,[4] Andrade and Escuder, in order. They had stone benches, but nothing else in their cells. Fortunately they didn't have to stay in that foul place for long. Nin had already been taken to —–[*5] no one knows where or what has become of him. There are all sorts of rumors, but really no one knows.

Upstairs we were crowded, almost a hundred in a place with thirty-five beds. The worst complaint up there was the lack of food – only two plates of soup and two pieces of bread per day. We got hungry before the first meal came at one thirty PM. There were prisoners up there who had been held without charges for weeks. There were men from the International Brigade, French, Belgian, Irish, Czech, Austrian, who were presumably being repatriated, but had landed at this station for a prolonged stay and without any reason. There was an Austrian worker who had come to Spain 'to help', but who happened to be coming on the ship 'Ciudad de Barcelona' when it was torpedoed by a submarine and sunk. He was picked up from the water and thrown into this hole to stay with no possibility of communicating with the outside, and no one to help him or even know him, if the word could be smuggled out. It was a nasty place; bed bugs crawled over the walls. We were very glad when they took us out that night.

About midnight they came and called a list of about thirty foreigners connected with the POUM. We marched out in a long line with two guards at the sides of each person. Silently we walked through the dark and narrow streets of the old town, with queer fears running through our heads. They took us to what was an ordinary building from the street, but had been a magnificent home of a fascist within – around a lovely courtyard hidden there in the center of town. Now the Catalan Service of Investigation had taken it over and constructed prison cells down in the servants' quarters.

The first eight men to walk in were the most fortunate. We were placed together in a room looking onto an air shaft. In the next room were placed eight women, including the wives of four of us. Downstairs the others were held, two and three in tiny cells, without good air or light. Oehler was singled out for special treatment, incommunicado from the other prisoners as well as from the outside world. He had little means either to read or write and doesn't know enough Spanish or Catalan to speak with the guards. We only saw him two or three times by accident, but I must say that he kept his spirit and stood up to the treatment like a good revolutionary.

Of the foreigners taken that first day, mostly of the POUM, were 8 Germans, 3 Americans, 3 French, 2 Dutch, 2 Italians, 1 Polish, 1 Austrian, 1 Albanian, 1 Greek, 1 Swiss, 1 Lithuanian and 1 Canadian. (Since then, dozens of foreigners of all political tendencies except Stalinists have been arrested. Besides many German Anarchists, we know of Belgian, American, Swiss, Scottish and French comrades being taken.) Several from the International Brigade were being held in the same prison. There were thirteen in a room below ours with whom we could speak. We also got communications with the women by forcing a crack in the nailed door. This was our telephone, or we could pass papers through.

The morale was excellent upstairs. We would pass the time singing revolutionary songs, which would spread through to the women, down to the soldiers and out to the guards. The whole prison together would sing the *Internationale*, *A Las Barricadas*, and *Auf, Auf, zum Kampf, zum Kampf*. We wrote the words in various languages all over the walls. We also organised political discussions in French and German in our cell.

Downstairs it was more difficult. There the comrades were held in smaller groups and had bad cell conditions. For several days they were out of touch with us. After repeated refusals to let them see anyone or write to anyone, to get a newspaper or even see the prison authorities to demand why they were being held, they presented a reasonable enough list of demands. These were: 1) to be accused or freed; 2) to see their respective national consuls; 3) to call a lawyer; 4) better cell conditions; and 5) more to eat. The majority (the Canadian, Greek, Albanian, Pole and Frenchman) agreed to start a hunger strike if no response came within two days. The four Germans, with their practical sense, voted against this. When we heard about this upstairs, we voted to ask them to postpone action, but they were resolved and four of them commenced the strike, one being excused because he broke down with tuberculosis during the two days between.

This was the Greek comrade, Witte, who is well known in revolutionary workers' circles as the head of the Greek Archio-Marxist Party.[6] Comrade Witte has suffered with tuberculosis before, and a few days after his imprisonment he commenced to hemorrhage. The doctor treated him very unkindly, insisting upon speaking in Catalan rather than Spanish, and pronouncing him well, though he was obviously pale and weak. After a third visit, they found the lesion and ordered him to the hospital, which the police authorities refused! For a week he was held in the most unfavourable conditions, in the same cell with two healthy men. If this should cost the life of this comrade, we will know who is to blame. (Compare the case of Bob Smillie, Scottish ILP comrade, held for weeks in the Valencia Model Prison, without charges, and when ordered to the hospital by the prison MD on account of an attack of appendicitis, was retained in prison by the police for another week and transferred only two hours before his death.[7]) When we left Spain on July 3rd, Witte had finally been sent to the hospital, as well as Krehm (of Toronto) and Joven (Albanian), who were weakened by their two weeks of fasting. Since leaving Spain, we have heard that over twenty of the foreign comrades have joined the hunger strike. This is probably true, since the general feeling in the prison had been that, although the original strike was called too precipitously, eventually, if no change came, all would have to join as the only possible protest against our unjustified detention.

Other persons were put with us, as spies, we suspected. One was a Russian. A woman was put among the women comrades for a couple of days. Two Italian comrades, who had formerly worked for the secret service of the Generality back when the POUM participated in the Justice and Public Order Department, recognised her as a policewoman. This stopped our 'telephoning' to the women comrades, but a Dutch comrade warned them by singing the message loudly to his wife.

There were Russians upstairs, directing the translating of our documents. When they took our finger prints (five copies) or asked us questions or finally let some of us speak with our consuls, a Russian was always present, as translator they said, though we could see no reason for translators when we spoke with our consuls. We knew he was Russian, because Polish comrades spoke with him in Russian. When one of the men from the International Brigade indignantly demanded to speak with a real communist, he was told that there was a real communist from Moscow upstairs.

The guard was changed daily. There were from 16 to 24 guards. Usually they were friendly and willing to talk, especially with the women. There were UGT and Stalinist guards from Valencia and sometimes Anarchists and POUM men among them. Many of them had been called directly from the Madrid front, drafted into this policing of Catalonia without any choice or questions. They couldn't understand why they should be brought there when they wanted to fight against the Fascists. When we pointed out that the Catalan police could not be trusted to persecute the workers, they would protest that they too were with the workers. They were confused and angry about this, but continued to patrol the streets and in fact supported the counter-revolution against their own will. They would try to redeem themselves by giving us cigarettes, newspapers and privileges, by telling us what information they had on our case, for example that we were supposed to be carefully watched because we were said to be a wiley lot. The guards sang revolutionary songs too, but they didn't dare let us speak with our wives too long for fear the superiors would come down.

The American consul was able to see us, though it seemed that the others were not allowed to see their nationals. It was doubtlessly due to the consul's pressure that they called upon my comrade and me one day to answer a cursory examination. The next morning at four o'clock they awakened us and set us free into the night without our passport or papers. [...]

57. *The May Days and My Arrest (by Lois Orr)*

George Tioli tried hard to be amusing.[8] [...] One day he came around to POUM headquarters to ask me, 'What would you like to have somebody bring you if you were arrested tomorrow?'

I thought that was the funniest thing he had come up with yet. Eileen said she wanted her toothbrush most of all. I coudn't bring myself to really think about such a silly thing, but finally said peaches, because I had seen some lovely ones the day before.

The next day, June 15, Nin and the entire POUM Executive Committee were arrested. The party headquarters was padlocked and all property seized by the police. At 2 AM Thursday, June 17, the police entered the Hotel Falcón and arrested everyone there. Later that morning, at 8 AM to be exact, they came to Argentina 2 bis to arrest us. There were four plainclothes men of the SIM[9] and four Assault Guards. They showed me a floorplan of the flat and a list of its occupants, Bill Krehm, the Greek, the Albanian, us, and even some of our Trotskyite friends who only visited there. Who had given them such a complete list? They picked up all my notebooks and journals. I was not allowed to take even a toothbrush, only the culottes and blouse I hastily put on.

They drove us to a jail on the Via Durruti, where we were held all day. There we saw Gorkín, Bonet, Andrade, Escuder and all the rest of the POUM Executive Committee except Nin. He had already been taken off to Madrid. At midnight, all foreigners were separated out and made to march out into the street. I was sure my end had come. The Moscow Trials and Souvarine's *Staline* had put a real horror of the stalinists in me, and I knew then that I was at their mercy. The blackout was on, and the torches of our guards flickered on the narrow streets of the Old Quarter to light our way – where? There were no Patrols out this night to save us from the counter-revolution. The thought crossed my mind that we should at least be singing revolutionary songs, something, so that we didn't just let them extinguish our lives silently, in this utter darkness. Nobody felt like singing, so we walked on in silence until we got to an old house the Russians had turned into a jail, Avenida Dr. Pavlov, 24.

They put all us women in a little, windowless room, about 15 feet square. One of us, Pauli, was an agent provocateur, although we did not know it until much later. The men also had a GPU spy in their cell. Friday, a Russian, who spoke French, German, English and Spanish, was put in with them. He told them he was 'in for the same reason you are.' Nobody believed him. They decided unanimously that he was a spy.

The communist press was all we were allowed to read. From *Treball* we learned that we were arrested as a foreign fascist spy ring. This absurd GPU fabrication was carried in the US by the AP, as well as the trusty correspondents in Valencia. 'Fascist Spy Ring Uncovered in Barcelona,' said the *N.Y.Times*, with our names and pictures.

I shouldn't complain about this lying article, since it helped save my life. Brown Ransdell, city editor of the Louisville *Courier-Journal*, had known me since I was eight years old, and knew I was no fascist. He alerted my parents and the senator from Kentucky when the story came over the AP wire. Senator Barkley had the consul in Barcelona inquiring about me Saturday, two days after my arrest. My American friends in Barcelona had already been to the Consul to report my arrest, and Barkley's intervention confirmed my identity. Somebody – was it Tioli? – was able to tell the consul which jail I was in. This was crucial as I was not in an ordinary government jail, but a new secret Russian-organised establishment, unknown officially. Thus, it turned out that George Tioli was wrong: at that time, and in that place – and perhaps thanks to him! – one American did lead a charmed life. What saved me from the death that met many friends was the blessed accident that I was an American citizen, not a German or Italian antifascist without a passport.

Meanwhile, in the jail on Saturday, a Russian took my fingerprints on five different forms. He spoke excellent English and frightened me to death by telling me what was to happen to each of these forms.

'One goes to Moscow, one to the FBI in Washington, one to the Valencia government, one to the Generality police, and one we keep here. You will never be able to escape from your crimes.'

I did not know what my crimes were, but a terrifying feeling of utter helplessness overcame me at the thought of such a far-reaching organisation determined to incriminate me. I was only one person, alone, in face of such power. The Russian succeeded in producing abject fear in me.

Saturday the American Consul came upstairs to ask about me, but I did not know it, or see him.

Sunday, a poor Belgian International Brigader, who had been here before we came, learned to his horror that there were now 'real Trotskyites' in jail with him. He was so incensed, and protested so long and hard, that the Guard finally took him upstairs to state his case to the final arbiter, a 'real Communist from Moscow.'

Monday the Consul came again. Still, I didn't see him. He brought some peaches for me, but no toothbrush. The peaches created a problem. We were sworn to share everything equally, but how could we divide two peaches among 8 women and 27 men? Reluctantly, we decided that the men must go without. There just wasn't enough. We cut each peach carefully into four parts, so we had two bites apiece. Our daily food ration of two bowls of watery soup, and two tiny hunks of moldy bread, made the peaches a Godsend. Even more beautiful to me than the fruit itself was the lovely wordless message they brought, the knowledge that only George could have sent them, that he knew where I was, and was trying to help me. Knight errant to the aid of a damsel in dickens, a fitting theme for a medieval troubadour, I realized later. George's touch was beyond me then.

Later that day, an English captain from the International Brigade, wounded, was put in with the men. Another bit of proof for our assumption that we were in a GPU prison. From some far-away part of the building we heard prisoners singing revolutionary songs in Dutch. That made at least three nationalities of International Brigaders imprisoned here, Belgian, Dutch and English. The Russian who had been put in with the men was very plausible, and we argued his story pro and con. He said he had been serving as a technical expert at Malaga, and had opposed the Popular Army's desertion of the city without a fight. For this, the Russian commanders of the Popular Army jailed him. Was it true? We knew that many loyal Stalinists were killed for the slightest opposition to the regime. Stalin's terror was at its height. Some loyal stalinist had drawn on the wall of our room a beautiful map of the Soviet Union, lovingly detailed with mineral deposits, industrial centers, mountain ranges and tundras. The men told us their quarters had a big picture of Stalin on the wall. These carefully executed wall drawings brought me much too close to the horror of the Moscow Trials, where you cravenly protest your love and faithfulness to those who falsely accuse and then murder you. Would I come to that? We all had a feeling of pity for the Russian, but what if he really was a GPU agent put there to spy on us?

We were thinking and acting as a group. It was this process the GPU wanted to know about. This cruel place made us lose great segments of our separate personalities and fused us into a common group personality. We pooled all our experiences, the life stories that had all ended simultaneously in this room. Thus we knew exactly what assets were available to us in each person. The one thing common to us all, that had led us by different life paths to this awful impasse, was our devotion to liberty, and hatred of the horrible bastard tyranny that the Russian Revolution had bred. We did not believe that any end could justify such means as the Russians were using in Spain. Beyond that, we had political divergences. I was the only one there who thought the workers should have seized power during the May Days. The rest were for a POUM-CNT government in the Generality.

We were all agreed that our only hope of self-respect and honesty was to live out our ideals in this prison until the guards stopped us. We would share everything, and not break our common front against the guards whatever happened. Pauli was the only foreigner with us who was not connected with the POUM. It never occurred to us she was a spy. Her husband was with the PSUC Column in Aragon. She said she was there for criticising the PSUC line. Why should we doubt her? Surely no one in their right mind would come to this awful place and eat that horrible soup by choice? [...]

Elsa,[10] a big raw-boned, brown-eyed German socialist emerged as the leader of the group. Her husband was with the POUM column in Aragon. She had been in exile in Paris for three years. Of the four Germans there, she had the most practical knowledge about jails and concentration camps. After hearing Elsa's horror stories about Nazi jailors who made you sleep with them before you could visit your imprisoned husband, our plain old Spanish Assault Guards were a blessing. They were not sadists, but quite human, and easy on us because we were women. We were lucky the Russians had to use Spaniards to do their dirty work. Our Guards told us they too were socialists, from Valencia. This seemed impossible, but we decided it was not the time to argue politics with them. They let us talk to the men through the doors, handed notes and papers back and forth between our cells, and even went out to buy us soap, which was at a premium in Barcelona.

The German girls and I made quite a ritual of stripping and washing every morning. We found a little balcony, sheltered by towering brick walls on each side, where we could have privacy. This bathing was precious to me. Once a day I could wash the filth and horror of that place off me, and for a few minutes I could feel clean. There was a slight suggestion of national, or cultural differences among us on the subject of this washing. The Frenchwoman, the Polish girl and the Rumanian did not care to join us in this. Nor were they enthusiastic about the daily exercises Elsa insisted on.

We must exercise every day to keep up our morale, was one of her maxims. Exercise our hearts, minds and bodies. Everybody took lessons from everybody else: we pooled our knowledge and special skills. I began studying German with Elsa, and dress design with the Polish girl. She had come to Paris as an antifascist refugee and found work with one of the great French couturiers. I did better in German than in dress design because the Polish comrade had so little good to say about American fashions – and my culottes! – that I was soon repulsed. I found I was not such an internationalist as I supposed, but had considerable latent national feeling.

They called me 'the baby' because my life story was so short, and mothered me kindly. I tried to help the one person who was worse off than I, Ella Koenig, wife of the German who had organised the POUM library. Ella could scarcely eat her watery rations. She couldn't make her throat work to swallow that hateful stuff. We all knew it was nasty, but she had to eat it to stay alive. So we worked with Ella, distracted her, and loved her, to get her to eat. She was a cultivated, beautiful Nordic woman, tall with lovely yellow hair that had turned almost silver since she left her beloved Berlin three years ago. She missed her modern, artistic Berlin so she didn't even want to live. At the library, I had watched her humpbacked husband, Peter,[11] reason gently with her when she told me of her imminent return to Germany in the spring. She could not, or would not, grasp the fact that she was an exile, a refugee, with a price on her head.

'You must come back with me in the spring, to see the plane trees,' she used to tell me when I came over from the Generality on my lunch hour to get books. 'Berlin is so beautiful in the spring. Unter den Linden, you know.' Of course I didn't know. She made me see them, and she made my heart ache at the awful sadness of exile from home.

When she talked about Berlin she would eat, so I drew her out, and coaxed down the food as Peter had learned to do. She pitied my ignorance of such a wonderful place and shared her love for Berlin with me – its theater of proletarian realism, its modern art, its wonderful kindergartens. She was a child psychologist of some sort. Soon, she even began teaching me German socialist songs.

We sang every day. French, German and even American songs from our room joined the far-off songs from the other cells full of International Brigaders. It was a form of sympathetic communion within the prison.

Tuesday the American consul called again. The Russians told him I didn't want to see him, which he, quite properly, insisted on hearing with his own ears. He demanded to see me, against my will, if necessary. He wasn't sure they hadn't killed me, he knew I was an American citizen, and he was there. His words took effect, I was hauled upstairs into a little room. I was never so happy to see anyone in my life.

'Where is your passport?' he asked me.

'They have it.' For one terrifying moment I was afraid the consul would refuse to accept me as an American because I didn't have my passport on me. I did not know that he had gone through this same routine with many deserters from the International Brigades whose American passports were highly valued by the GPU. This Russian passport-stealing annoyed him immensely, so he immediately took my citizenship for granted – blessed man! – and jumped all over the Spanish officials. The Russian who had terrified me so was conspicuous by his absence.

'You can't treat American citizens like this. What kind of justice does your Spanish Republic practice? What have you done?' to me.

'Nothing but try to help the antifascists. Please get us out.'

'I'll see what I can do.'

The interview was over. I was led back downstairs.

The next day we read the full accusation against us in the Barcelona press. It was a classic GPU frame-up: The secret network of foreign agents working for Franco and Trotsky would be brought to trial in specially created espionage courts.[12] The communists dotted the i's and crossed the t's. We tried to think of an appropriate inscription to put under the big picture of Stalin in the men's cell in light of this latest crime. Our imagination failed us before such infamy. Instead we wrote the words to revolutionary songs on our walls, our small addition to the hopes and dreams buried in that black silent place. I looked at those dirty, worn walls – there was nothing else to see – and thought of all the prisons in Russia, in Germany and Italy with just the same kind of walls, and the same kind of humans staring at them. [...]

Friday, the Spanish officials brought me upstairs and took a short affidavit – where I was born, when, why I came to Spain, what I had done here. 'We will check this against your diaries and journals,' one of them said. 'Everything will be done in a proper and legal way. We Spaniards understand justice. We have specialists in all languages in Valencia right now, preparing for your trial, translating everything you foreigners have written.'

Was this poor soul embarrassed at the barbarous GPU methods? In any case, I was never tried at all, simply let out into the street at 4 am the next morning, without passport or papers. 'Come back tomorrow when the office is open and get your papers,' the guard said.

For once I did not worry about being out at night without any documentation. Nothing worse than what I had escaped could possibly happen to me. The dark streets looked sweet and friendly as I walked home to Argentina 2 bis. It seemed as if I had been away for years, not just ten days. My thoughts were very clear. [...]

I didn't want to go back to Av. Dr. Pavlov again, ever. How did I know they wouldn't arrest me all over? It would be no more impossible than my first arrest. Against my every instinct, I went back to that street.

In the daytime it looked almost ordinary. The front door of No. 24 looked like any other door. Who would guess from the outside the horror of those black walls deep within. I felt the hopeless misery and agony radiating from the building so strongly that I could not stir. How could those black-clad women across the street quietly wait for milk in their queues just as if this place didn't exist? What right had I to be out, not in? There, but for the grace of God, was I imprisoned. Still, I *was* out, at least part of me was. My feelings and heart were still in the cell downstairs with Ella and Elsa and the rest. Who would make Ella eat?

I made myself go up the steps for my passport by thinking, it really isn't right for me not to be in jail. If they put me back in, that's where I belong anyway, not out here. If I do get my passport, and get out of Spain, I will do everything I can to make it up to those still imprisoned by telling the TRUTH about the Loyalist Government. With this prayer I went back into the door of that reeking house.

The Spanish official was more apologetic than before. Between yesterday afternoon and this morning, I was somehow tried and found Not Guilty of fascist spying. Shades of Kafka. [...] He gave me my passport.

From Av. Dr. Pavlov I went to the American Consulate. That dear man arranged to evacuate us from Barcelona July 3rd by boat to Marseilles. Next, I tried to see what I could do to help my friends in jail. The outside world was not quite real to me yet. I found Negrete,[13] Skippy Escuder, Eileen and all my friends working overtime to keep informed about who had been arrested, where they were, and what they needed. The entire POUM organisation was in jail. It was a nightmare. Shortly after I was released my comrades were moved to another private jail in the Calle Corsica, where their conditions were much worse. The POUM had a relief service functioning, underground of course because the party was now illegal. Stalinist normality prevailed; no opposition allowed. Women members took blankets and food to their husbands and sons when they could locate them. The network of secret prisons made this difficult. Fortunately, the people had eyes and ears everywhere. [...]

After an aeon, July 3rd came, I was at the port saying goodbye to the two Georges, Tioli and Kopp. They really made a queer pair – the gross, ruddy Flamand, still pot-bellied though Spanish diet had cost him 40 pounds, and the elegant, spare, Italian gentleman, immaculate in his white linens.

Tioli, as usual, was giving me his last bit of unheeded, but good advice. He was saying that Pauli was a spy and would turn up in Paris. (She did.) I wasn't paying him any mind at all. My whole attention was fixed on two Swiss Trotskyites boarding the boat with us. The sinister nightmare I was fleeing reached toward me again as I saw two SIM men stop them on the gangplank and take them back to a car.[14] I was terrified. I didn't feel safe until I saw the green water spreading wider and wider between me and the dock.

I did not stay on deck to wave goodbye or take a last look at the city ringed by green hills. I went downstairs to the restaurant to eat – French butter, brioche, and strawberry jam. In face of death, affirm life. At a wake, eat.

58. *List of foreign detainees – facsimiles (by Lois and Charles Orr)*

AUSTRIAN
8 — Julia Landau, Der Funker
NORWEGIAN
                (Fritz Sanders) German SAP

SINCE JUNE 17
            Georges Kopp, Belgian
            Harry Milton, American, Socialist Party
            Nicolas Sindlowitch
July 2   Talman, Swiss
July 2 Mrs. Talman, Swiss, Bolshevik-Leninist
July   Ethel MacDonald, Scottish (freed July, by Brockway)
July 7-28 Margot Tiety Ant-Parliamentarian
Also many German Anarchists and many POUM Shock batalion
Before July 9: Hans Reiter
                Walter Schwarz
                Carl Mobb: 8 French + 1 Italian (one was Marcel Colin)
Those wanted, but still free (There was a list of about 50 in hands
                of the port customs.)

Max Ratel
Kurt Landau
Eva Settig
    Balduini
Rosa Winckler
    Trusco
Camille
Dr. Carlotta Margolin
    Moulin
    Pepito
Auger
Gisola
Asetin Guadell

Other foreigners in danger
Dr. Davis
Charles Doran
Harvey Buttonshaw
Hugh McNeil
Douglas Stearns
        Orlando
            Frankfort
            Ritchie
Harry Webb
Mike Wilton
    Braithwaite
David Crooks
George Tioli
Ethel McDonald
Charles Segalis
    Forster
Mrs. Marchi and children

German

Richard Tietz — July 8 (militia) taken at Guadalajara (Carcel Modelo) S.F.I.

Franz Gerstner
Horst Lichtenstein   — S.A.P. } about July 25 in automatic Br.
Hans Wielgud   all in Shock Batallion
Georg Gernsheimer
Max _____
Richard (K.P.O.)   — about July 26 (Shok Bat.
           Monden

Swiss
Zita Schultz — (Swiss) taken in émigré house
                about June 20 (?) Her husband was in
                — In Women's Prison   the C.N.T. militia

D oste.
Fred
     Ilynberg   } 7. D.A.S. now all taken to Valencia
Egon
Michel
___

59. Letter fragment from Paris, January 1938 (by Lois Orr)

You meet more nice people here in Paris.[15] Americans and English most of them. The French remain very unsociable. Altho we know a lot of nice comrades of the IVth International movement. One of them, a marvelously pretty lad, with hair the color of honey and very pretty, was in Catalonia in the Anarchist International Brigade. He's only 19. He said that the corpses and the wounded men and that sort of thing were the worst part of the whole business. Once, they had been attacking and hadn't had anything to eat for three days, marching in the sun; the only thing they had to drink was *anis dulce* (which is very sweet and very strong liqueur). So, after three days, he drank two glasses – you usually drink it in finger-size glasses – and got horribly drunk. But kept on marching. Everybody else being more or less in the same condition. Another time at night they saw some peasants cutting their telephone wires – all the peasants around there were for Franco, and one of the men, formerly a customs guard, shot the guy right thro the neck; the kid thought it wasn't necessary and that the guard just wanted to show off what a good shot he was.

There is a very nice German comrade, who is very very big and tall with a shiny child's face. He has adopted the name Camille,[16] which of all the names under the sun doesn't fit him at all.

[...]

This afternoon I had dinner with Molins,[17] Skippy and a Catalan comrade who has just come from Barcelona.[18] He crossed the mountains with another guy, and it took them 15 days on foot, through snow up to their knees. He came with another POUMist who was the chief of police in Barcelona in the days when there was a revolution there. This latter has TB and his legs are absolutely raw up to the knees from that trip. The kid we ate with was in jail since June; he used to be the judge of the Popular Tribunal (set up by the revolution) in Lérida – a POUM town. Some of the stories he tells –

It is nice fresh cloudy spring weather here. Hearing all this Catalan around me reminds me so vividly of Barcelona. In the spring and summer it was so nice. Every Sunday morning, when we lived in the Hotel Falcón, there was an organ grinder who would come around while we were still in bed and play the gaiest bubbling songs. Spanish songs have an air and swing to them that is unique. *Molt bi* (pronounced mul bay) is Catalan for 'very good;' and *molt guapa* means 'very good-looking,' or 'hot,' or something to that effect. What a screwy but nice language.

[...]

I have already made three outlines for this book, and am now going to rewrite the main one, and try to organise it more thoroughly.[19]

Notes

1. This memory protocol was written soon after Lois and Charles were released from prison.
2. Julián Gorkín was amongst the founding members of the Spanish Communist Party. Along with many others of this generation of Spanish Communists, he soon joined the anti-Stalinist opposition and eventually became a leading member of the POUM.
3. Arthur Lewin emigrated to Barcelona in 1933, where he played a major role in the local German Anarchist group. After the defeat of Republican Spain, Lewin moved to France, where he was arrested and sent to Auschwitz in 1942. He died in Paris in 1976.
4. Jordi Arquer, David Rey (pseudonym of Daniel Rebull) and Pedro Bonet were leading members of the POUM. Manuel Maurín, who died in prison, did not count amongst the prominent members of the POUM, but he was the youngest brother of Joaquín Maurín and therefore captured as well.
5. Note by Charles Orr: 'Andrade had news, just before he was arrested, that Nin was in Murcia, Checka stronghold.'
6. Witte was the pseudonym of Demetrious Giotopoulos; at the time, he was a leader of the Greek Archio-Marxists, an organization which, in the early-to-mid-1930s, had been one of the largest dissident communist groupings in Europe with several thousand members and a solid implantation in several Greek industrial centres.
7. An interesting recent exchange regarding the circumstances of Bob Smillie's death in a Valencia prison took place in the pages of the British *The Historical Journal* (THJ); see Tom Buchanan, 'The Death of Bob Smillie, the Spanish Civil War, and the Eclipse of the Independent Labour Party', *THJ*, 40 (1997), 435–461; John Newsinger, 'The Death of Bob Smillie', *THJ*, 41 (1998), 575–578; and Tom Buchanan, 'The Death of Bob Smillie: A Reply', *THJ*, 43 (2000), 1109–1111.
8. First sentence of Chapter 16 of Lois' 1961 manuscript, *Spain, 1936–1937*, available in the Orr Papers of the Labadie Collection at the University of Michigan in Ann Arbor. Chapter 16 begins on p. 317 and recounts the May Days from Lois' after-the-fact perspective. The reproduced portion of her text begins on p. 330 of her 1961 manuscript.
9. The *Servicio de Investigación Militar* (SIM), founded as a counter-espionage service by the Republican government, soon became dominated by the Stalinist apparatus and turned into a willing tool for Soviet designs in Republican Spain.
10. Elsa Hentschke was released in late November 1937 only to be kidnapped and rearrested again one week later. She was finally released and expelled to France in late January 1938. On Elsa Henschke's fate in Spain, see Hans Schafranek, *Das kurze Leben des Kurt Landau: Ein österreichischer Kommunist als Opfer der stalinistischen Geheimpolizei* (Vienna: Verlag für Gesellschaftskritik, 1988), pp. 494–495, 510–511.

11. Here, Lois' memory appears to be failing her. Ella Koenig's husband was Ewald Koenig.
12. The various attempts by the Soviet leadership to stage such an international show trial are conveniently surveyed in the special edition of the *Cahiers Léon Trotsky*, 3 (July–September 1979), *Les Procès de Moscou dans le monde*, particularly the section entitled 'Procès manqués', 121–200. For an important update, see Reiner Tosstorff, 'Ein Moskauer Prozess in Barcelona: Die Verfolgung der POUM und ihre internationale Bedeutung', in his *Die POUM in der spanischen Revolution* (Cologne: ISP, 2006), pp. 126–170.
13. Rosalio Negrete was the pseudonym of Russell Blackwell.
14. This Swiss couple, Clara and Paul Thalmann, survived their period in jail and were released on 30 August 1937. The episode of their capture is narrated, from the perspective of the two Swiss, by Paul Thalmann in his autobiography, *Wo die Freiheit stirbt* (Olten: Walter, 1974), pp. 205–206.
15. Third full paragraph of a letter fragment with handwritten notation, 'Jan. 9 1938', written by Lois during their stay in Paris. It is the sole letter from their stay in Paris included in the holdings of the Labadie Collection.
16. A handwritten notation explains that this was the pseudonym for Leon Sedov, 'Trotsky's son'. Leon Sedov (1906–1938) was a key activist within the Trotskyist movement throughout the 1930s. He had accompanied his father, Leon Trotsky, into exile in 1928. He subsequently had his home base in Berlin and then Paris, where he died in February 1938. His death while undergoing an emergency hospitalization remains shrouded in mystery. A well-planned murder by Stalinist agents remains a widespread explanatory theory, but a careful reconstruction of the medical evidence surrounding Leon Sedov's emergency hospitalization by two French Trotskyist medical experts suggests an ill-attended appendicitis. See Jean-Michel Krivine and Marcel-Francis Kahn, 'La mort de Leon Sedov', *Cahiers Léon Trotsky*, 13 (March 1983), 44–54.
17. Narcis Molins i Fàbrega was a leading activist in dissident communist circles in Spain (and subsequently in exile) throughout the 1930s and 1940s.
18. Top paragraph of third page of letter fragment written by Lois. A handwritten notation states, 'Jan. 14, 1938.'
19. This is a reference to the first of three manuscripts on the history of the Spanish Revolution written by Lois in the course of her life.

9
(Auto-)Biographical Notes by Lois Orr

The following paragraphs provide elements towards a personal-political biography of Lois Orr. Except for the first two brief statements, they are transcripts of an interview held on 9 January 1983 in Louisville, Kentucky. I thank Ellen Poteet for transcribing the tape for me, which is held in the Labadie Collection at the University of Michigan's main Ann Arbor library. To convey some of the flavour of the interview and the personality of the main protagonist of this book, Lois Orr, here are some comments Ellen Poteet, a southerner herself, wrote as an introduction to her transcript:

> *The interviewer was Paul Garing (sp.?). There was one other man present who was not identified. He appeared to be either a friend or relative of Orr. All quite informal. Throughout, the sound of the interviewer lighting another cigarette and taking that first long puff. Then, with the second side of the tape, began the background sound effects of ice chinking against glasses. And there is this way that ice sounds in a glass when iced tea is at issue, and when gin and bourbon are at issue, and in this case Sir Lipton was not profiting. Orr has a long southern drawl. At the beginning of the interview she drew out each word sotto voce so that one had to strain to hear. But she became more forceful in tone as the interview continued, though the unhurried rhythms were constant.*[1]

At an early stage in my efforts to reconstruct the life and times of Lois and Charles Orr during their stay in Barcelona and in subsequent years, a relative of Lois suggested that she might write up a short biographical sketch. Alas, this idea was never translated into reality. Therefore, the following sections of the interview provide otherwise unavailable data on the circumstances of Lois' life after her (and Charles') narrow escape from the Stalinist prison complex erected in Republican Spain. The opening portions of the interview transcript also cast cursory light on the prehistory of Lois' activist engagement in the process of the Catalan Revolution and revolutionary politics in subsequent years. Two very brief sections of her 1961 book manuscript provide additional insights into Lois' pre-1936 personal politics as well as her own assessment of a major turning point in her commitment to the anti-fascist and revolutionary cause while in Catalonia.

* * *

'In 1932 I had supported Norman Thomas in a high school debate.'[2]

On 23 November 1936, Buenaventura Durruti, who had been killed by a stray bullet three days earlier while fighting in Madrid, was buried in a public ceremony in Barcelona. Contemporary accounts list the number of onlookers, who came to bid the popular anarchist the last farewell on his way to the Montjuich cemetery, as numbering between 200.000 and 500.000. Lois Orr was amongst the crowd. Her 1961 reflections include the following passage:

> In the immensity and power of that demonstration I completely lost the nagging sense of my own unimportance and insignificance that had been my constant companion for so many months. I lost my "self" in a tremendous sense of identification with these swarthy, silent, wonderful people. I felt for them, I loved them, I wanted to be one of them. This feeling had never come from the hundreds of newspaper articles or manifestos exalting the antifascist cause. It first stirred in me the night Rosas was bombed – Durruti's funeral brought it to full consciousness. From this day on I was emotionally and intellectually committed to the antifascist revolution as a noble and wonderful human experiment and the last doubts and reservations were swept away.... Not that my daily life changed much after my emotional rededication. I just *felt* differently about what I was doing.[3]

* * *

Interview Transcript

(Q.: When were you born?) I was born in Louisville, Kentucky, April 23, 1917, at the Jewish hospital.

(Q.: What caused your first interest in left politics?) My mother. The Depression. My mother began to take the *New Republic*.[4] I was in high school and I was on the school paper. And then came the elections of 1932, and we had to have somebody do an article for Hoover, Roosevelt and Norman Thomas. So, having heard my mother talk about Norman Thomas, I said I would do the one for the socialists. And from then on I began to be more aware of the socialists. And when I went to university, I declared myself a socialist. And Charles was indeed a socialist. And they had some kind of meeting. It was an anti-war meeting, and I went and that's where I met Charles. And I became active.

(Q.: Were you ever a member of the Communist Party?) The only organisation I belonged to was the Student League for Industrial Democracy,[5] the Louisville Chapter. Charles was a member of the Socialist Party.

(Q.: Did you ever carry a weapon?) No. Theoretically I was a member of the POUM female militia. That was how I got my meal ticket. But I never carried a weapon.

(Q.: What did you do in Paris?) That was 1937/38. Charles worked on his Ph.D. thesis at the Bibliothèque Nationale. Pierre Naville[6] got me these files of anarchist papers, and I made notes about what happened in the first days of the revolution. That's what I did. We spent our time with Trotskyists. David Rousset[7] and his wife Leah ... Skippy Escuder. We circulated on the edges of the POUM refugee circle. While we were in Paris, Trotsky's son was killed by the KGB. They kill people. Like the Pope.

We were denounced to the police and that's why we had to leave Paris. The Stalinists. [...] France was not nice to refugees. They said, sure come, open arms. But they didn't want you. They had a socialist government with some communists. They didn't want to make the Soviet Union mad at them. Our papers were perfectly in order, so we got out. We didn't want to fool around with any more jails.

When we came back to the United States, Charles worked his way back on a ship and went to Texas, and I rode across as a passenger on a freighter and landed in Newfoundland. I came down to New York City, and I spoke at a mass meeting. And there were a whole lot of people there from the Trotskyite party, like Irving Howe[8] ... and Jim Cannon[9] who was to have been the featured speaker at this meeting, but since I showed up they had me talk about Spain. And that was how I met Jim Cannon.

(Q.: [Did you use any] pseudonyms?) Miriam Gould. Miriam. I wanted to be Jewish, so I said Miriam.

(Q.: When did you use the pseudonym?) Only while I was in Texas. In 1937 we were in Paris. In 1938–9, Texas.[10] Charles had gone back to teaching Economics. He felt I was so radical that he didn't want me on the campus of the University of Texas. He lived in Austin, and I lived in Houston where I helped the CIO organise Houston Milling, and a few other places like that. And I got a job at Houston Milling. Under my own name. The owner was some tall, gorgeous French Jew. He had taken all his capital out of France and put it into Houston Milling, which was a very wise move, because this was '38. So he was walking through his factory one day in one of those white smocks like European managers wear. I was filling cornmeal boxes. He looked at me and said, 'Fire that girl.' He picked up on the vibes. I was there to organise for the union. But the superintendent was a real country boy, harassed with wife and children. Real hillbilly. So he hid me in a job where this guy would never see me. [Laughter] But that's why I used a pseudonym – because Charles did not want to lose his job. I was so wild and radical that he knew if I was allowed to meet ordinary people I would get him fired.

We didn't organise it [Houston Milling]. I didn't last too long. I did a lot of work for the Steelworkers. I tried to get another job to help the Amalgamated, but it was not too good of times, and I couldn't get another job, so I spent my time writing leaflets, picketing, and stuff like that for the Steelworkers. I only stayed in Houston for a year and then told Charles I didn't want any more of it.

(Q.: [On her visit to Mexico and Leon Trotsky]) He was very charming. Nice house. Well, he was just utterly superior. What you got from him was the impression of an older statesman who just knew and who had so much more experience than you had. This is what he put out. Now this is all vibes, not necessarily anything he said. He was very polite, but he just – from the wealth and depth and height of his experience – he just knew you were wrong. And he could listen to you a little bit, but he didn't want to hear very much. [...] Charles did all the talking. Trotsky had arranged a debate between Charles and his guards, who were followers of Cannon. Charles and I by this time were Shachtmanites.[11] We had the debate. Trotsky decreed we were wrong. And shortly thereafter that man put an ax in his skull. We were in Mexico the summer of 1940, the summer Trotsky was killed.

(Q.: [On her acquaintance with C.L.R. James[12]]) Oh, Jimmie Johnson! David [Lois' and Charles' son] was born in 1942. I lived in St. Louis. I was an active Trotskyite. Charles and I both worked as organisers for the Amalgamated Clothing Workers, and on the side there was an active Trotskyist group in St. Louis, the SWP.[13] This group was busy organising sharecroppers in southeast Missouri with the help of the CIO council. CLR James came down to help us. He has made great capital on that. Had this Oxford accent. He was an upper-class Jamaican Black, a revolutionary. He didn't know anything. We knew what we were doing.

(Q.: [On the prehistory of her various manuscripts on the Spanish Revolution]) I started making notes for the book in Paris that whole year. I worked some on it in Houston. When my employment got slack, I worked on the book. I finished the first draft, I think, in '42. I was pregnant with David.

Notes

1. Letter from Ellen Poteet to editor, 22 May 2003.
2. Lois Orr, *Spain, 1936–1937*, unpublished 1961 manuscript, p. 79.
3. Orr, *Spain*, pp. 190–191.
4. *The New Republic* published its first issue in November 1914 as a progressive magazine. In the interwar period it was generally broadly sympathetic to the Soviet Union and Soviet politics, an attitude which changed only with the outbreak of the Cold War.
5. The Student League for Industrial Democracy emerged as the youth section of the League for Industrial Democracy, a social democratic organization founded under a different name in 1905 by prominent socialists, including the novelists Upton Sinclair and Jack London. Many decades later, after a period of relative quiescence, the Student League changed its name to Students for a Democratic Society (SDS) and became the most prominent US student organization associated with the New Left of the 1960s.
6. After an early period of intense interest in surrealism, Pierre Naville (1906–1993) became a member of the French Communist Party. A meeting with Trotsky in Moscow in 1927 convinced him to join the Trotskyist Left Opposition. He remained part of the international leadership of the Trotskyist movement until the Second World War period. He became a well-known academic sociologist, and he remained engaged in activist politics in various Left socialist organizations in post-war France.
7. David Rousset (1912–1997) began his political engagements in the ranks of the French Socialist Students in 1931. In the second half of the 1930s he became a leading figure in the French Trotskyist movement. A Trotskyist resistance activist in the Second World War, he was captured and tortured in 1943 and survived a series of concentration camps. He obtained a certain degree of fame as a writer with the 1946 publication of his *L'Universe concentrationnaire*. He separated from the Trotskyists by 1947 and joined up with Jean-Paul Sartre in the short-lived episode of the 'Third Force' *Rassemblement Démocratique Révolutionnaire*. Already in the late 1940s, David Rousset became a leading critic of the Soviet practice of prison camps. He remained a

writer and journalist for much of the post-war period, sympathized with the Gaullist movement in the 1960s, but remained sympathetic to the political Left.
8. Irving Howe (1920–1993) entered politics as a member of the YPSL, then joining Max Shachtman's Workers Party. He later founded the magazine *Dissent* and became one of the United States' most famous literary critics.
9. James P. Cannon (1890–1974) was socialized into radical US politics within the ranks of the Industrial Workers of the World (IWW). A Socialist Party member since the age of 18, he led the pro-Bolshevik faction within the Socialist Party, and in 1919 he became the first national chairperson of the Communist Party, then still called the Workers Party. A leading American Communist in the ensuing decade, James P. Cannon became attracted to the Trotskyist critique of Soviet politics while attending the Sixth Congress of the Communist International as a party delegate in 1928 in Moscow. He remained a leading figure of American and international Trotskyism until the end of his life.
10. In fact, Lois Orr employed the same pseudonym at other points in her activist life as well. For instance, the index of articles published in the American Trotskyist journal, *The New International*, between 1940 and 1946, includes several articles written by Lois Orr and published under the identical pseudonym: 'Lessons of the Spanish Commune', *New International*, 75 (May 1943); 'Spain 1936 – A Study in Soviets', *New International*, 85 (April 1944); 'Spain 1936 – A Study in Soviets – II', *New International*, 86 (May 1944); 'Women, Biology and Socialism', *New International*, 104 (February 1946); and 'Profits and the Housing Crisis', *New International*, 105 (March 1946).
11. Max Shachtman (1904–1972), after an early period in the American Communist Party, became a leading member of the Trotskyist Socialist Workers Party and editor of its theoretical journal, *The New International*. Together with many other intellectuals, he developed differences with the orthodox Trotskyist view on the class nature of the Soviet Union and officially broke with the Socialist Workers Party in 1940. He helped found the Workers Party and retained control over *The New International*, which for some time became the leading American Marxist periodical. In later decades, Max Shachtman moderated his views and, together with his followers, Shachtman developed close links with certain Left-leaning circles within the Democratic Party.
12. Cyril Lionel Robert James (1901–1989) was one of the twentieth century's most famous Black writers. Born in Trinidad, he moved to England in 1932 as a cricket journalist. He spent most of his subsequent years in Great Britain and the United States. He joined the British Trotskyist movement in 1934 and remained in various Trotskyist groupings, taking on prominent political and journalistic roles, for the ensuing 15 years. Moving to the United States in 1938, he joined up with Max Shachtman and the Workers Party in 1940. Disillusioned with Leninist vanguard politics by the late 1940s, he was deported from the United States to England in 1952. Within the Workers Party, he adopted the pseudonym J.R. Johnson.
13. In fact, the Orrs were members of the Workers Party, the section of the SWP which had split off in 1940, in the wake of growing disagreements over the nature of the Soviet regime.

Index

Note: Locators in bold refer to footnote explanations of the biography of a particular person

Andrade, Juan, 46, 80, **108**, 117, 135, 158, 185, 189

Blackwell, Russell, 46, 104, **111**, 119–20, 132, 137, 138, 139, 151, 173, 195

Companys, Lluís, 6

Dos Passos, John, 46, 158, **173**, 180–1

Erber, Ernest, 46, 56, 68, 69, 70, 73, 79, **106**
Escuder, Josep and Skippy, 127, 137, **145**, 166, 185, 189, 195, 199

Fields, B.J., 80, **109**
Fletcher, Edwin 'Ted', 80, 84, 92–3, 102, 104, **109**

Giral, José, 4, 6
Goldman, Emma, 36, 46, 68, 70, **106**

Hentschke, Elsa, 192, **200**

James, C.L.R., 205–6, **207**

König, Ewald and Ella, 132, **146**, 193
Kopp, Georges, 80, **109**, 141, 158, 163, 195
Krehm, William, 81, **109**, 124, 132, 134, 151, 156–7, 187, 189

Landau, Kurt, 169, **175**
Largo Caballero, Francisco, 6, 8, 9, 173
Lichtveld, Lou, 77, 79, **108**

Low, Mary (Mary Breá), 40, 42, 56, 71, 72, 79, 81, 86, 87, 89, 93, **107**, 115

Marckwald, Willi, 46, 77, 94–5, 102, 103, 104, **108**, 114, 115–16, 117, 126, 132, 145, 160
Marzani, Carl, 39, 114, **144**
McGovern, John, 96, 97, 98, **110**
McNair, John, 36, 55, 106, **111**–12, 116, 142, 151, 156, 159, 168, 176, 177, 178
Miravitlles, Jaume, 120, **145**, 169
Molíns i Fàbrega, Narcis, 199, **201**
'Moulin' (Hans Freund), 46, 55, 73, 100, 104, **107**, 135, 136

Naville, Pierre, 204, **206**
Negrín, Juan, 8, 173, 183
Nin, Andreu, 46, 80, **108**, 158, 180, 182, 183, 189

Oehler, Hugo, 137, 139, **146**, 151, 185, 186
Orwell, George (Eric Blair), 40, 42, 159, 174, 176–81
O'Shaughnessy, Eileen (Mrs. Eric Blair), 55, 137, 138, 142, **146**, 147, 152–4, 159, 163, 176, 178–82, 195

Piscator, Erwin, 46, 102, 103, **111**
Prieto, Indalecio, 9, 173

Rousset, David, 204, **206**

Sedov, Leon ('Camille'), 199, **201**

Smillie, Bob, 80, 86, 104, **108**, 120, 144, 158, 168, 187, 200

Thalmann, Paul and Clara, 36, 37, 39, 195, **201**

Thomas, Norman, 80, **109**, 169, 203, 204

Tioli, George, 147, 152–4, 156, 160, 176–7, 181–2, 189, 191, 195

Weisbord, Abe, 162, 169, **174–5**

'Witte' (Demetrious Giotopoulos), 187, **200**

The manufacturer's authorised representative in the EU is Springer Nature Customer Service Centre GmbH, Europaplatz 3, 69115 Heidelberg, Germany. If you have any concerns regarding our products, please contact ProductSafety@springernature.com

Printed and bound by CPI Group (UK) Ltd, Croydon, CR0 4YY

23/03/2026

02076744-0010